GCSE ENGLISH LITERATURE

Julie Grover

Longman

Longman Group UK Limited,
Longman House, Burnt Mill, Harlow,
Essex CM20 2JE, England
and Associated Companies throughout the world.

First published 1988

British Library Cataloguing in Publication Data

Grover, Julie
English Literature. — (Longman GCSE revise
guides).
1. English Literature — Study and teaching
(Secondary) — England 2. General Certificate of
Secondary Education — Study guides
I. Title
820′.76 PR51.G7

ISBN 0-582-01574-X

Set in 10/12pt Century Book Roman

Printed and bound in Great Britain by
Thamesmouth Printing Group, Basildon, Essex.

CONTENTS

EDITORS' PREFACE

Longman Revise Guides are written by experienced examiners and teachers, and aim to give you the best possible foundation for success in examinations and other modes of assessment. Much has been said in recent years about declining standards and disappointing examination results. While this may be somewhat exaggerated, examiners are well aware that the performance of many candidates falls well short of their potential. The books encourage thorough study and a full understanding of the concepts involved and should be seen as course companions and study guides to be used throughout the year. Examiners are in no doubt that a structured approach in preparing for examinations and in presenting coursework can, together with hard work and diligent application, substantially improve performance.

The largely self-contained nature of each chapter gives the book a useful degree of flexibility. After starting with Chapters 1 and 2, all other chapters can be read selectively, in any order appropriate to the stage you have reached in your course. We believe that this book, and the series as a whole, will help you establish a solid platform of basic knowledge and examination technique on which to build.

Geoff Black & Stuart Wall

AUTHOR'S PREFACE

I hope this book will help you throughout your GCSE course and enable you to be successful, whether you are assessed by coursework or by examination. There are no correct answers in English Literature but there are questions that can be usefully asked. The first aim of this book is to show you the right kinds of questions to ask about poetry, plays and novels. This will enable you to develop your own ideas and your own response. The second aim is to help you write interestingly and appropriately about the literature you have studied.

The first chapter shows what is expected by each examining board. Advice on how to approach coursework, on the different types of question set and on how to prepare for examinations is provided in Chapter 2. Each remaining chapter deals with an important aspect of poetry, drama or prose. Every chapter contains passages from texts, which can be used as exercises to test your understanding, as well as examination questions with suggested answers. The passages quoted are from a great variety of works, many from set books. I hope that these will give you a taste of a range of literature and stimulate your interest and appetite.

I have received a great deal of help and support while I have been writing this book. I am particularly grateful to Stuart Wall for his encouragement, to Stuart Sillars for his careful scrutiny of my text and the many suggestions he made to improve its clarity, and to my husband, Philip, for countless discussions about literature.

Julie Grover

ACKNOWLEDGEMENTS

We are grateful to the following Examination Boards for permission to reproduce questions which have appeared in their specimen examination papers. Whilst the Boards have granted permission to reproduce their questions, I accept full responsibility for the answers provided.

The London and East Anglian Examining Group, The Midland Examining Group, The Northern Examining Association (comprising the Associated Lancashire Examining Board, Joint Matriculation Board, and the North, North West and Yorkshire and Humberside Regional Examinations Boards), The Northern Ireland Schools Examining Council, The Southern Examining Group, The Welsh Joint Education Committee.

We are grateful to the following for permission to reproduce copyright material:

Faber and Faber Limited for an extract from 'Lullaby' by W.H. Auden; A.D. Peters and Co. Ltd. and George Duckworth and Co. for 'The Midnight Skaters' from *Collected Poems* by Edmund Blunden; Methuen, London Ltd. for an extract from *The Caucasian Chalk Circle* by Bertolt Brecht, translated by James and Tanya Stern; David Higham Assoc. Ltd. for an extract from 'Timothy Winters' by Charles Causeley; the author for 'A Child Half-Asleep' by Tony Connor; Harper and Row Inc. for 'Yet do I Marvel' by Countee Cullen © 1925 renewed 1953 by Ida M. Cullen; Carcarnet Press Ltd. for an extract from 'Anger Lay By Me' from *Selected Poems* by Elizabeth Daryush; The Society of Authors and the literary trustees of Walter de la Mare for an extract from 'The Dove said, "Coo"'; Methuen, London Ltd., for an extract from *A Taste of Honey* by Shelagh Delaney; Harvard University Press and the President and fellows of Harvard College for extracts from *The Complete Poems of Emily Dickenson* ed. Thomas H. Johnson; Faber and Faber Ltd. for an extract from *The Waste Land* by T.S. Eliot; Century Hutchinson Ltd. for an extract from 'The Future' by Ruth Fainlight; The Bodley Head Ltd. for an extract from *The Great Gatsby* by F. Scott Fitzgerald; Edward Arnold Ltd. for an extract from *A Passage to India* by E.M. Forster; Jonathan Cape Ltd. and the estate of Robert Frost for an extract from 'Out Out' from *The Poems of Robert Frost* edited by Edward Connery Latham; Faber and Faber Ltd. for an extract from *The Lord of the Flies* by William Golding; William Heinemann Ltd. and The Bodley Head Ltd. for Extracts from *Brighton Rock* and *The Power and the Glory* both by Graham Greene; Penguin Books Ltd. for 'A Thousand Years' by Lady Heguri, translated by Geoffrey Bownas and Anthony Thwaite, from *The Penguin Book of Japanese Verse*; HMSO for extracts from the National Criteria, by permission of the controller of Her Majesty's Stationery Office; Michael Joseph Ltd. for an extract from *A Kestrel for a Knave* by Barry Hines; William Heinemann Ltd. for an extract from *The Long and the Short and the Tall* by Willis Hall; Faber and Faber Ltd. for 'The Jaguar' from *The Hawk in the Rain* by Ted Hughes; William Heinemann Ltd. for an extract from *To Kill a Mockingbird* by Harper Lee; The Hogarth Press for an extract from *Cider With Rosie* by Laurie Lee; The New Directions Publishing Corp. and the author for 'Fragrance of Life, Odor of Death' by Denise Levertov; Elaine Green Ltd. and Penguin Books for extracts from *The Crucible* (1952/53) and *Death of a Salesman* (1949) both by Arthur Miller;

Curtis Brown Ltd. and Little, Brown and Co. Ltd. on behalf of the estate of Ogden Nash for 'The Octopus'; Heinemann Educational Ltd. for an extract from *Spring and Port Wine* by Bill Naughton; the estate of the late Sonia Brownwell Orwell and Secker and Warburg Ltd. for an extract from *Animal Farm* by George Orwell; Methuen, London Ltd. for an extract from *Look Back in Anger* by John Osborne; the author's literary estate and Chatto and Windus Ltd. for 'Exposure' from *The Collected Poems* by Wilfred Owen; Methuen, London Ltd. for an extract from *The Caretaker* by Harold Pinter; Harper Row Publishers Inc. and Ted Hughes for an extract from 'Poppies in October' by Sylvia Plath; A.D. Peters and Co. Ltd. for an extract from *An Inspector Calls* by J.B. Priestley; Laurence Pollinger Ltd., Alfred A Knopf Inc. and Random House for an extract from 'Blue Girls' from *Selected Poems* by John Crowe Ransom; Robson Books and the author for 'Growing Pain' by Vernon Scannell; The Society of Authors on behalf of the estate of Bernard Shaw for an extract from *Pygmalion*; Oxford University Press for extracts from *The Complete Works of William Shakespeare* ed. Wells and Taylor; William Heinemann Ltd. for an extract from *Of Mice and Men* by John Steinbeck; David Higham Assoc. Ltd. for extracts from 'The Force that through the Green Fuse Drives the Flower' and 'Do Not Go Gentle Into That Goodnight', both by Dylan Thomas; Jonathan Cape Ltd. for an extract from *I'm Talking about Jerusalem* by Arnold Wesker; Blackie and Son Ltd. for an extract from *Billy Liar* by Keith Waterhouse and Willis Hall; the estate of Tennessee Williams, for an extract from 'The Glass Menagerie' (1945); A.P. Watt Ltd., Michael Yeats and Macmillan London Ltd. for 'At the Grey Round of the Hill' from *The Dreaming of the Bones* by W.B. Yeats.

SOME USEFUL TERMS

Here are the definitions of some useful terms. They appear in the book but are brought together here for easy reference.

ALLITERATION: the repetition of the same consonant sound, as in 'Billy the Bully'.

AMBIGUITY: a word or phrase which has a double meaning.

ASIDE: when a character in a play turns away from the action on stage and speaks directly to the audience, as though the other characters cannot hear.

ASSONANCE: the repetition of vowel sounds, as in 'green trees'.

BALLAD: a poem that tells a story in a simple and straightforward way, usually in four-line stanzas.

CHORUS: a character, or a group, in a play who comments on the action.

COMEDY: nowadays a work that makes you laugh, but it used to mean a work with a happy ending.

COUPLET: two lines of verse which rhyme.

DIALOGUE: two or more characters speaking to each other. We also speak about the 'dialogue of a play', meaning all the words that are spoken.

DICTION: the words a poet chooses to use.

DRAMATIC IRONY: occurs when a character says something that has a different meaning for the audience from the one it has for the character. This happens when the audience knows more about a situation than the character who is speaking.

FICTION: anything that is not fact,

FIRST PERSON: using 'I' in speech or writing, as in 'I shall tell you the story of what happened to me when I was six'.

FREE VERSE: verse that has neither rhyme nor rhythm.

GENRE: a kind of writing. Poetry is one genre of literature, plays are another, prose is a third genre.

IAMBIC PENTAMETER: a line of poetry made up of ten syllables, with alternating light and heavy beats, as in: 'Is this the face that launched a thousand ships?' A great deal of English poetry has been written in iambic pentameter.

IMAGERY: writing that creates a picture in your mind, usually through the use of comparisons.

IRONY: saying one thing but meaning the opposite, as in Jane Austen's famous opening sentence of Pride and Prejudice: It is a truth universally acknowledged that a single man in possession of a good fortune, must be in want of a wife.

JUXTAPOSITION: putting two things side by side in order to show a relationship between them.

METAPHOR: a comparison that says one thing is another thing, rather than saying one thing is like another, as in: She was a rose of fairest hue.

METRE: a regular rhythm in verse.

NARRATIVE: a story. It can be a novel, short story, poem or simply spoken.

NARRATOR: someone who tells a story.

NOVEL: a long fiction story in prose.

ONOMATOPOEIA: a word which shows its meaning through its sound, as in 'plop'. We sometimes say the sound echoes the sense.

PERSONIFICATION:writing of things or ideas as if they were persons, e.g. Old Father Time.

PROSE: any piece of continuous writing that is not verse or dialogue.

QUATRAIN: four lines of verse.

RHYME: words which have the same sounds, except for the first consonant, as in 'hot' and 'pot', placed at the end of the lines in poetry, or sometimes at fixed points in the middle.

RHYTHM: the movement of language in speech, verse or prose. It does not have to have a regular beat.

SIMILE: a comparison which uses like or as, as in: 'My love is like a red, red rose'.

SOLILOQUY: a speech in a play which represents the character thinking. It is usually spoken when the character is alone on stage.

SONNET: a poem of fourteen lines, rhyming in a particular way (see Ch.6).

STANZA: the correct term for the groups of lines a poem is divided into, often mistakenly called a verse.

SYMBOL: a thing which stands for something else. A flag stands for a country and is a symbol that everyone recognizes. Writers invent their own symbols.

THEME: the central idea of a piece of writing.

TRAGEDY: a play, or sometimes a novel or a poem, with an unhappy ending. It must be serious and it usually shows the sufferings of a good or great character whose life is spoiled by a weakness or by the workings of fate.

VERSE: the proper word for poetry.

EXAMINATION
REQUIREMENTS

GENERAL AIMS
SPECIFIC AIMS
ASSESSMENT
TYPES OF EXAM
    QUESTIONS
COURSEWORK
BOARDS:
    LEAG
    MEG
    NEA
    NI
    SEG
    WJEC
    IGCSE

GETTING STARTED

This book sets out to help you develop the skills you need as a candidate for GCSE English Literature. It will explain the concepts you need to understand and help you to study effectively the three areas of literature – poetry, drama and prose. It will also suggest how to write assessed coursework units and answer examination questions. No matter which Board's examination you are taking you will find every chapter relevant. You can turn to a particular chapter to help you with a specific problem; but if you work your way through the whole book, it will help you to answer all the required questions and to write the required coursework units.

AIMS OF GCSE IN ENGLISH LITERATURE

1 > GENERAL AIMS

The kind of *skills* which an English course should aim to develop have been agreed nationally. They are to enable candidates to:

➤ communicate accurately, appropriately and effectively;
➤ understand and respond imaginatively to what they hear, read and experience in a variety of media;
➤ enjoy and appreciate the reading of literature;
➤ understand themselves and others.

These are the *general* aims. In your English Literature course you will pursue these aims by studying the three areas of literature – poetry, drama and prose. (Prose is any piece of continuous writing, like a novel or a short story.) These areas of study are often called 'genre' and the books are called 'texts'.

2 > SPECIFIC AIMS

You will be expected to know the content of each text and show you have understood what you have read. You will also be expected to show an appreciation of the texts. This means being able to write about what is interesting in each text. In practice this means writing about the characters, the writer's ideas, and the way the book is written. Finally you will be expected to have your own views and feelings about the text.

Here is the way the examination boards set out these *more specific* aims. You will be expected to:

➤ acquire a firsthand knowledge of the content of literary texts;
➤ understand literary texts in ways which may range from a grasp of their surface meaning to a deeper awareness of their themes and attitudes;
➤ recognize and appreciate ways in which writers use language;
➤ recognize and appreciate other ways in which writers achieve their effects (e.g. structure, characterisation);
➤ communicate a sensitive and informed personal response to what is read.

These objectives are of equal importance and carry equal weight. Notice though how *three* of them are concerned with *appreciation and understanding* and only *one* with the *content* of literature. The key words in relation to *personal response* are 'sensitive and informed'. This means your opinion must be thought through and properly backed up by evidence from the text. The purpose of this book is to show you ways of developing an appreciation and understanding of literature so that you can then apply these skills to any book on any syllabus.

3 > ASSESSMENT

The examination takes the form of a written exam paper and/or a number of written coursework units. There is no oral exam for English Literature.

The percentage of marks awarded for coursework and examination varies from Board to Board. Some Boards have two or three schemes which allow for a greater or lesser stress to be placed on coursework. If you are studying at school or college, your Board and probably your syllabus will have been chosen for you. It is important you should know how many assessed coursework units will count towards your final grade and how much depends on the final exam. The requirements for each of the Boards is set out in Table 1. 1.

TABLE 1. 1

Contribution of Exam & Coursework to Final Mark					
Board	Exam	%	Length	Coursework %	No. of units
LEAG	1	50	2 hrs 15 mins	50	5
	2	—	—	100	10
MEG	1	60	2 hrs 15 mins	40	4–6
	2	60	2 hrs	40	4–6
	3	—	—	100	10
NEA	1	40	2 hrs	60	5
	2	—	—	100	10
N I		70	2 hrs 15 mins	30	3
SEG	1	45	75 & 90 mins	55	6
	2	—	—	100	10
WJEC	1	50	2 hrs 30 mins	50	5
IGCSE	1	100	3 hrs	—	—
	2	75	2 hrs 15 mins	25	4

There are provisions for **external** candidates who are not in full-time attendance at schools or colleges and are not able to comply with coursework requirements. Some Boards (e.g. MEG and NEA) have set papers for such candidates. If you are such a candidate you should write to the Boards for details of their papers and the places where you can sit their exams.

TYPES OF WRITTEN EXAMINATION

You also need to know what to expect when you get into the exam room. There are **two** types of paper:

➤ The **traditional** type of paper. Here you have to learn all you will need as you are not allowed to look at any books.
➤ The **open-book** or **plain-text** paper. Here you are allowed to take set books, unmarked with any notes, into the exam room. You can look at the set books when answering the questions.

Some Boards set open-book questions for one area (e.g. prose) but not for other areas. Table 1. 2 shows you which boards set open-book questions on which areas.

1 ▷ TYPES OF EXAM QUESTIONS

SET BOOKS

All the Boards, except LEAG, set a syllabus of a short list of books to be studied for the written exam. Some Boards set poetry, prose and drama books. Some set only two of the three genre for the written exam and examine the third through the coursework. Table 1.2 shows you which areas are covered by which method. Questions on set books take two forms:

(i) **Extracts**. A passage taken from the book will be followed by a number of short questions based on the passage. At least one of the questions will ask you to relate the quoted passage in some way to the rest of the book.
(ii) **Essays on plot, characters, etc**. The LEAG have a long list of suggested texts to choose from. Their questions are therefore very general in scope. These general essay questions can be applied to whichever books you have chosen to study.

TABLE 1. 2

TYPES OF ASSESSMENT														
Examining Board	LEAG		MEG			NEA		NI	SEG		WJEC	IGCSE		
Alternatives	A	B	A	B	C	A	B		A	B		1	2i	2ii
Coursework **Individual Texts:**														
Prose	✓			✓		✓			✓	✓	✓			
Drama	✓	✓		✓		✓			✓	✓	✓			
Poetry	✓			✓		✓			✓	✓	✓			
Wider reading:														
Prose	✓	✓	✓	✓	✓	✓	✓	✓	✓	✓	✓			✓
Drama	✓	✓	✓	✓	✓	✓	✓	✓	✓	✓	✓			✓
Poetry	✓	✓	✓	✓	✓	✓	✓	✓	✓	✓				✓
Unseen	✓		✓	✓	✓	✓	✓		✓					
Supervised Writing	✓	✓	✓	✓					✓	✓				
Extended essay	✓	✓	✓	✓	✓				✓	✓				
Written Exam **Set texts:**														
Prose		✓	✓	✓		✓			✓	✓	✓	✓	✓	✓
Drama			✓	✓		✓			✓	✓	✓	✓	✓	✓
Poetry			✓	✓					✓			✓	✓	✓
Unseen poetry		✓				✓	✓	✓			✓		✓	
Unseen prose								✓					✓	

UNSEENS

These are passages of poetry or prose which you have not seen before. Several boards set unseens. You are not expected to have any advance knowledge of the poem or prose passage printed on the exam paper. The questions, usually quite short ones, test your ability to respond by using the skills you have built up during the course. If no unseen question is set on the **exam paper** there is always a requirement for one in the **coursework**.

2 ⟩ COURSEWORK

COURSEWORK UNIT

A coursework unit is a piece of writing of between 400 and 600 words. Because there is no pressure of time, as in an exam, a high standard of presentation (grammar, spelling, punctuation and legibility) is looked for. Usually a unit is a continuous piece of writing, like an essay, but can sometimes be a set of short answer questions. It is not called an 'essay' because the opportunity is offered to do other kinds of writing if you wish. Chapter 2 shows you how to go about writing a coursework unit. Suggestions for the kind of work that can be done are made in the final section of each chapter of this book. The coursework units allow you to show your understanding and appreciation of works of literature without the burden of having to learn and remember all the details of a book. You are also expected to show your wider reading, so some of your coursework units should refer to more than one book.

EXTENDED ESSAY

Some Boards suggest that candidates may wish to do longer pieces of writing on one topic. This could then be considered the equivalent of two coursework units. (See Table 1.2 for the Boards that offer this choice.)

SUPERVISED WRITING

Some Boards insist that one or more units should be written in the classroom under the teacher's supervision. See Table 1.2.

UNSEENS

Some Boards insist that one (or two) units should be unseens, i.e. writing on unprepared material. This would also be written in the classroom under the teacher's supervision.

Every Board asks you to do a different number of questions of each kind. The requirements for each board are set out below. Read carefully the requirements of your Examination Board so that you understand exactly what coursework you have to produce and exactly what you will have to do in the exam.

REQUIREMENTS OF THE BOARDS

1 LONDON AND EAST ANGLIAN GROUP (LEAG)

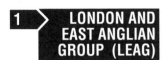

SCHEME 1

50% Written exam, 50% Coursework.

(a) Written Exam

You must answer 2 questions.

(i) Unseen poetry

(ii) Essay on novel or short stories from advisory book list. Choose 1 question from 7 provided.

(b) Coursework

5 units; 1 must be supervised.

(i) Drama – at least 2 units. You can study one or two plays.

(ii) Open Study – at least 2 units. Must show wider reading. You can choose poetry, prose or drama. Can be an extended essay (i. e. equivalent to 2 units).

SCHEME 2

100% Coursework – 10 units.

(a) Coursework

5 units, the same as (b) in Scheme 1.

(b) Coursework

5 units. 1 unit in each area must be a minimum of 500 words. Other units may be a number of shorter related pieces.

(i) Poetry – at least 2 units. 1 must be an unseen.

(ii) Prose – at least 2 units.

2 MIDLAND EXAMINING GROUP (MEG)

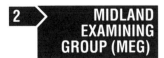

SCHEME 1

60% Written exam – open book, 40% Coursework.

(a) Written exam

You must answer questions on 3 set books.

(i) Choice of 4 questions on each set book; 2 are on extracts (not printed on the paper you so must have a copy of the book with you) 1 of your 3 answers must be on a passage.

(ii) In your 3 answers you must cover 2 of the 3 areas – poetry, drama, prose.

Dictionaries may be used.

(b) Coursework

4–6 units; 1 must be an unseen.

(i) You must not write on any set book studied for the written exam.

(ii) You must cover all three areas of poetry, drama and prose.

(iii) You may write an extended essay, counting for more than 1 unit.

SCHEME 2

60% Written exam, 40% Coursework

(a) Written exam

You must answer questions on 3 set books.

- (i) Choice of three questions on each set book. May be either general essays or based on extracts.
- (ii) In your 3 answers you must cover 2 of the areas – poetry, drama, prose.

Dictionaries may be used (***NOT TEXTS***: this is not an open-book exam).

(b) Coursework

The same as for Scheme 1.

SCHEME 3

100% Coursework – 10 units; 1 must be an unseen; 2 must be supervised writing.

- (i) 6 units must show detailed study of individual books.
- (ii) At least 3 books must be studied.
- (iii) At least 2 of the areas – poetry, drama, prose – must be covered.
- (iv) 4 units must show wider reading (at least 3 more texts). All 3 areas must be covered.
- (v) You may write extended essays, counting as more than 1 unit.

3 NORTHERN EXAMINING ASSOCIATION (NEA)

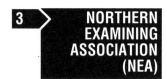

SCHEME 1

40% Written exam, 60% Coursework.

(a) Written exam

You must answer 2 questions.

- (i) Choice of 2 questions on each set book. May be either general essays or based on extracts.
- (ii) You must answer one question on drama and one on prose.

(b) Coursework

5 units. 1 must be an unseen

- (i) Poetry – 2 units must be on poetry. 8-10 poems must be studied in detail. These poems should be by one poet, or based round a theme, or a selection of a type of poem e. g. narrative poems or a recognized selection
- (ii) Wider reading – 2 units must show wider reading in poetry, prose and drama so one of these units must deal with texts from 2 areas. You must not write on texts studied either for the written exam or for the coursework units on poetry.

SCHEME 2

100% Coursework – 10 units. 1 must be an unseen.

- (i) At least 3 texts, including poetry, drama and prose must be studied in detail.
- (ii) You must write at least 6 units on texts studied in detail.
- (iii) At least 3 units must show wider reading in all three areas – poetry, drama and prose.

4 NORTHERN IRELAND SCHOOLS EXAMINATION COUNCIL (NI)

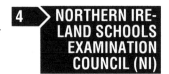

70% Written exam, 30% Coursework.

(a) Written Exam

You must answer 3 questions. Poetry ***ONLY*** is open book.

- (i) Unseen poetry or prose – compulsory question
- (ii) Prose – choice of 2 questions on each set book. May be either general essay or based on extracts. You may answer 1 question.
- (iii) Drama – choice of 2 questions on each set book. May be either general essay or based on extracts. You may answer 1 question.
- (iv) Poetry – open book. Choice of 5 general essay questions. You may answer 1 question.

(b) Coursework

3 units. Total length about 1500 words. You must show wider reading in all areas – poetry, drama, prose. The 3 units should be linked by a theme.

5   SOUTHERN EXAMINING GROUP (SEG)

SCHEME 1

45% Written exam, 55% Coursework

(a) Written Exam

2 Papers.

> *Paper 1* – You must answer 2 questions.
>
> (i)   Prose. – Choice of 2 questions on each set book. One general essay and one based on an extract. You must answer 1 question from this section.
>
> (ii)   Drama – Choice of 2 questions on each set play. One general essay and one based on an extract. You must answer one question from this section.
>
> *Paper 2* – 2 compulsory unseens: 1 passage of prose and 1 of poetry.

(b) Coursework

6 units; 2 must be supervised writing.

> (i)   Poetry – 2 units must be on poetry.
>
> (ii)   Prose and Drama – at least 1 unit must be on drama and one on prose. You must write on at least 4 books. These may or may not be taken from the list of set books.
>
> (iii)   You must write 4 units on texts studied in detail.
>
> (iv)   You must write 2 units to show wider reading

SCHEME 2

100% Coursework – 10 units; 2 must be supervised, 1 an unseen.

> (i)   You must write 6 units on texts studied in detail, 2 on poetry. 2 on prose, 2 on drama.
>
> (ii)   Remaining units must show evidence of wider reading. You must cover all 3 areas – poetry, prose, drama.
>
> (iii)   You may write an extended essay, counting as 2 units.

6   WELSH JOINT EDUCATION COMMITTEE (WJEC)

50% Written exam, 50% Coursework

(a) Written Exam

You must answer 3 questions.

> (i)   Poetry: 1 compulsory unseen
>
> (ii)   Drama: 1 question from a choice of 2 on each set book.
>
> (iii)   Prose: 1 question from a choice of 2 on each set play

(b) Coursework

5 units.

> (i)   2 units must be on poetry
>
> (ii)   2 units must show wider reading of prose and drama

7   INTERNATIONAL GCSE: CAMBRIDGE LOCAL

LITERATURE 1

100% Written exam

(a) Paper 1

Core Curriculum (for Grades C – G only) You must answer 4 questions.

> (i)   You must answer 3 questions on set books. 1 must be on drama and 1 must be on prose.
>
> (ii)   You must answer 1 question based on an extract from a set book. This can be on either drama or prose

(b) Paper 2

Extended Curriculum (for Grades A – E only) You must answer 3 questions.

> (i)   You must answer question 1 based on an extract from the set book of poetry.

(ii) You must answer 1 question on drama and 1 on prose. The questions are based on extracts from the set books.

(c) Paper 3

For both Core and Extended Curricula. You must answer 1 question. There is a choice of 5 essay questions, each one on a set book. Core curriculum students must not answer the question on the poetry set book.

LITERATURE 2
Scheme 1

100% Written Exam – Paper 1: English texts; Paper 2: French texts; Paper 3: Spanish texts.

(a) Paper 1, 2 or 3. You must answer 3 questions.
  (i) You must answer 1 question on prose, 1 on poetry and 1 on drama.
  (ii) Choice of 3 questions on each set text, 2 general essays and 1 based on an extract. At least 1 of your answers must be on an extract-based question.

(b) Paper 2. 1 unseen. The passage set may be either poetry or prose.

Scheme 2

75% Written Exam, 25% Coursework

(a) *Written Exam*: Paper 1, 2 or 3 as in Scheme 1.

(b) *Coursework*: 4 units.
  (i) The units must show wider reading in all 3 areas – poetry, drama, prose.
  (ii) You must not write on any of the set books you have studied for the written exam.
  (iii) You may write units in your own language.

G   R   A   D   E   S

These grades apply to all boards. Your final grade will depend on your overall performance throughout the exam. Above-average work in one area can compensate for below-average work in another. The grades range from A to G. Very detailed criteria have been laid down to determine the level of skill required for each grade.

Each grade requires a slightly higher *level of competence*. For Grade G you have to show you have understood the text. For instance for a novel you would have to be able to write about the story and the characters and say what the book meant to you. For Grades F – C you have to be 'competent' at writing about the book. For Grade B you have to show a 'high level of competence'. For Grade A you have to show 'expertise'.

There is also a gradual progression in the *range of skills* expected as you move to the higher grades. As well being able to write about story and character you have to be able to write about themes, language and structure. You have to be able to illustrate your points with details from the text. Finally, for Grades A and B you have to be able to 'evaluate' what you have read. This means forming a sound judgement on what the book is about and the way it is written. The details of the criteria for the grades are set out below for you to see but do not worry too much about the fine print of what is required at each grade. This is a much bigger problem for the examiner than it is for you.

GRADE G

You will have to show
➤ an understanding of the basic events in the text;
➤ a recognition of the broad features of characters involved;.
➤ a personal view or response to texts you have studied.

GRADE F

You will have to show you are competent at

➤ giving a straightforward account of the content of literary texts in terms of narrative and situation;

➤ understanding the surface meaning of texts;

➤ recognising obvious differences in the way authors write;

➤ recognising other obvious aspects of the texts studied, such as characterisation;

➤ communicating a straightforward response to the texts.

GRADE E

You will have to show you are competent at

➤ giving a broad account of the content of literary texts with reference to narrative and situation;

➤ understanding the surface meaning of texts with some awareness of themes and attitudes;

➤ recognising some of the basic features of the way authors write;

➤ recognising important aspects of texts such as characterisation;

➤ communicating a basic personal response to the texts studied.

GRADE D

You will have to show you are competent at

➤ giving an account of the content of literary texts with some reference to narrative and situation;

➤ understanding literary texts in a way that shows a basic recognition of themes and attitudes;

➤ recognising some of the significant ways in which writers have used language in the texts studied;

➤ recognising some other aspects of texts used by authors to present ideas;

➤ communicating a personal response which shows that some significant points have been considered.

GRADE C

You will have to show you are competent at

➤ giving an account of the content of literary texts, with detailed reference, where appropriate, to narrative and situation;

➤ understanding literary texts at a deeper level and showing some awareness of their themes, implications and attitudes;

➤ recognising and appreciating specific ways in which the writers have used language in the texts studied;

➤ recognising and appreciating the significance of other ways (e.g. structure, characterisation) in which the writers studied have achieved their effects;

➤ communicating an informed personal response to the texts studied.

GRADE B

You will have to show a *high level of competence* in

➤ giving an account of the content of literary texts, with appropriate reference to narrative and situation, supported by quotation;

➤ understanding literary texts at a range of levels showing some emphasis on interpretation and evaluation with a recognition of themes and attitudes;

➤ recognising and appreciating, to a considerable degree, the ways in which writers have used language in the texts studied;

➤ recognising and appreciating other significant ways (e.g. structure, characterisation, imagery) in which the writers studied have achieved their effects;

➤ communicating a well considered personal response to the texts studied.

GRADE A

You will have to demonstrate *expertise* in

➤ giving an account in appropriate detail of the content of literary texts, with well chosen reference to narrative and situation, properly supported by quotation;

➤ understanding literary texts at a range of levels with due emphasis in interpretation and evaluation and a thoughtful recognition of both themes and attitudes;

➤ recognising, appreciating and evaluating the ways in which writers have used language in the texts studied.

➤ recognising, appreciating and evaluating other significant ways (e.g. structure, characterisation, imagery) in which the writers studied have achieved their effects;

➤ communicating a considered and reflective personal response to the texts studied.

You should also note that you can only achieve a high grade if the books you choose to write on in your coursework units are of the same level of difficulty as the set books. If you are not sure whether a book is of a suitable standard you should ask your teacher or lecturer. All the texts mentioned in this book are of the same level of difficulty as the set books.

CHAPTER 2

COURSEWORK & EXAMINATION TECHNIQUES

READING WELL

PERSONAL RESPONSE

MAKING NOTES

ESSAYS

SHORT QUESTIONS

OTHER KINDS OF WRITING

UNSEENS

PREPARATION

TYPES OF QUESTION

OPEN-BOOK EXAMS

IN THE EXAM

GETTING STARTED

English Literature is not a subject that depends on learning a particular set of facts. One of the good aspects of GCSE is that it clearly recognises this, so that the amount you have to *memorize* is cut to a minimum. If you are being assessed entirely by coursework it is cut out altogether. Lucky you! Instead you are asked to *demonstrate various skills* and to show you have *understood and appreciated* the literature you have read. *You* – not the teacher. To do this you need to read attentively and write effectively about what you have read.

P R E L I M I N A R I E S

1 > READING WELL

We read all the time. We learnt how to do this when we were six. Nothing to it! However, reading literature is vastly different from the sort of reading for information that we do most of the time. Literature uses words at full stretch and *every single one* has to be attended to. It's no good 'skipping', that is reading to get the gist, or general meaning, and being happy to miss chunks out. You have to read *all* the book, carefully, to the end.

Develop good reading habits from the beginning. First of all turn off the radio, television or stereo. People who claim to work better with them on have never found out what real concentration is and do not realize what they could do if they tried it. Read with a pen and notebook at your side and a dictionary handy. There are bound to be words you do not understand and have to look up. If you do not want to interrupt yourself jot the word down and look it up at the end of the chapter, scene or poem. Do not put it off and forget.

Everybody has their own reading speed but you must be careful not to read too fast. Gobbling a book leads to indigestion. By all means read the book quickly through to the end if you wish – but if you do this you will have to go back and read it again more thoroughly.

Pause at the end of a chapter or scene to let it sink in. Think about what you have read. If it raises questions in your mind jot them down too. If you are studying the book in class, raise the questions with your teacher and discuss them with your friends. The more people there are contributing thoughts and queries on a work, the more everybody will get out of it.

If you find your mind wandering, have a rest. Maybe you are not used to reading for long stretches of time, if so do not try to. Read for 20 minutes with real attention and then stop. Do something different. Come back to the book later and do another concentrated stint. You will soon find you can concentrate for longer.

When you have read to the end, re-read – but not immediately. Plan to have enough time to leave a gap between one reading and the next. Literature matures in the mind, like wine in a cellar. The second tasting is better when you have left it for a while.

Poetry, in particular, needs careful reading in the first place, and many re-readings. Do not always expect to understand it straightaway. A lot of poetry is concentrated stuff. That is its point.

2 > PERSONAL RESPONSE

One of the main things the examiners are looking for is *your personal response* to literature. This can be learned from nobody and it is the reason why *your own* careful reading and questioning of the text is so important. What you can learn are various ways of looking at a text; and techniques and vocabulary to use when writing. This book will help you with both those aspects, but in the end what matters is what happens as the book passes through *your* mind. It is this that produces your own personal reaction and enables you to write about the book satisfactorily.

A word of warning, though, 'personal response' does not mean writing, 'I like this book very much because it reminds me of the great time I had when I went. . .' The thoughts and feelings about a book must be yours, but they must also be *disciplined*. That means they must be based on the *text* and not on personal experiences. There are topics you will be expected to cover, like character, theme and language. No one, however, can tell you what *you* feel about the text. The only requirement is that you must be able to defend your opinions with *evidence* from the text. For instance, you cannot claim that you feel a character is a liar and a cheat if there is nothing in the text to suggest it.

3 > MAKING NOTES

Whether you are preparing for an exam or studying a text in detail in order to write a coursework unit you will need to *make notes*. These should be *sufficient*, *but brief.* Do not let yourself get bogged down in wads of paper. Some people's notes are as long as a book in themselves and take ages to read through. You are better off spending your reading time actually reading the text itself and spending your writing time actually writing essays. It is also a good idea just to sit and think about what you have read. However some notes are necessary to record the work you have done and to allow you to organize your thoughts.

At the end of each scene of a play, or chapter of a novel, make a very brief *summary* of the plot. A few sentences will usually do. This will help keep the important events and the proper sequence in your mind and can be referred to quickly when writing essays. When you read a poem summarize the content in the same way.

Other notes are even more important. The chapter titles of this book show you the kinds of notes you should be making.

For a poem you should make notes under the headings *diction and imagery, figurative language, rhyme, rhythm and sound* and *overall effect*.

For a play you should make notes under the headings *staging, conventions, character, plot, theme* and *language*.

For a novel or short story you should make notes under the headings *narrative, plot, character, setting, theme* and *language*.

Not all these aspects will be equally important in every poem, scene or chapter, but if you get into the habit of *listing* these headings and asking yourself questions about these areas you should have a useful set of points at the end. These notes will then help you to write your coursework or do your revision. The chapters in this book will tell you the kind of questions that are useful to ask, in the section headed 'Essential Principles'.

C O U R S E W O R K

All the Boards ask you to produce a folder of *coursework*. The number of units you have to write will depend on your syllabus. A unit is a piece of writing of about 500 words, that is about two sides of A4 in ordinary handwriting. You will have to cover poetry, drama and prose. You may have to do an unseen. Some texts you will have to look at closely. Others will not need to be considered in so much detail. This is to give you the chance to read more widely. Chapter 1 told you precisely what coursework is required by each Board. The following pages tell you exactly what is meant by these requirements and the sort of work you will be expected to produce.

 1 ⟩ ESSAYS   You will probably be given *essays* to write about the books you are studying in class. For example, suppose you have been discussing characters and then you are given the essay title:

Sheila alters a great deal during the course of the novel. What are these changes and what causes them? Do you feel sympathetic towards her?

Your work on the essay will have three stages:
➤ Preparation
➤ Writing
➤ Revision

If you have made notes on Sheila as you read each chapter you will have a *record* of the changes in her character and feelings and when they happened. Take out this information from the notes you made on character and plot. (If you did not make notes as you went along you will have to go back through the book and make them now.) This gives you the material to write on the first part of the question – 'What are these changes and what causes them?' Since this question is about *change* you have to begin with what the character is like to start with. Your first notes on the character should tell you this.

Make a *list* beginning with what Sheila is like in the opening chapter. Then note the major changes and the events of the novel which show them taking place. For example:

(i)   Sheila is selfish, rude and spoilt. Party at Manor. Presents.
(ii) Cannot accept difference when Father leaves. Lies to Elizabeth and Miss P. Taunts Anne.
(iii) Becomes very lonely; feels friendless. Outing to Port Merillon.
(iv) Realizes mistakes but unable to change. Meeting with Peter. Works alone.
(v)   Success makes her realize her own worth; becomes more relaxed but still cautious with others. Work with Mr. Gulliver.

Now look at the second part of the question. It asks if you feel 'sympathetic' towards Sheila. This does not mean whether you pity her but whether you are able to understand what she feels and share that feeling. You have to decide what you think about Sheila. Alongside your first list jot down your response to Sheila at each stage of her development. For instance:

(i)   Author presents Sheila in a very bad light. I feel no sympathy.
(ii) Her reactions are understandable but so extreme that the other characters seem right to despise her.
(iii) The author makes me feel that she deserves to be isolated because of her behaviour.
(iv) I begin to understand why she reacts in the way she does.
(v)   Finally I understand her attitude and sympathize with her difficulties. I feel she has become a different and more likeable person and will eventually develop good relationships with others.

It will be difficult to answer this if you have no strong reactions to the character. Try not to get into the position of having to write about something you have no particular response to. Ask for an alternative title. Or go and discuss it with someone. Ask them what they think and decide whether you agree. Your own opinion may emerge as you talk. If you disagree, argue your point.

Now you are ready to *write*. Your *opening paragraph* should make a general statement on how Sheila changes.

Then you should work down your list using the *events* of the novel to illustrate what you see as the *changes* in the character. You should not just tell the story – that is not what the question asked you to do. You have to *select* events that show how Sheila has changed. Do not forget that you are writing about a character invented by an author and not a real person. So mention the author from time to time. You can say 'The author shows how Sheila suffers when her father goes away', or 'Elizabeth Green depicts Sheila as a proud and deceitful girl, who is humbled by experience'. Remarks like this show you are aware of the book as a piece of literature.

Include your *own reactions* as you go along. This is better than lumping them together at the end and you will find more to say. Try not to keep repeating the words of the question, as in, 'I feel sympathetic because. . . ' This becomes irritating. Say what you feel and why. Always support your points by reference to the text itself.

For your *conclusion* give your general verdict on the character's behaviour.

Finally *revise* your work. Read it through carefully. Is it clear? Have you made your points about the character strongly? Have you included enough evidence? Look particularly at your opening. Sometimes the essay does not quite come out the way you expected because your thoughts develop as you go along. Then you will have to change the introduction to fit the essay you actually wrote, rather than the one you thought you were going to write.

This is the pattern you should adopt for all your writing. Plan, write, revise. No one can just sit down and write a good essay. They may say they can – but they cannot. The planning has gone on, even if it is only in their head. The more you do your planning on paper the easier and quicker it becomes. Writing, too, becomes easier the more you do.

Instead of an essay you may be set a number of **short questions** around a topic or about a text you have studied. For example:

   (i)   What are your first impressions of Dick?
   (ii) What kind of person is Judith?
   (iii) How and why do Judith's feelings about Dick change?
   (iv) Dick and Anderson are very different. What do you think about them both?
   (v)   What are your reactions to the end of the play?

   You may find this an easier assignment because you will not have to write so much for each question. Taken together your answers should add up to the usual coursework unit length of about 500 words. Look on each short question as a miniature essay question and go through the same stages: look through your notes and plan; write; revise.

One of the advantages of coursework is that you can do different kinds of writing from the traditional essay. If you have been to see a play you might decide to write a **review**. This gives you a chance to give your own opinions of the play but you must, of course, make sure that those opinions are supported by evidence. You should start by giving a brief account of the plot of the play. Then you can go on to discuss the actors' interpretation of the characters, the way the play was staged, including comments on the set, costume and lighting. Then briefly sum up your opinion of all you have seen with a general comment about the production. You could do the same for a play you have seen on television.

   A review of a novel you have read would follow the same pattern. In this case you should comment on the way the story is told, the background, the characters and your response to the author's ideas.

   A quite different approach would be to take a work **written in one form and change it into another.** For instance you could turn a chapter of a novel into a scene from a play, or a scene into a short story.

   When turning prose into drama you should keep the same characters and use any dialogue the author has written. You will need to add extra dialogue, in appropriate language, to convey thoughts and feelings which the author has described the characters as having. What cannot be put into dialogue has to be put in stage directions. Stage directions also need to include the setting of the scene. When turning a scene from a play into a short story the stage directions become description and you should write as though seeing it all in your imagination, describing the characters' actions as though happening before your eyes.

   Imaginative writing is not ruled out either, but it has to be firmly linked to the text you are studying. If you take characters from a play of a novel and write an extra scene or episode you must make it fit in with the original. You must show you understand the characters and not distort them completely. If you are really adventurous you could try writing in imitation of the author you are studying. It is not a good idea to write more than one or two assignments of this kind.

Everyone has to do at least one **unseen**, either as part of your coursework or in an exam. You are given a poem or a passage of prose which you have never seen before. You answer the questions on it, usually several short questions, without any preparation or instruction from the teacher. Clearly you will need plenty of practice to feel confident about doing this kind of question. Here is an example:

   Read the following poem carefully; then answer the questions that follow:

vigorous actions

noise

'If you'll give me a kiss and be my girl
Jump on my bike and we'll do a ton.
We'll *explode* from the city in a cloud of dust
And *roar* due west to the setting sun.

We'll *bounce* the days all over the beach
Pop them like seaweed and scatter ourselves
Careless as *kids with candyfloss*
Into the shapes of all the shells.

fun and childish pleasures

We'll go as giddy as *merry-go-rounds*
Bump with a *crash* like *dodgem cars*
{ Float in a basket of coloured balloons
Or jump in a rocket and whizz for Mars.

excitement

action

noise

If you love to *be blown* by a *roar of wind*
If you love to *twist and spin and twirl*
If you love to *crash on the shore* like waves
Then give me a kiss and be my girl. '

'I love to be blown by a roar of wind
But I love to *watch* the sea asleep
And breathe in salt and fresh-caught shrimps
As we *wind our way through snoring streets*.

quiet

I'll jive in a cellar till the band *drops dead*
But I want you to *sing* on your own guitar
For *no-one* but me and a *moonlight oak*
Then dive in the silent lake for a star.

} romantic pleasures

alone and private

I love to twist the night away
But I love to *hold you dark and still*.
I love your kick that drives us for miles
But I love the *view* from the top of a hill.

thoughtful

But if you give me the crashing waves
And *sing me the blues* of the sea as well
Then, whether there's candyfloss or not,
I'll give you a kiss and be your girl. '

(i)   In the first four verses (lines 1-16) the boy speaks. Read the lines carefully. Then note down all the things that the boy wants to enjoy with his girl-friend. (3 marks)
(ii) In the last four verses (lines 17-32) the girl replies to the boy. Read these lines carefully. Then note the **different** things the girl wants to enjoy if she agrees to be his girl. (4 marks)
(iii) How different are the boy and the girl as people? (5 marks)
(iv) What do you think about this poem? You may, if you wish, write about the effect on you of the way the boy and the girl speak to each other, any words or phrases you particularly enjoyed, the effect on you of the rhythm, rhyme and the shape of the poem. (8 marks) (WJEC)

I have made quite a mess on the paper, underlining and joining things up with lines. This is my way of picking out the points for each question and organizing them before I start to write. If this book was printed in colour you would see that I have used blue for the first four verses and red for the last four. This means all the material to answer question (i) is in blue and all the material for question (ii) is in red. You don't have to do it this way. You may develop quite a different method that suits you better. But you must find *some* way of picking out the relevant details to use in your answer.

The first question is simple – and a bit deceptive. You have to do more than just list what the boy says in the poem. Some of the things he says he wants to do cannot be taken literally. For instance, 'jump in a rocket and whizz for Mars'. You have to decide what is behind this and find a way of expressing what he is talking about. At other times he seems to be talking about things they might really do, like going on a merry-go-round, but when you read it carefully you see that he is not saying that. He is comparing himself and his girl-friend to these fairground things to show the fun they are going to have. I have collected the things he wants to enjoy into three groups: noise, activity, excitement. Having done that I would write this paragraph in answer to question (i):

The boy loves noise and vigorous activity. He wants to roar off out of the city on his motor-bike and feel the wind against them. He wants to dash around on the beach, tumble around on the sand and feel free, 'crash on the shore like waves'. He wants to forget about being grown-up and behave like a kid. He likes fun and excitement because he describes their day together as being like a fun-fair. He is prepared to do anything as long as it is exciting, 'jump in a rocket and whizz for Mars'.

This is the kind of process to go through with all the parts of the question. In question (ii) you must make sure that you write about the *different* things the girl likes:

The girl likes more gentle things like watching the sea when it is peaceful, going home at night through the quiet streets and looking at the view from the top of a hill. She wants sometimes to be alone with her boy friend because she talks of him singing to her alone and says she loves to hold him 'dark and still'. She likes romantic places like woods by moonlight and would like him to be romantic too: 'dive in the silent lake for a star'.

The things I underlined for questions (i) and (ii) also help to answer question (iii). The boy and girl are different because he likes noise and action and while she likes those things too, she also likes quieter and more private things. Therefore we can say that he seems to be a lively and energetic person. She is not dull, because she is prepared to join in with his activities, but she also has a calmer, more reflective side. Making these points would probably earn you 3 out of the 5 marks. To earn the final 2 you would have to indicate what in the poem shows you these things. We see that the boy is lively and energetic because his language is full of words of action: verbs such as 'jump', 'explode', 'bounce' and 'bump'. The girl's quieter nature is shown in words and phrases like 'watch', 'wind our way' and 'sing me the blues'.

The last question is probably the one that you will find most difficult. Whether you are doing an unseen in an exam or in the classroom, you will not have a great deal of time to look at the poem in detail. You should say whether you like the poem or not and *give a reason*. Then you should comment on some or all of the things suggested in the question. This would be my answer, but there are many other points to be made:

I like this poem because the language is simple and direct, like a boy and girl talking to each other. The rhymes are simple, too, like a ballad. The rhythm has a strong regular beat which gives an energy and drive which suits the subject and reflects the character of the boy. The poet uses several interesting metaphors. He compares the boy and the girl leaving the city on their bike to an explosion to convey the noise of the bike and the speed and energy. The holiday atmosphere is conveyed by comparing what they will do with their days to bouncing a ball. They can be frittered away in fun: 'Pop them like seaweed'. Both the boy's and the girl's desires are expressed through metaphors and similes. The boy compares the fun they will have to a fun-fair, to floating in a basket or whizzing off to Mars. Then he likens them both to the waves crashing on the beach. The girl compares whatever romantic, pretty thing he might do for her to diving into a lake to bring back a star.

When she speaks of candyfloss it becomes an image for all the silly frivolous things that are nice to have and to do but which she can do without.

The most important thing is to look at the poem as closely as you can and comment in detail on some lines and phrases. Chapters 3 and 4 will help you to choose words and phrases that are interesting and show you the kinds of things to say about them. Chapter 5 will tell you about rhyme and Chapter 6 about rhythm.

You will find many passages in this book to practise on. Almost every chapter has an exam question based on a poem or a passage from a book or a play. If you have not read the book from which they are taken, these passages will be unseens for you. The suggested answers are there to help you, but you should read them *only after* you have made your own attempt.

E X A M I N A T I O N S

1 > PREPARATION

You have read and re-read your books. You have made notes. So what is left to do? In the exam room the emphasis will be on *speed*. You will have little time to think, therefore you should do as much organising of your thoughts as you can *before* you get there.

Go over your notes carefully. Make a *list of possible questions* on each set book. There are exam questions at the end of each chapter in this book. Your teacher can give you others. If you are studying alone you can look in the local library for specimen papers, or you can write direct to your Examination Board. Do not just look at questions for your own set books. Questions on other books will show you other things that are likely to be asked. Adapt questions on other books to your own set books. Simply *doing* this makes you think about the works you have studied.

Work out the *answers* to a number of these questions. Take some as far as the planning stage. Write out others in full. Try to do a variety of different kinds of question. As you do this work it will become clear that some passages in your texts are particularly important because they keep cropping up in your answers. Go back to the texts and read these passages carefully.

You will be expected to be able to *quote from plays.* Compile a list of useful quotations to illustrate character, theme or language and memorize these. Quotations should only be one or two lines long.

To revise poems you should read through each one, in full, alongside your notes. You need to be able to *quote from poems* too. Choose quotations which show a particular point about the subject or the language of the poem and memorize them.

Finally you need to practise answering questions *in the time allowed*. This is usually 40 minutes for each question. When you have done all your other revision on a text, choose a question, make sure you will not be interrupted, set the alarm clock and write your answer. If you do this several times for different texts you will develop a feeling for the length of time a question takes and you will have far less trouble in the exam room. All this is hard work and, above all, takes time. Do not think you can skimp on the time and get a good grade. Do not be fooled by people who say they are not doing any revision. They probably are, in secret. Most of us have to work hard to get through exams.

2 > TYPES OF QUESTION

On the exam paper you should expect *three* types of question on the set books.
  (i)   The traditional essay.
  (ii) An extract, followed by short questions
  (iii) A structured question, often with a short extract.

THE TRADITIONAL ESSAY

For this you are given a title, which you then have to plan and write as you did for coursework. This may be a general title that could apply to a number of texts. For instance, 'Relationships between people are often difficult. Write about a book you have read where there is a difficult relationship and show how it develops'. You could write about an enormous variety of books under this title. Otherwise, instead of a general title, there will be a choice of titles of titles specifically on the set texts on your syllabus. There are usually two, sometimes three, on each text. For both kinds of title you will have to make a plan, as you did for coursework but, this time from memory, before you begin to write. Planning is vital so do not try to miss it out because you want to get on quickly. Read the question two or three times to make sure you realize what it is you are being asked to do. It is very easy in the stress of the exam to assume the question is asking one thing, when in fact the examiners want something slightly different. Many candidates fail to do themselves justice because they do not answer the question in front of them. So take your time. Read the question carefully. Think. Plan.

QUESTIONS ON AN EXTRACT

One of the two questions on each set text is often based on an extract from the text. You are asked to read a passage, either printed on the paper, or from the book itself, if it is an open book exam, and then answer a series of short questions. They will be questions like:

(a)   What do we learn from this passage about the characters involved?

_____ **(6 marks)**

(b)   Look at lines 37-39. What do they tell us about Peter's attitude?

_____ **(2 marks)**

(c)   How do you think the dramatist creates suspense in this scene?

_____ **(4 marks)**

(d)   Most of the other characters dislike Peter. What do you think of Peter's behaviour towards them throughout the play?

_____ **(8 marks)**

The first thing to do is read the passage carefully. Even if you recognize it immediately because you have done your revision well, you should still do this. Look at the number of marks for each short question. This shows you the amount of time you should spend on each. You do not want to write a page on a question that can only earn you two marks. Notice the last question which relates the passage to the rest of the play. There is always one like this – just in case you feel tempted to live off your wits and not read the whole play or novel. Each chapter of this book has a section on examination questions. You can practise answering this kind of question from the examples you will find in each chapter.

STRUCTURED QUESTIONS

These questions suggest some areas to be covered in your essay. For example:
Boxer is obviously very popular with the animals. How do you think he will be remembered by the animals? In your answer, you may wish to consider some or all of the following:
  Boxer's character;
  his actions;
  his attitude to the revolution;
  his relationships with the other animals.
  '"Alfred Simmonds, Horse Slaughterer and Glue Boiler, Willingdon. Dealer in Hides and Bone-Meal. Kennels Supplied." Do you not understand what that means? They are taking Boxer to the knacker's! A cry of horror burst from all the animals. At this moment the man on the box whipped up his horses and the van moved out of the yard at a smart trot. All the animals followed, crying out at the tops of their voices. Clover forced her way to the front. The van began to gather speed. Clover tried to stir her stout limbs to a gallop, and achieved a canter. 'Boxer!' she cried. 'Boxer! Boxer! Boxer!' And just at this moment, as though he had

heard the uproar outside, Boxer's face, with the white stripe down his nose, appeared at the small window at the back of the van. 'Boxer!' cried Clover in a terrible voice. 'Boxer! Get out! Get out quickly! They are taking you to your death!' (SEG)

In this case the passage is a way of jogging your memory and stimulating some thoughts about the subject of the essay. In effect, the form of the question has done some of your planning for you by suggesting topics to write about. Notice that you do not have to cover **all** the topics suggested, nor do you have to give them equal weight in your answer. But they do provide you with a very helpful outline to follow if you wish. You should write your answer as an essay. Each chapter of this book has a section on examination questions where you will find more examples of this type of question.

Unseens: As well as questions on the set books some exam boards set an unseen, either poetry, or prose, or both. Look back at the section on Coursework to see what these entail and how to approach them.

3 ⟩ OPEN-BOOK EXAMS

The difference between an open-book exam and a traditional exam is that you take a copy of your texts in with you. That copy has to be unmarked by any notes. It is there for you to refer to so that you can refresh your memory of passages you want to use as illustration. It also means that for the second type of question described above, the extract-based questions, the passage will not be printed on the exam paper. You will be asked instead to look it up in the text you have. Having the text there with you is comforting but not as useful as you might at first think. You can spend an awful lot of time looking through a text for a particular passage if you do not know precisely where to look. So you have to know your text just as thoroughly as for a traditional exam. One advantage is that you can look up quotations and so quote them accurately.

4 ⟩ IN THE EXAM

If you stay up late the night before the exam, or get up at crack of dawn to do some last minute revision, you will not be at your best during the exam itself. Try to arrive feeling relaxed and refreshed. Make sure you have everything you need with you: pens, dictionary if you are allowed one and texts if it is an open-book exam. Wear comfortable clothes.

When you are shown your place try to settle down and shut everything else out of your mind before you are told to start.

Look through the paper and find the questions on your set books. Read all these questions carefully and decide which ones you are going to answer.

Most important **do the right number of questions**. Read the directions carefully. In preparation get to know what your exam paper will look like by working through specimen papers or past papers. Every year candidates do badly because they do not finish the paper. Do not let yourself spend so long on one question you have not time to do the required number of questions. Good luck!

READING
TO
UNDERSTAND:
POETRY

DICTION
TONE
ASSOCIATIONS
AMBIGUITY
IMAGERY
RESPONSE

GETTING STARTED

Poetry is often considered to be the most difficult part of an English Literature course. It is felt by many people to be strange and alien. This is hardly surprising. Poetry is not part of our everyday experience nowadays, though it used to be. Ballads were once popular entertainment and right up to the present century poets were valued as storytellers. What is more, it is not always immediately clear what a poem is about; even when we understand all the words separately we may not understand the way the poet has put them together. The first requirement of the examiners is that you should be able to give an adequate account of the surface meaning of a poem. If even this is difficult, how can you hope to go beyond to the deeper meaning and develop the personal response that the examiners are looking for?

The first thing to accept is that if you cannot grasp a poem on first reading you should not give up in despair or dismiss it as rubbish. Poetry is the most intense and concentrated language there is. It yields up its meanings, its many meanings, slowly. We have to read and re-read and read again. You should try to begin by reading aloud and after that to hear the poem in your head as you read.

Secondly, reading poetry is, in a sense, a different skill from ordinary reading and so we have to learn to do it. You may wish to learn how for the purposes of the exam but you will discover that, like any skill, it will stay with you. The impressions made on us as we read are created by the kinds of words the poet uses. This chapter will help you to begin to read poetry with understanding by showing you some of the things you should be looking for.

ESSENTIAL PRINCIPLES

1 ▷ DICTION

The words which poets use, the vocabulary, is frequently called the ***diction***. The choice of diction gives a poem its character – elevated and lofty or colloquial and down to earth, serious or lighthearted.

A great deal of the mood of a poem comes from the impression we receive from the diction.

Poets writing in English have half a million words to call on. They may resurrect a long dead word if it suits them or on other occasions invent words and leave the reader to work out the meaning. Shakespeare was the greatest such inventor and many of his words have since passed into the English language. Do not assume a word is invented, though, until you have scoured the dictionary. Newly coined words, or the archaic ones dug up from past centuries, stand out because they are unusual. They surprise us, which is presumably why the poet went to the trouble of using them.

Here are two contrasting styles. One has very elevated formal diction, the other colloquial and conversational:

> *(i)* ***Avenge, O Lord, thy slaughtered saints, whose bones***
> ***Lie scattered on the alpine mountains cold.*** (John Milton)
> *(ii)* ***Lawd, Son, whut um go do with you?***
> ***You makes me so mad***
> ***I don't know whut to do!*** (Betty Gates)

The first poet has a different purpose from the second. Milton is addressing an all-powerful God. A poet could address God in the way that Betty Gates talks to her son in the second extract but we would then get a very different impression of the relationship between the poet and God.

One of the first things to note about a poem is the general effect of the diction. You should note all unusual words and ask yourself what their effect is.

> ❝ Do you have a good dictionary? Always have one near when you are reading or writing. ❞

2 ▷ TONE

Growing out of the poet's choice of diction is the **tone** of a poem. You may find it helpful to think of it as tone of voice or to imagine the poet speaking. The question to ask is 'What is the poet's attitude to the subject?'. This may change as the poem progresses, as the tone is not necessarily the same all the way through. Tone often changes from stanza to stanza and sometimes single lines have a marked tone of their own. Finding words for the tone demands careful distinctions. Can you briefly describe the tone of these lines?

> *I have had playmates, I have had companions*
> *In my childhood days, in my joyful schooldays*
> *All, all are gone, the old familiar faces.* (Charles Lamb)

'Regret for the past' would sum it up adequately. The tone of the next poem is also regretful but it is different:

> *A thousand years you said*
> *As our hearts melted.*
> *I look at the hand you held*
> *And the ache is hard to bear.* (Lady Heguri)

Here the regret is more painful and there is also a suggestion of resentment at betrayal. These distinctions are important.

When you study a poem hear it in your head. Try to decide what the poet's tone is, and if it changes during the course of the poem.

> ❝ Ask your teacher or local library if there are recordings available of the poems you are studying. ❞

3 ▷ ASSOCIATIONS

Poets choose their words with extreme care so we must look at them with equal care. Ordinarily we use words to convey information in a fairly straightforward way. But words are loaded. They communicate shades of meaning and feelings. Would you rather be described as 'skinny' or 'slim'? Words with more or less the same literal meanings carry senses which make us react differently. Some words seem naturally attractive because of their **associations**, some equally naturally unattractive. 'Golden' would be an example of the first, 'murky' an example of the second. Poets make use of this ability of words to prompt particular **reactions**: they choose words very deliberately for their associations and connotations. When the sun is described as blood-red we feel there is something dangerous or sinister about it because of the associations of blood. A sun that is as red as a poppy has more comfortable associations.

Here is a description of a dead lamb:
> ***I saw on the slant hill a putrid lamb,***
> ***Propped with daisies***. (Richard Eberhart)

The poet chooses 'putrid' because he wants to show the dead animal as unpleasant. He could have achieved a quite different effect by describing the lamb as though it were asleep. Why, though, does he decide to include 'daisies'? They are pretty, charming little flowers, often associated with children. The poet seems to be deliberately bringing together the prettiness and nursery rhyme associations of the daisies (and lambs) with the horrid associations of 'putrid'. It is the associations which make the lines more than just a statement about a lamb lying dead on a hillside because they affect your reactions to the words.

Try to be aware of the associations of words as you read and the reactions they provoke in you.

4 ⟩ AMBIGUITY

Double meanings, or **ambiguities**, abound in poetry because the poet tries to concentrate a great deal into a few words. It is one of the ways that poetry is made so rich and complex. When Robert Frost writes:
> ***And miles to go before I sleep***.

he means both that he has a long way to ride and that he has many more things to do before the end of his life.

You must always be on the look out for words which mean more than at first appears. On the other hand you do not need to look on the whole of poetry as a trap, with double meanings lurking everywhere.

5 ⟩ IMAGERY

This is one of the most frequently used terms in talking about poetry. Put simply it means using language to convey sense impressions. An **image** will do more than just state that we can see, hear, feel, smell or taste something. The poet will try to create the experience in our imagination. Wordsworth describes how, while he is rowing across a lake at night, he suddenly becomes aware of a huge cliff:
> ***the huge cliff***
> ***Rose up between me and the stars, and still,***
> ***With measured motion, like a living thing,***
> ***Strode after me.***

This immediately conjures up a picture of the rock towering over him and seeming to move with him. **Visual** imagery of this kind is very frequent in poetry.

But poets are concerned with all five senses so imagery can also be **aural**, to do with sound:
> ***Listen! you hear the grating roar***
> ***Of pebbles which the waves draw back, and fling,***
> ***At their return, up the high strand,*** (Matthew Arnold)

Here we are invited to imagine the sound of the pebbles which the poet creates with the words 'grating roar' before we are given a picture of the waves flinging them up the beach.

Imagery can be **tactile**, to do with touch:
> ***Against the rubber tongues of cows and the hoeing hands***
> ***of men***
> ***Thistles spike the summer air*** (Ted Hughes)

Calling the cows' tongues 'rubber' gives us a very strong impression of what the touch of the thistles against them would be like. The language is both visual and tactile because we can both see and feel the spike of the thistles.

Imagery can be to do with *smell*, as in this description of a fight between a knight and a mythical beast:

> *Therewith she spew'd out of her filthy maw*
> *A floud of poison horrible and black,*
> *Full of great lumps of flesh and gobbets raw,*
> *Which stunke so vildly, that it forst him slacke*
> *His grasping hold, and from her turne him backe.* (Edmund Spenser)

The poet says that the beast's vomit 'stunke so vildly'. But it is the associations of words like 'spew'd', 'filthy', and 'poison', together with the visual images of 'great lumps of flesh and gobbets raw', which turn our stomach in disgust.

Taste is notoriously difficult to describe and taste is probably the sense referred to least in poetry. Here is one example:

> *O, for a draught of vintage! that hath been*
> *Cool'd a long age in the deep delvèd earth,*
> *Tasting of Flora and the country green,* (Keats)

Perhaps only drinkers of Elderflower or Cowslip wine can really appreciate the flavour of Keats' vintage. More likely, he was not really expecting to create the sensation of taste but relying on the power of association with flowers and the countryside to produce an effect.

On many occasions poets will use imagery referring to *several senses* to express their meaning. Notice how in the following stanza the poet uses four of the five senses to evoke the purity and beauty of his lady:

> *Have you seen but a bright lily grow*
> *Before rude hands have touched it?*
> *Have you marked but the fall of snow*
> *Before the soil hath smutched it?*
> *Have you felt the wool of the beaver,*
> *Or swan's down ever?*
> *Or have smelt o' the bud o' the brier,*
> *Or the nard i' the fire?*
> *Or have tasted o' the bag of the bee?*
> *Oh so white, oh so soft, oh so sweet is she!* (Ben Jonson.)

Sometimes poets will deliberately *jumble the senses*. They may talk about sights in terms of sound, or touch in terms of taste. To speak of 'bitter sorrow' is to transfer taste sensations to an emotion. In these lines Elizabeth Barrett Browning uses a colour to describe a voice which she hears answering her:

> *'Guess now who holds thee?'– 'Death,' I said. But there,*
> *The silver answer rang,– 'Not Death, but Love. '*

Colour is quite frequently used like this. We often talk about feeling blue when we mean sad. It is not a great step from that to imagine the colour of the sound of trumpets – many of us might say red. This technique (called synaesthesia) is yet another way of intensifying expression and making it fresh and new.

Look at the kinds of images used in a poem. Which of the senses is the poet appealing to? When you have looked at individual images in a poem you should notice if any of them can be grouped together. Many poems have clusters of images of the same kind. There may be a contrast between two images or sets of images.

6 > RESPONSE

The examiners are looking for a *personal response* to poetry. This does not just mean asserting opinions – 'I think this is a good poem' is not going to get you very far. If you can say 'This is an interesting poem because . . . ' and then give some reasons for your reactions, that is far better. In theory it is just as valid to say 'I don't like this poem because. . . ', but in practice it is rather difficult to write well about negative responses.

The techniques mentioned in this chapter should begin to give you an idea of what to look for and what to base your opinions on. While you are reading a poem try to keep in mind the various attributes of poetry mentioned in this chapter. At the same time notice if the poem stirs in you any particular feelings or responses. If it does, try to decide which of the poet's words, phrases or ideas are responsible for the effect. If it does not, do not worry. We cannot feel things to order and it may be that studying the poem will awaken a response. At the very least, study will give you an appreciation of the poet's skill and provide you with material for your writing.

7 ▷ SUMMARY

➤ The poet's choice of diction gives the poem its character and tone.
➤ Meaning comes through associations as well as the literal meaning of words.
➤ Double meanings or ambiguities give poetry richness and complexity.
➤ Visual imagery creates pictures in the mind but imagery can appeal to all five senses.

ADDITIONAL EXAMPLES

Use the following examples as exercises to see if you have understood everything so far. Work through them and then read the Key at the end.

1. What can you say about the diction and tone of this stanza?

> *Fear no more the heat o' the sun,*
> *Nor the furious winter's rages;*
> *Thou thy worldly task hast done,*
> *Home art gone, and ta'en thy wages;*
> *Golden lads and girls all must*
> *As chimney-sweepers, come to dust*

2. Explain the ambiguity of this line:

> *He that is down needs fear no fall,*

❝What senses is the poet appealing to? What are the contrasts? ❞

3. What kinds of imagery are used here?

> *Fragrance of Life, Odor of Death*
> *All the while among*
> *the rubble even, and in*
> *the hospitals, among the wounded,*
> > *not only beneath*
> > *lofty clouds*
>
> > > *in temples*
> > > *by the shores of lotus-dreaming*
> > > *lakes*
>
> *a fragrance:*
> *flowers, incense, the earth-mist rising*
> *of mild daybreak in the delta – good smell*
> *of life.*
>
> *It's in America*
> *where no bombs ever*
> *have screamed down smashing*
> *the buildings, shredding people's bodies,*
> *tossing the fields of Kansas or Vermont or Maryland into the air*
> *to land wrong way up, a gash of earth guts...*

it's in America, everywhere, a faint seepage,
I smell death.

1. ***William Shakespeare.*** The diction is fairly simple, easy to understand and down to earth, but quite formal. Several words (o', thou, art) show that it was not written in this century. The tone is grave and calmly philosophical: he speaks of death as taking wages and going home, the end of life as completing a task. The phrase 'Golden lads and girls' is warm and affectionate.

2. ***John Bunyan.*** 'He that is down' could mean both physically down – on his knees, or in the gutter – or it could mean mentally or spiritually down, perhaps depressed or humble. Such a person need have no fear of falling down physically or from a mental height, whether of excitement or of pride. In the case of a word like 'down', which can have so many applications, we need the rest of the poem to show us which particular meaning, or meanings, the poet is thinking of. The next line of Bunyan's poem is 'He that is low, no pride', which shows us how to take the first line. Because the poem opens with the general word 'down' we think of all sorts of interpretations before the second line points us towards a specific one. This ambiguity gives a depth and richness to the lines.

3. ***Denise Levertov.*** A great many of the images in this poem are of war-smashed buildings and shredded bodies; the land devastated and in chaos. Most of these are visual images, though there is one sound image of bombs screaming. However, the poem is organized around two contrasting smells, which the poet equates with life and death, as the title tells us. The poet evokes the first, the fragrance of life, with strong images of the scent of flowers, particularly the lotus, incense and the smell of the damp earth rising in the morning mist. The second odour she evokes indirectly in 'a gash of earth guts'. This, too, is a visual image but the associations of the dreadful pungent smell of guts are strong, especially when she states, 'I smell death'. This is the smell that seems to be buried in America and is seeping out everywhere.

EXAM QUESTION

The following question is an unseen from an LEAG paper. You can use it as practice for an unseen (either the ones you may have to do in class or in the final exam). Unseens are explained in Ch. 2. The following is half of the poetry question on the paper. Since the whole question should take 40 minutes you should aim to do this part in 20 minutes, eventually. Writing takes practice so you probably will not be able to finish in time at first. Do not worry. You will get quicker as you do more questions.

Growing Pain – Vernon Scannell

The boy was barely five years old.
We sent him to the little school
And left him there to learn the names
Of flowers in jam jars on the sill
And learn to do as he was told.
He seemed quite happy there until
Three weeks afterwards, at night,
The darkness whimpered in his room.
I went upstairs, switched on his light,
And found him wide-awake, distraught,
Sheets mangled and his eiderdown
Untidy carpet on the floor.
I said, 'Why can't you sleep? A pain?'
He snuffled, gave a little moan,
And then he spoke a single word:

> **Are you hearing the poem in your head?**

> *'Jessica. ' The sound was blurred.*
> *'Jessica? What do you mean?'*
> *'A girl at school called Jessica,*
> *She hurts –' he touched himself between*
> *The heart and stomach '– she has been*
> *Aching here and I can see her'.*
> *Nothing I had read or heard*
> *Instructed me in what to do.*
> *I covered him and stroked his head.*
> *'The pain will go, in time,' I said.*

The Boy: Write about the boy. You may wish to consider the following:
- the problem that prevented him sleeping;
- the words or phrases used to convey to you his disturbed state of mind;
- why he is so upset.

The Parent: Write about the father. You may wish to consider:
- the father's attitude towards his son and towards school in the first part of the poem;
- his reaction to his son's problem;
- any change in his attitude caused by the experience.

The Poem: Write about the poem. You may wish to consider:
- any phrases lines or ideas which you feel are interesting;
- how the ones that you select have helped to convey the feeling of the poem or have helped you to understand what the poet is trying to explain;
- your views about the way the poet has expressed himself.

NOTES AND TUTOR'S ANSWER

 **NOTES**

Read these notes through, then write your own answer before reading the one below.

This question is set out very well because it directs you to the things that the examiners are expecting, and gives you a ready-made outline for your answer. They want you to write about the ideas, feelings and language of the poem and they have given you useful headings to start you thinking. In your writing they want you to show your personal reaction to the poem and have shown you how to do this by asking you to select interesting words, phrases and lines. Use what you have learnt in this chapter to help you make interesting choices.

1. Read through the poem, slowly, at least twice. If you are not in a position to read aloud try to hear the poem in your head.
2. Read through all the questions.
3. Go back over the poem and underline words and phrases relevant to each question. You may find it useful to jot notes in the margin.
4. Write your answer in three paragraphs, following the questions on the boy, the parent and the poem.

2 SUGGESTED ANSWER

The boy is prevented from sleeping by a bad dream. Jessica, a girl at school, has a pain and the thought of this is upsetting him. The first sign of his disturbed state is 'darkness whimpered' which conveys his distress and fear. We are told he is 'distraught' and the description of his bed:

> *Sheets mangled and his eiderdown*
> *Untidy carpet on the floor*

shows he has been tossing in his sleep. When he speaks he snuffles and moans as though he is almost crying.

The father was obviously apprehensive about his son starting school because he seemed so young to be left there. He seems worried that his son will now have to learn to accept the teacher's discipline and is relieved when the boy seems happy. He does not know what to do but tries to comfort the boy. He feels sad that the boy must learn to cope with painful experience and knows that, as he grows older he will become less sensitive and sympathetic to others.

The last line of the poem is interestingly ambiguous. It could be referring to Jessica's pain or to the boy's distress. Jessica may get better, or she may die. Either way the pain will go. If she dies the boy will have to come to terms with death. The boy's pain will go in time too – he will forget Jessica and later will become hardened to others' suffering. The poet has packed a great deal into this line, which is very poignant and sad. I find two images very striking, 'darkness whimpered' and the pictures of the rumpled bed. In the first the poet writes as if the darkness itself is making the sound rather than the boy. This creates the situation powerfully because it is exactly how it would seem to someone standing listening in the dark. It also evokes the anxiety of the listener by making the sound foreign and unrecognisable at first. In the second the word 'mangled' is very expressive. It is as though the boy has been fighting with the sheets, like an animal mangling the body of its prey. The eiderdown has fallen so far across the floor that it has become a carpet.

SUGGESTIONS FOR COURSEWORK

1. You can use the exam question as a model for writing about other poems.
2. Make a study of the kind of diction and imagery a poet uses in several poems. Use this material in a coursework unit where you write about these poems and your response to them.
3. Choose a theme and find poems on it written at different times, or in different places. Go back as many centuries as you can. Include in your comments on the poems whatever differences you can see in the kind of language used and the tone.

STUDENT'S ANSWER – EXAMINER'S COMMENT

Here is a general essay on the poetry of Wilfred Owen and Siegfried Sassoon.

Question

In what ways do Owen and Sassoon treat the ordinary soldier in their poetry?

"A good introduction, giving a brief and clear response to the question asked."

Wilfred Owen served in the War, like many of the young soldiers he wrote about. He later served as a company commander, and it is evident, through an extract of a letter he wrote to his mother that he cared for the soldiers:

> 'I came out in order to help these boys: directly, by leading them as well as an officer can: indirectly, by watching their sufferings that I may speak of them as well as a pleader can.'

He portrays this same attitude of care and responsibility towards the soldiers in his poetry. For example, in his poem, 'Dulce et Decorum Est', he writes with distress when he describes how he was helpless to aid a dying soldier:

"A good choice of poem to illustrate the point made in the introduction. Good quotations."

> 'In all my dreams, before my helpless sight,
> He plunges at me, guttering, choking, drowning.'

In the ensuing verse of this poem he speaks to the reader, warning him not to mislead soldiers - as many did - with false pretence of glory, because that means luring them to their death - a death filled with only terror. This verse shows Owen's concern for the soldiers. He speaks of them as:

> '.....children ardent for some desperate glory.'

This portrays his pity for those unsuspecting, innocent youths.

In his poetry, Owen is realistic, and many of his poems describe the horrific and terrifying lives the pitiful, and helpless soldiers led. None of his poems portray any happiness they experienced at war - implying there was none to be found. He writes in this way, to arouse sympathy for the soldiers, so, obviously he himself harboured great sympathy. In his poem, 'Anthem for Doomed Youth', he emphasizes their deprivation:

"Brings in a second poem, but too briefly to say anything effective."

> 'What passing bells for those who die as cattle?
> Only the Monstrous anger of the guns.'

In the poem, 'Exposure', he exposes the reality of their life: the child-like longings they felt for their homes, and the appalling conditions under which they suffered:

> 'Our brains ache, in the merciless iced east winds that knive us....'

The poem, 'The Sentry' also describes the terrible conditions, and even the suicidal thoughts of a soldier (probably one of many):

"The quotation does not illustrate the point about the terrible conditions. There are better ones available."

> 'And one who would have drowned himself for good'

So, overall, he paints a picture of horror, and presents it to the readers: portraying his great sympathy and feeling for those soldiers, who have surrendered their lives for what seemed to be a futile exercise. Through his poetry, he seems to pose the question, 'Why did it happen?' in the reader's mind, as he did in his poem, 'Exposure':

> 'What are we doing here?'

Siegfried Sassoon does not describe the devastating conditions and appalling lives the soldiers led in as much detail as Owen, although he does touch upon it in several of his poems. For example, in his poem, 'Aftermath', he writes:

"Good. Introduces the second poet and notes the difference between the two poets named in the question."

> 'Do you remember the rats, and the stench
> Of corpses, rotting in front of the front-line trench'

Sassoon portrays his sympathy in a different approach, by describing the soldier's feelings rather than the ......

"This essay continued to display a high standard of analysis and expression. The points made were, on the whole, well supported by apt quotations."

FIGURATIVE LANGUAGE

GETTING STARTED

Most questions on poetry ask you to make some comment on the poet's use of language. It is often the case that the way in which ideas are expressed in a poem is more important than the ideas themselves. This chapter and the next three will deal with different aspects of the language of poetry. If you work your way through all four chapters you should be equipped to deal with any question which asks for a comment on the poet's use of language. We begin with figurative language, or figures of speech, because without an understanding of this kind of language a great deal of poetry is a closed book to the reader. We have seen how poetry works through association and suggestion. Its purpose is not primarily to convey information but to suggest mood and atmosphere, pictures and impressions, attitude and emotion. Above all, perhaps, pleasure in itself. Because it has so much to do at once, much poetic language is highly concentrated and so sometimes puzzling at first. Many of the puzzles can be solved by understanding figurative language and why a poet uses it.

SIMILE
METAPHOR
PERSONIFICATION

ESSENTIAL PRINCIPLES

1 ▷ SIMILE

A simile is a comparison. We all know and use hundreds:

➤ She looked as white as a sheet.
➤ My feet are like blocks of ice.
➤ She was as cool as a cucumber.
➤ He's like a bear with a sore head.

The essential elements in a simile are the two things that are being compared, and a word or phrase which links them. In the above examples the link is 'as' or 'like'. It could also be 'seemed' or 'resembled' or a phrase like 'similar to'.

When we are telling others about something we have done we are often asked, 'What was it like?' In reply we may struggle to find a comparison that will convey the experience we want to describe. Sometimes a ready-made simile is usefully to hand. 'It was like an oven in there', we may say, to convey the heat of a room. When there is no off-the-peg comparison available we often resort to a general description like, 'It was awful', or 'Great!' No poet can duck out like that. Faced with the same need to convey experience the poet has to try to avoid old similes and invent something fresh and new that really brings the comparison and the experience alive. When Robert Burns wrote:

> *My love is like a red red rose,*

it probably did not seem the stale cliché that years of Valentine verses have made it. Even so, Robert Browning's comparison of a woman to a flower is more original and precise:

> *On her neck the small face buoyant, like a bell-flower on its bed.*

> **❝Don't confuse every use of the word 'as' with a simile; look for two things which are being compared.❞**

This is not to say the Browning is better than the Burns. They have different effects. Burns is simple and direct. Browning's picture of the little head carried on the slender neck like a flower on a stem in a garden bed is more complicated. Nevertheless he is still comparing a woman to a flower. Some similes present us with comparisons that only the poet could have thought of and we have to pause and consider the validity of:

> *There's a certain Slant of light,*
> *Winter Afternoons –*
> *That oppresses, like the Heft*
> *Of Cathedral tunes.*

Here Emily Dickenson is comparing two things which oppress her: the light on a winter afternoon and a tune like those played in church. The church tune has a heaviness ('Heft'); the winter light also strikes her as heavy. Both things weigh on her feelings in a way that is purely personal. The sense of heaviness that comes from the cathedral tune is probably more general and easily understood. She tries to communicate the despair that the slant of light on a winter afternoon brings to her soul by comparing the feeling that they both produce. This is a simile that we have to work at a little, but if we do so we add something of Emily Dickenson's experience to our own.

Look at the similes in the poems you are studying. Are they good and original? Do they make you see things in a new way?

2 ▷ METAPHOR

A Metaphor is also a comparison, but in this case the linking word is omitted so that the two things being compared become even more closely identified. Instead of saying 'the girl is like a flower', we say 'the girl *is* a flower'. This is much more forceful.

We find ourselves using metaphors in everyday situations when we want to express extremes. We might exclaim, 'I'm starving' or 'I'm dying for a drink'. We are really comparing the intensity of our hunger or thirst with that of a dying person. How many times have you heard the expression, 'at the end of the day'? This is a metaphor, and a very overworked one, which compares reaching a conclusion, or coming to the end of something, with the day ending.

Poets tend to use metaphors more than similes because they are more forceful and more concise. We understand them in the same way as similes. Look at the two parts of the comparison presented and ask what similarity the poet has seen there. Marianne Moore says:

the sea is a collector, quick to return that rapacious look

She does not explain why. We have to work out how the sea can be greedy and a collector. Perhaps because it takes lives. The poem is called 'A Grave' which would point to the same meaning. Titles often give clues to meaning.

Here is an effective use of quite common metaphors:

Old age should burn and rave at close of day

There are two metaphors here. The first compares the anger of the old with a fire, by using the word 'burn'. The second compares the end of life with the end of a day. The poet, Dylan Thomas, increases their effectiveness by coupling the two metaphors together and by using the word 'burn' alone. He doesn't add 'with anger' but leaves the reader to work out what old age should burn with. This leaves the meaning open. The burning might be with pride or hatred as well as anger. Or it might simply mean that the old should carry on living as strongly and intensely as ever, refusing to give in.

Metaphors are often contained in single words, as in Andrew Marvell's:

My vegetable love should grow

This is startling. In what way can his love for a woman be like a vegetable? Does he mean that love is like a seed: once planted it takes root and grows? Why not a weed then? A vegetable has to be cultivated. Perhaps his love is more like a cultivated plant than a weed; earthy but cultivated. This is the way we have to work towards the poet's meaning – by looking at all the possibilities that the comparison throws up and selecting those that are helpful in the context of the poem.

In the following poem Stevie Smith appears at first to be writing about a man who is literally drowning:

Nobody heard him, the dead man,
But still he lay moaning:
I was much further out than you thought
And not waving but drowning.

Poor chap, he always loved larking
And now he's dead
It must have been too cold for him his heart gave way
They said.

Oh, no no no, it was too cold always
(Still the dead one lay moaning)
I was much too far out all my life
And not waving but drowning.

But by the time we reach the end we realize that the whole poem has to be read metaphorically. When the poet writes 'I was much further out than you thought' she seems to be describing a man in the sea. When we come to, 'I was much too far out all my life', it is clear that the sea has become a metaphorical one – the sea of life, if you like. In the light of this we look back and find other metaphors which we took for literal statements: not the sea but the whole of life was 'too cold'; 'his heart gave way' not from coronary thrombosis but a spiritual heart failure – he lost the heart, the will, to go on. This makes the poem much more poignant.

I admire the skill with which Stevie Smith utilizes metaphor here, so that the poem has to be read on two different levels.

Once you become accustomed to reading in this unliteral way, much difficult poetry becomes easier. Even so do not expect everything to be made suddenly easy. Understanding metaphor may be a key, but the locks still have to be worked at.

Do the poets you are reading use metaphor a lot or a little? What kinds of comparisons do they make?

3 ▷ PERSONIFICATION

Personification is a particular kind of metaphor in which inanimate objects or abstract ideas are spoken of as if they are people. Death is often personified, and so is time. Often, but not always, they begin with a capital letter when they are personified. Ruth Fainlight personifies the future and speaks of it as a timid woman:

> *The future is timid and wayward*
> *and wants to be courted, will not*
> *respond to threats or coaxing,*
> *and hears excuses only*
> *when she feels secure.*

The poem goes on to picture this shy person, the future, frightened by aggression, lurking in a corner like a nun.

Keats uses personification in '*Ode to Melancholy*' to bring to life a number of abstractions. He speaks of Melancholy as 'she':

> *She dwells with Beauty – Beauty that must die,*
> *And Joy, whose hand is ever at his lips*
> *Bidding adieu; and aching Pleasure nigh,*
> *Turning to poison while the bee mouth sips:*
> *Ay, in the very temple of Delight,*
> *Veiled Melancholy has her sovran shrine,*

This method of personification allows Keats to create a series of images. By calling Melancholy 'she', and by saying she lives with Beauty he creates a nebulous sense of two goddess-like beings. The next line has a more specific image: Joy is seen as a man who seems to be forever caught in the act of kissing his fingers in a gesture of farewell. A little later Melancholy is pictured shrouded in a veil.

In Keats' famous '*Ode to Autumn*' the season is personified in a number of ways. The seasons are favourite subjects for personification, so are the months – May is often seen as a young girl, December as an old man. Wind, rain and the sun are frequently personified. Personification enables a poet to develop a character and a personality for any idea or object.

4 ▷ SUMMARY

➤ A simile is a comparison, using the words 'as' or 'like'.
➤ A metaphor is a comparison which does not use these words.
➤ Personification compares things to people.
➤ Poets use these comparisons to show the nature of their subject, often in ways we have not thought of before.

ADDITIONAL EXAMPLES

Identify the similes, metaphors and personifications in the following lines by writing down the two things that are being compared. Notice how the poet chooses unusual or out of the ordinary objects and try to explain why:

1. *Anger lay by me all night long,*
   His breath was hot upon my brow,
   He told me of my burning wrong,
   All night he talked and would not go.

2. *Ears like bombs and teeth like splinters,*
   A blitz of a boy was Timothy Winters.

3. *White poems*
   are daggers. guns. cops.
   piercing hearts in weird designs
   Black poems are beautiful

egyptian princesses.

4. *Day after day, day after day,*
   We stuck, nor breath nor motion,
   As idle as a painted ship
   Upon a painted ocean.

5. *Nothing is so beautiful as Spring –*
   When weeds in wheels shoot long and lovely and lush;
   Thrush's eggs look little low heavens, and thrush
   Through the echoing timber does so rinse and wring
   The ear, it strikes like lightnings to hear him sing

6. *Poppies in October*

   Even the sun clouds this morning cannot manage such skirts
   Nor the woman in the ambulance
   Whose red heart blooms through her coat so astoundingly –

1. Elizabeth Daryush personifies anger as a man who lies beside her all night talking to her of his grievances. By doing this she makes anger into something outside herself, a persistent presence over whom she has no control.

2. Charles Causeley's similes comparing Timothy Winters' ears to bombs and teeth to splinters are not visual images. It is not helpful to picture large black objects on the side of Timothy's head. Rather they give a general impression of the boy's untidiness and neglect. This is summed up in the metaphor 'a blitz of a boy'. This suggests two things. Firstly, Timothy himself looks as though a bomb has hit him. Secondly, his behaviour is so unrestrained that other people feel he is like a bomb about to go off. The whole stanza portrays someone in need of loving care.

3. Ahmed Alhamisi's first metaphor compares poems written by white people to three threatening things: daggers, guns and cops, to show how he feels threatened and oppressed by white culture. He picks up the idea of daggers again when he speaks of 'piercing hearts'. That is, he extends the original metaphor and shows how the poems, like daggers, can hurt.

His second metaphor compares black poems to Egyptian princesses. By doing this he makes black poems seem exotic and rich and rare. Princesses have a high status so the comparison confers that same status on the poems. He makes the princesses Egyptian because he wants a connection with the African continent and Egypt is a part of Africa with a long and distinguished culture.

4. Coleridge's simile compares a becalmed ship to a painting. He suggests the absolute stillness of the ship and the sea. It seems that, as with a painting, there is no possibility of movement.

5. Gerard Manley Hopkins' first simile compares weeds, perhaps grasses, to wheels. They grow from a centre point and spread in a circle on the ground. Secondly he compares the blue of thrush's eggs to the blue of the sky. Both these are visual images which encourage us to picture the Spring but the next metaphor is an aural or sound image which suggests the sound of Spring. He compares the thrush's song to something which rinses out and wrings the ear. This makes the song very pure and clear. The simile comparing the effect on the ear to lightning adds force and directness to the purity.

6. Sylvia Plath's title is important because without it we would not know she was talking figurative about poppies. The first line is complicated by a double metaphor. She sees the red petals of the poppy as skirts. The red swirling clouds of the sunrise also remind her of skirts. But the red of the sunrise is not so vivid as the poppies. The next lines are very unexpected. What is the connection between poppies and the woman in the ambulance? And why does it seem that we can see her heart through her coat? The connection is in the phrase 'red heart blooms'. We take 'red' to be the colour of blood and therefore of life. Despite being in the ambulance the woman is full of life, she is blooming. So much so that we can imagine her heart beating. Even so, she is not so vibrantly alive as the poppies. 'Blooms' is the meta-

phorical word. If the poet had used 'beats' the connection with the poppies would have been lost.

EXAM QUESTIONS

Whether you are answering an exam question on an unseen poem or on a set text, you will very frequently have to comment on figurative language, usually as one part of a question. Examiners have always complained that candidates answer this sort of question badly. Because it is recognized as difficult you can earn high marks with a good answer.

Questions on language can be phrased in various ways. Here are some examples.

1. Comment on any use of language or other poetic qualities that you find interesting.
2. Write about the poem. You may wish to consider the following:
   any phrases, lines or ideas which you feel are interesting;
   how the ones that you select have helped to convey the feeling of the poem or have helped you to understand what the poet is trying to explain;
3. Comment on the effectiveness of the language used.

All these questions are basically the same and can be asked about any poem. Choose one and apply it to the following poem:

If you have not read this poem before, use it as a practice for an unseen.

The Jaguar

The apes yawn and adore their fleas in the sun.
The parrots shriek as if they were on fire, or strut
Like cheap tarts to attract the stroller with the nut.
Fatigued with indolence, tiger and lion

Lie still in the sun. The boa constrictor's coil
Is a fossil. Cage after cage seems empty, or
Stinks of sleepers from the breathing straw.
It might be painted on a nursery wall.

Are you hearing the poem in your head?

But who runs like the rest past these arrives
At a cage where the crowd stands, stares, mesmerized,
As a child at a dream, at a jaguar hurrying enraged
Through prison darkness after the drills of his eyes

On a short fierce fuse. Not in boredom –
The eye satisfied to be blind in fire,
By the bang of blood in the brain deaf the ear –
He spins from the bars, but there's no cage to him

More than to the visionary his cell:
His stride is wildernesses of freedom:
The world rolls under the long thrust of his heel.
Over the cage floor the horizons come.

NOTES AND TUTOR'S ANSWER TO QUESTION 3

1 > NOTES

Read these notes and then attempt your own answer to Question 3 before reading the answer below.

You would have 15 to 20 minutes to answer this part of a question in an exam but do not attempt to limit your time yet. Once you have had plenty of practice in answering questions you can start to practise answering to time. If you are writing a coursework unit then time does not matter.

1.   Underline words and phrases that you think are worthy of comment.

2.   Identify similes, metaphors and personification by a note in the margin. (S, M, or P will do, with a line drawn to the relevant phrase).

3.   Think back to what you learnt in Ch. 4 and underline anything else you think worthy of comment.

4.   Try to write something about everything you have underlined but do not simply say, 'This is a simile', 'This is a metaphor'. Instead use your knowledge of figures of speech to pick out interesting phrases to comment on. You will get marks for good choices. You will get more marks for being able to say what the effect of the poet's comparisons are.

5.   Do not worry if it does not come easily at first. Go back and reread the chapter, several times if necessary.

You will probably have underlined some or all of the following:

Similes – as if they were on fire, strut like cheap tarts, lie still as the sun, painted, as a child.

Metaphors – coil is a fossil, prison darkness, drills of his eyes, fuse, blind in fire, wildernesses of freedom, rolls.

Other Evocative Language – yawn, shriek, stroller with the nut, stinks of sleepers, breathing straw, enraged, bang of blood, spins, long thrust, horizons come.

In the first part of '*The Jaguar*' Ted Hughes creates a picture of the typical zoo. The atmosphere of languid afternoon is set at the beginning by the word 'yawn'. The apes are seen as so engrossed in their own fleas that they seem to adore them. A series of comparisons evokes images of the animals. The plumage of the parrots is so bright they look as though they have been set on fire, and their raucous call is like a shriek for help. Their awkward walk is compared to that of tarts soliciting for custom. The tiger and lion are, aptly, as 'still as the sun' because neither they nor the sun can be seen to move and, by associating them with the sun, Hughes reminds us of their natural habitat. The boa constrictor is so absolutely still, as it sleeps curled up in a coil, that it might have been turned to stone centuries ago. In an evocative phrase, 'breathing straw', Hughes reduces the animals to characterless heaps in the corners of empty cages where the only sign of life comes from the slight movement of the straw. The general effect of lifelessness is given by comparing the whole scene to a painting in a child's room.

The second part of the poem becomes more metaphorical to express the intensity of the jaguar's rage at being caged. To be kept in captivity is like being in perpetual darkness. His eyes become drills boring through the darkness as though through stone and the phrase 'short fierce fuse' suggests he will explode with rage. The strength of his passion to be free is also expressed in 'blind in fire' and 'the bang of blood in the brain'. He is not conscious of the crowds who come to stare at him like children because his eyes seem blinded by the desire to be free and the blood throbbing in his ears shuts out the noise of the zoo. 'Wildernesses of freedom' shows how he strides about his cage like an animal roaming freely but the word 'spins' depicts the ferocity with which he turns at the bars. The images of the last two lines convey the difference between the animal's actual imprisonment and his imagined freedom. By saying 'the world rolls' under his feet Hughes suggests the little exercise wheels given to small pet animals in cages but the jaguar can only behave as if his treadmill brings the horizons of his imagination closer.

If you managed to write as much as this in an exam you would be doing very well indeed. If you find yourself with more to say than you have time for, get down the main points and leave a space in case you have time to come back to the question when you have finished the paper. You should *never* leave yourself with too little time to do the required number of questions.

SUGGESTIONS FOR COURSEWORK

1. You should try to include writing on figurative language in one of your coursework units. The question and answer above can be used as a model for part of a unit. This answer is nearly as much as the amount you should try to write. Material on other aspects of the poem can be added when you have studied the chapters on rhyme and rhythm.
2. Make a study of the work of one poet. Look at the way he uses language in several poems.
3. Make a comparison of two or more poems on the same topic by different poets. Include comments on the different way they use figurative language.

STUDENT'S ANSWER – EXAMINER'S COMMENTS

Question
Comment on the language used in the poem 'Incendiary'.

Good. Notices and explains the metaphor comparing the fire to a tiger.

The poem creates a fierce, uncontrollable fire that refuses to be extinguished. A metaphor is used because the fire is a 'flame-fanged tiger'. The 'tiger' is an animal which refuses to be tamed. It seems very frightening because words like 'fierce' 'huge' 'hungry' 'brazen' 'frightening' and 'roaring' are used. It must also be very big because it has the ability to destroy 'Three thousand guinea's worth of property and crops at Godwins farm on Saturday'. The fire also gives the impression of being 'nasty' because it seems to 'set the sky on fire and choke the stars to heat' even though in reality this would not be at all possible but in the boys mind it would be and maybe this sentence is used to create an even larger inferno.

A good choice of words and phrases in giving an impression of the boy.

The small boy seems to be deprived of a normal home and family. He seems very frightened and unhealthy but with an air of determination about him and maybe even anger.
I think he is unhealthy and deprived because he has a face like 'pallid cheese' and 'burnt out little eyes' and he also has 'such skinny limbs'. He seems deprived because all he wants is one warm kiss but there is nobody to give it to him.

Here the essay goes beyond what was in the poem. There is no foundation for these opinions.

He has obviously been looking for such love and attention for a while. (Maybe this is why he starts the fire to get some attention.) He is frightened that he, such a small boy, could start such a large inferno. I suspect that he started the fire out of anger and revenge to the people who should have been giving him the love he so sought after. Maybe he is jealous at the people who live at Godwins farm for perhaps they have a very 'tight-knitted' family.

Good. Notices the repetition of the word 'frightening' and suggests a reason for it.

The poem repeats the word 'frightening' a number of times which gives the word more effect. The boy may have been not only frightened physically of the fire he started but maybe mentally of all the pent-up emotions. He must have been

66 **There is no evidence in the poem that the boy is an orphan.** 99

scared that, he, such a small young boy could have such rage, anger, jealousy and need for revenge. He may be frightened of the consequences, again physically and emotionally. Physically because if he is caught and taken to an orphanage (as I suspect he is an orphan) or the people who may have been hurt or killed. And mentally of all the guilt he will feel over such damage and destruction that may haunt him for the rest of his life.

I feel the word 'frightening' is not the strongest or most final feeling in the poem and feel that the boy's loneliness and deprivation is the most 'real' and stronger emotion. The fire is the 'reality' and action which brings the fire to a climax but the emotions of the boy are the final feelings and the most upsetting.

66 **Overall, good use of figurative language. However, this could have more closely related to what was <u>actually</u> in the poem.** 99

RHYME

GETTING STARTED

This chapter, like the following one, sets out to help you to appreciate an important technical aspect of poetry. Understanding rhyme will enable you to answer those questions in the exam which ask you to comment on the language and form of a poem. It will also provide you with interesting ways of looking at poetry which will be useful for your coursework.

Do not confuse rhyme with rhythm. Some people tend to mix them up, perhaps because of the spelling. Rhyme is two words which sound the same except for their first consonant, like 'meet' and 'feet'. Rhythm will be dealt with in the next chapter.

For several centuries far more poetry was written in rhyme than was not, so that poetry and rhyme were thought of as almost synonymous (meaning the same thing). But poetry does not have to rhyme and in this century many poets have chosen to write unrhymed verse. In fact, if your reading has been mainly of twentieth century poetry you may need to accustom yourself to rhymed verse so you can appreciate it properly.

We learn to use rhymes very early in life and most little children take a delight in rhyming, so that later on we may come to think of rhyme as 'childish', Of course it is not. We also hear rhyme used in other places, by advertisers for instance and in games and jingles. If your experience of rhyme is limited to such things then you might find it difficult to accept its use for more serious purposes. The remedy is to widen your experience. The following poem by William Blake has a lot in common with a jingle but is clearly profoundly serious.

> *My mother groan'd! My father wept*
> *Into the dangerous world I leapt:*
> *Helpless, naked, piping loud:*
> *Like a fiend hid in a cloud.*
>
> *Struggling in my father's hands,*
> *Striving 'gainst my swaddling bands,*
> *Bound and weary I thought best*
> *To sulk against my mother's breast.*

If at the end of the first stanza you are thinking of 'Twinkle Twinkle Little Star' that is because Blake's poem rhymes in the same way and has the same rhythm as the nursery rhyme. The poem is also about a baby. But nothing else about it is pretty or nurserylike. Read it through several times and pay attention to the harsh words the poet uses. They may make you feel quite uncomfortable about this particular baby. Look at a general collection and you will find more poems written in a simple style which nevertheless are very serious.

ESSENTIAL PRINCIPLES

1 ▷ THE PURPOSE OF RHYME

> ❝Note the spelling of rhyme. Many students spell this wrongly.❞

If you have ever tried to write to a rhyme scheme, particularly a complicated one, you will know how difficult it can become. Finding the word that fits the rhyme and the meaning often proves to be such a struggle that inexperienced or less skilful poets fail in the attempt. They cannot find a perfect rhyme, the meaning becomes twisted or lines have to be padded out with vague phrases. Even very good poets sometimes seem to have chosen a word because it fits the rhyme scheme and not because it really says what the poet means. The French poet Valery put it like this:

> *I seek a word*
> *A word which is feminine*
> *has two syllables*
> *contains 'p' or 'f'*
> *ends in a mute vowel*
> *is synonymous with the word 'brisure'*
> *which is not a learned or an unusual word.*
> *Six conditions at the very least.*

So if it is so difficult why do they do it? Why not simply choose to write unrhymed or free verse? Or, to put it another way, what is the purpose of rhyme?

STRUCTURE

Rhyme helps to give the poem *shape* and *pattern*. The human mind appreciates pattern. Perhaps you can even say we are genetically programmed to do so by the symmetry of our bodies. Certainly we quickly learn to respond to shape and pattern. Our lives follow a pattern of days and nights, of weeks, months and years. In all probability the room you are sitting in contains many patterns – on the walls or floor, in the arrangement of the furniture.

Rhyme appeals to this love of pattern. It gives a structure to the poet's thoughts and ideas by arranging them in lines and stanzas. After we have read the first stanza of a poem our ear knows what to expect. We read with the expectation of the rhymes coming again in the same places in the following stanzas. To have this expectation satisfied is pleasurable in itself. If the poet is using an odd or unusual rhyme scheme that may give an added pleasure.

Of course not all poets want this kind of structure to their verse. They may find it too rigid. They may want to sound more conversational.

PROMINENCE

When the reader is expecting a rhyming word it gives that word extra *prominence*. Because we are waiting for the rhyme to end the line, we notice it much more strongly. Rhyme also enables us to remember words much more easily. The poem can take advantage of the ability of rhyme to get words noticed by using them to carry important ideas. In some poems you can get a good idea of the meaning of a stanza just by looking at the rhymes, because the poet has used the rhymes so forcefully. It is as though the rhymes are a summary or a memory aid for the meaning of the whole line.

BRINGING TOGETHER

Because they sound the same, rhyming words are *brought together* as a pair. In the poem this pair of words may be separated by two or even more lines but we still hear them as a pair. The sound, which pairs them, also makes us think of their meanings together. Some rhyme pairs seem to go together very naturally, like defend/friend. We would defend a friend; someone who defends us would be a friend. Some rhyme pairs make a very strong contrast, like death/breath. Breath can be thought of as the essence of life; death is the absence of life and breath.

Hence the contrast. Poets sometimes use rhymes to introduce or emphasize points of association, comparison or contrast like these. Some have been used so often, like trees/breeze, that the connection seems very stale and adds little to the poem. Other rhyme pairs are original, and make us think carefully about the words and their meanings. Andrew Marvell, writing about a little girl in a garden, says:

> *And there with her fair aspect tames*
> *The wilder flowers, and gives them names.*
> (A Picture of Little T.C. in a Prospect of Flowers – Marvell)

This is an affectionate picture of a small child inventing her own names for the flowers. This is how she makes them familiar to herself or 'tames' them as the poet puts it. In fact, when we think about it, the comparison between taming and naming is valid in all sorts of ways. Once something has a name we feel safer and more at ease with it. But it is a connection we might not have thought about until the poet's rhyme drew our attention to it.

A rhyme pair might direct us to a meaning which is stated nowhere else in the poem. Here is a simple example from Thomas Hardy's **'The Darkling Thrush'**:

> *I leant upon a coppice gate,*
> *When frost was spectre-gray,*
> *And Winter's dregs made desolate,*
> *The weakening eye of day.*

The poem tells us that everything is covered with a gray frost. The rhyme gray/day adds to this. Without having to take the time actually to say so the poet tells us that the whole day has been gray. Because we associate the two words through sound, we also associate their meaning. Gray can mean 'sunless' or 'depressing'. We realize from the context of the poem that the day has been both.

HUMOUR

We must not forget that poets use rhymes for *fun*. Here Lord Byron is poking fun at a contemporary:

> *Shut up the bald coot bully Alexander,*
> *Ship off the holy three to Senegal,*
> *Teach them that sauce for goose is sauce for gander*
> *And ask them how they like to be in thrall.* (Don Juan – Byron)

We know that Byron is going to have a go at Alexander when he calls him a 'bald coot'. The rhyme adds to this humour because it seems to compare Alexander with a gander.

Always ask yourself what the purpose of the rhymes are? Are they to give pattern and structure? Do they give prominence to certain words and show the connections between them? Are they for fun?

MASCULINE RHYME

The simplest form of rhymes are words of one syllable, like rang/sang, or mad/bad/sad. You will immediately be able to think of dozens of examples like this. These rhymes, called *masculine* rhymes, give a clean, definite ending to a line.

FEMININE RHYME

Less numerous are words rhyming on two syllables, like pester/fester or gory/story. These are called *feminine* rhymes and give a lighter ending to the line or a sense of continuing, of something more to come.

TRIPLE RHYME

A rhyme on three syllables, or *triple* rhyme, is quite unusual but you do find it used occasionally. Thomas Hardy uses it extensively in '*The Going of the Battery*', often splitting the rhyme between two words, as in gleaming there/seeming there.

If you have a passion for labelling things you can use these names. If they confuse you, do not worry. Much more important than knowing the names is knowing what rhymes do, and being able to write about their effect.

There are three other types of rhyme which you should be able to recognize.

EYE RHYME

These are words which look as though they should rhyme from their spelling but in fact are pronounced differently like love/move or through/bough.

HALF RHYME (OR PARARHYME)

The vowels in the middle of the rhyme words are different but the opening and closing consonants are the same, like stroked/streaked, battle/bottle or cope/cape.

The use of eye rhyme in a poem may indicate that the poet has given up the search for a perfect rhyme. On the other hand it may be used deliberately to disturb the perfect harmony of the rhyme and give a sense of discord or roughness in the sound. Half rhyme is also used for this purpose.

INTERNAL RHYME

All the rhymes we have been discussing so far have been identified by their sound. Internal rhyme is distinguished by its position. It occurs in the middle of a line rather than at the end. When the lines are very long, as in the following example, it almost has the effect of cutting the line in half:

> *Thou hast conquered O pale Galilean, the world has grown grey with thy breath,*
> *We have drunken of things Lethean, and fed on the fullness of death.*

Why, we might ask, does the poet not turn this into a quatrain of 4 short lines instead of a couplet of 2 long ones? The answer must be that he wants two points of emphasis – the rhyme in the middle and the rhyme at the end. He saves for the end rhyme two words that are very important to his meaning. He also wants the longer unfolding, the expansiveness, the greater span for the rhythm to push forward, that the long line allows. A short line would be much more clipped and constrained.

Look at the *types* of rhyme the poet uses. Do they relate to the mood or meaning of the poem?

3 ▷ PATTERNS OF RHYME

When writing in rhyme a poet is committed to writing to a pattern, which gives the poem a shape. We describe these rhyme schemes by using letters of the alphabet – A for the first rhyme, B for the second and so on with a new letter for every new rhyming sound until we come to the end of the stanza. At the beginning of each stanza we go back to A.

There is no point at all in writing about a rhyme scheme unless you can say something about its purpose or effect.

COUPLETS

The simplest rhyme scheme is two lines rhyming, or *couplets*, like this one by Ogden Nash:

> *Tell me O octopus I begs*   A
> *Is those things arms, or is they legs.*   A

Couplets are very useful for wrapping up a thought neatly and concisely in a tidy package. They are often used at the end of a stanza or a poem or even scenes in plays to give a sense of finality. But they also lend themselves to being added to indefinitely – AABBCCDD and so on, as long as the poet wishes. Many long poems are written in couplets.

QUATRAINS

Four line stanzas, *quatrains*, are probably the most common in English poetry. A quatrain may be two couplets, AABB, or it may be alternate rhyme, ABAB:

Love seeketh not itself to please,	A
Nor for itself has any care,	B
But for another gives its ease	A
And builds a Heaven in Hell's despair.	B

(William Blake)

Notice how this stanza is also a complete sentence, but the use of four lines allows complications in the thought to be introduced – the words at the beginning of the lines show this. Each line begins a new clause. Notice too how the stanza is divided into two halves by the rhyme. The first two lines tell of what love does, or rather does not do for itself. The second two lines tell of what love does for another, the loved one. The poet has built his sentence around the pattern of the rhyme. This is one of the important uses of rhyme. To clarify an idea by making the structure of the expression clear.

A quatrain may be in the form of a couplet enclosed between another rhyme, like this:

Practise your beauty, blue girls, before it fail;	A
And I will cry with my loud lips and publish	B
Beauty which all our power shall never establish,	B
It is so frail.	A

John Crowe Ransom, who wrote this stanza, follows the rhyme structure with his sentence structure. The two inner lines go together and are not broken by punctuation. The two outer lines are brought together by the sound of the rhyme, making us link 'fail' and 'frail'.

Poets do not always link rhyme structure with sentence structure. It would be monotonous if they did. One of the ways in which they bring variety into their poems is by making the sentence structure follow the rhyme scheme sometimes and at other times compete with it.

A quatrain may also follow the pattern ABCB, as in this anonymous poem:

Western wind when wilt thou blow	A
The small rain down can rain.	B
Christ that my love were in my arms,	C
And I in my bed again.	B

Ballads are often written in this way, as in the following example:

The king sate in Dumfermline town
Drinking the blude-red wine;
'O whare will I get a skeely skipper
To sail this new ship o' mine?'

OTHER STANZA FORMS

There are many other stanza forms which are less frequently used, some of which have names. ***Rime Royal*** has seven lines rhyming ABABBCC. ***Ottava rima*** has eight lines rhyming ABABABCC. Of course poets do not have to stick to any previously used pattern, they can invent their own. However, in the course of the centuries every conceivable rhyme scheme has been used so that it would probably be impossible now to devise a pattern that had not been used at sometime by someone.

> **Note where the poet ends his sentences and where the pauses are. It is better to use the words 'pause' and 'sentence structure' in your writing, than to talk about commas and full stops.**

SONNET

This is one of the most widely used forms in poetry. It is such an important form and can show us so much about the workings of rhyme schemes that we must look at it in some detail. It has 14 lines and there are two traditional rhyme schemes, called after poets who used them.

The Petrarchan Sonnet

ABBAABBACDECDE. Milton, who often adopted this scheme, used it in '**On His Blindness**':

When I consider how my light is spent,	A
Ere half my days in this dark world and wide,	B
And that one talent which is death to hide	B
Lodged with me useless, though my soul more bent	A
To serve therewith my maker and present	A
My true account, lest he, returning chide.	B
'Doth God exact day-labour, light denied?'	B
I fondly ask. But patience to prevent	A
That murmur, soon replies: 'God doth not need	C
Either man's work or his own gifts; who best	D
Bear his mild yoke, they serve him best. His state	E
Is kingly: thousands at his bidding speed,	C
And post o'er land and ocean without rest;	D
They also serve who only stand and wait.	E

Look at how the rhyme scheme divides the sonnet into two parts. The first eight lines, or octave, uses two rhyming sounds, A and B. The last six lines, or sestet, uses three more rhymes, C, D, E. Now look at the meaning.

Milton spends the first part of the poem musing on his own blindness, his inability to use the one talent God has given him, and wondering what God expects of him. In the second part he answers himself. The transition in the argument can be seen quite clearly in 'Patience to prevent that murmur soon replies'(Lines 8-9). The poet has used the rhyme scheme to organize the argument of his poem.

The Shakespearian Sonnet

ABABCDCDEFEFGG. There are more rhyming sounds used in this type, which divide it into three quatrains and a couplet:

Like as the waves make towards the pebbled shore,	A
So do our minutes hasten towards their end;	B
Each changing place with that which went before,	A
In sequent toil all forward do contend.	B
Nativity, once in the main of light,	C
Crawls to maturity, wherewith being crown'd,	D
Crooked eclipses 'gainst his glory fight,	C
And Time that gave doth now his gift confound.	D
Time doth transfix the flourish set on youth	E
And delves the parallels in beauty's brow,	F
Feeds on the rarities of nature's truth,	E
And nothing stands but for his scythe to mow:	F
And yet to times in hope my verse shall stand,	G
Praising thy worth, despite his cruel hand.	G

The opening quatrain tells us that the subject is time. It compares the inevitable progress of our lives towards death with the inevitability of the incoming tide. Each quatrain advances the argument a stage further. The second tells how Time gives, as Man grows to maturity, and then begins to take back those gifts. The third gives examples of the way Time works. The final couplet concludes the argument with a twist: despite the cruel work of Time Shakespeare's verse will survive. A proud boast – but one that has been justified! Once again we can see how the poet uses the rhyme scheme to support the development of his ideas.

The sonnet has proved to be so effective a form that poets have gone on using it for centuries and still do so. Sometimes the form is changed a little. For instance by using ABABABABCDCDEE the poet can have the advantage of an octave, as in the Milton sonnet, change the argument when the rhyme changes to CDCD and still have the benefit of a clinching couplet at the end.

The rhyme scheme the poet chooses allows the ideas to unfold in a particular way. When you work out the rhyme scheme of a poem look at the way it gives an outline or structure for the poet's thoughts.

---

4 ▷ SUMMARY

➤ The purpose of rhyme is
  to give a structure to the poet's thoughts;
  to give prominence to important words;
  to show connections between words, lines and ideas;
  to provide humour.
➤ Different types of rhymes give a different character to the line endings and can relate to mood and meaning.
➤ Different rhyme schemes, like the couplet, quatrain and the sonnet, can show the unfolding of the poet's ideas in different ways.

ADDITIONAL EXAMPLES

Use these examples as exercises to see if you have understood the chapter so far. Work them out yourself first before looking at the key at the end. For each poem write down the rhyme scheme and types of rhymes used then try to say what their purpose, or effect, is. Look back at the previous section if you have any difficulties.

1. *When Molly smiles beneath her cow,*
   I feel my heart, I can't tell how;
   When Molly is on Sunday dressed,
   On Sundays I can take no rest.

   What can I do? On working days
   I leave my work on her to gaze.
   What shall I say? At sermons I
   Forget the text when Molly's by.

   Good master curate teach me how
   To mind your preaching and my plough:
   And if for this you'll raise a spell,
   A good fat goose shall thank you well.

2. *I doubt not God is good, well-meaning, kind,*
   And did he stoop to quibble could tell why
   The little buried mole continues blind,
   Why flesh that mirrors Him must someday die,
   Make plain the reason tortured Tantalus*
   Is baited by the fickle fruit, declare
   If merely brute caprice dooms Sisyphus*
   To struggle up a never ending stair.
   Inscrutable His ways are, and immune
   To catechism by a mind too strewn
   With petty cares to slightly understand
   What awful brain compels His awful hand
   Yet I do marvel at this curious thing:
   To make a poet black, and bid him sing! (Countee Cullen)

---

*These are figures from Greek mythology. Sisyphus was doomed always to push a boulder up a hill. Tantalus was doomed to try, but fail, to reach some fruit which dangled 'tantalizingly' just out of reach.

3. *Oh it was sad enough, weak enough, mad enough*
Light in their loving as soldiers can be –
First to risk choosing them, leave alone losing them
Now, in far battle, beyond the South Sea!...

1 KEY TO THE EXAMPLES

1. Rhyme scheme: Quatrains rhyming AABB. Types: All masculine. Purpose: The anonymous poet uses each couplet in stanzas 1 and 3 for a single statement. This is varied in stanza 2 where each couplet contains a question and explanation. (If you look at the punctuation you will see how each couplet ends in a full stop, semicolon or colon.) Each stanza concentrates on a different aspect of the subject: Molly herself, the speaker of the poem, the curate. Thus we can say that the purpose of the rhyme scheme is structural. But there are also several rhymes which emphasize the meaning of the lines: 'days/gaze' sums up the way in which he spends his days gazing at Molly; 'how/plough' sums up the speaker's plea to the curate to tell him how to keep his mind on the things he should be doing rather than on Molly.

2. Rhyme Scheme: Sonnet, ABABCDCDEEFFGG. Types: Masculine except for Tantalus/Sisyphus which is triple rhyme and also half rhyme. Purpose: The rhyme scheme divides the sonnet into two parts. The octave uses alternate rhyme and the sestet uses couplets. The subject of the octave is to suggest that God must have reasons for all the pain that man and animals have to endure. The sestet says that man cannot hope to understand the marvellous ways of God. The final couplet declares that of all the marvels the most difficult to understand is how God expects anyone who is black to overcome the difficulties of their life and write poetry. This sonnet uses the rhyme scheme to organize the thought but not as closely as the other sonnets we have looked at. The effect of the half rhyme Tantalus/Sisyphus is to introduce a note of discord or difficulty which is appropriatc to the trials of Tantalus and Sisyphus.

3. Rhyme Scheme: ABAB. Types: mad enough/sad enough is internal rhyme and also triple rhyme; be/sea is masculine; choosing them/ losing them is also internal triple rhyme. Purpose: The poet, Thomas Hardy, uses the contrast between the masculine rhymes and the triple rhymes as one of the ways of showing the contrast between the men and women in the poem. The lines which talk about soldiers and battle end on the firm masculine rhymes. The rest have unstressed endings appropriate to the feminine speakers of the poem. The choosing/losing rhyme brings out a contrast which the women feel. When a woman chooses a husband it should be for life but they are losing their husbands prematurely.

EXAM QUESTION

You may be specifically asked to comment on rhyme in a question about the language of a poem (see the question on the unseen in Ch.2). Even when rhyme is not specifically mentioned in the question you should not omit to comment on it if you have something interesting to say.

Questions on language and form will give you the opportunity to use the skills you have learnt concerning rhyme and the opportunity to comment on any interesting aspects of rhyme which you may have discovered in studying poems.

Rhyme schemes are part of the form of a poem and also part of its poetic qualities. Whenever you are asked about these things, or about the way the poem is written, or what you think of a poem, you can include comments on rhyme.

In the following question you are asked to write about form, tone and language. What you have read in this chapter will help you answer, but since tone and language have already been dealt with in earlier chapters you can use this question to apply what you have learnt there as well.

Compare the following poems. Show how the two poems are similar or different in their form, tone and language.

(i) **The Midnight Skaters**

The hop-poles stand in cones,
The icy pond lurks under,
The pole-tops steeple to the thrones
Of stars, sound gulfs of wonder;
But not the tallest there, 'tis said,
Could fathom to the pond's black bed.

Then is not death at watch
Within those secret waters?
What wants he but to catch
Earth's heedless sons and daughters?
With but a crystal parapet
Between, he has his engines set.

Then on, blood shouts, on, on,
Twirl, wheel and whip above him,
Dance on this ball-floor thin and wan,
Use him as though you love him;
Court him, elude him, reel and pass,
And let him hate you through the glass.   (Edmund Blunden)

(ii) *Because I could not stop for Death –*
He kindly stopped for me –
The carriage held but just Ourselves –
And Immortality.

We slowly drove – He knew no haste
And I had put away
My labor and my leisure too,
For his Civility –

We passed the School, where Children strove
At Recess – in the Ring –
We passed the Fields of Gazing Grain –
We passed the Setting Sun –

Or rather – He passed Us –
*   The Dews drew quivering and chill –*
For only Gossamer, my Gown –
My Tippet – only Tulle –

We paused before a house that seemed
Swelling of the Ground –
The Roof was scarcely visible –
The Cornice – in the Ground

Since then – 'tis Centuries – and yet
Feels shorter than the Day
I first surmised the Horses' Heads
Were toward Eternity –   (Emily Dickenson)

NOTES AND TUTOR'S ANSWER

Read these notes and then write your own answers to the question before reading the answer below.

1 ▷ NOTES

This kind of question is often set as part of a question. In an exam look at the number of marks for each part of the question and work out about how long you should spend on each part.

At the moment you do not have to worry about time. Write as much as you can.

1. Work out the rhyme scheme of each poem. Look at the types of rhyme used. Ask yourself if the scheme of any of the rhymes has a particular purpose.
2. Decide what the poet's tone is – what is the poet's attitude to the subject?
3. Make a note of all the metaphor, similes, personification, association, evocative words and phrases and imagery (the aspects of language you read about in Ch. 4 and Ch. 5).

2 ▷ SUGGESTED ANSWER

(i) Rhyme Scheme ABABCC. Types – regular pattern of masculine and feminine or triple rhyme.
Tone – Warning of danger, excitement, defiance.
Language – <u>Metaphor</u>: steeple, thrones, parapet, engines, blood shouts, dance, ball-floor, court him. <u>Personification</u>: Death, Earth. <u>Other Evocative Words</u>: sound gulfs, black bed, secret waters, twirl, wheel and whip.

(ii) Rhymes – sometimes 2nd and 4th lines rhyme imperfectly.
Tone – acceptance, regret.
Language – <u>Metaphor</u>: Extended metaphor of ride with Death; School, Fields, Sun, Dews, Gown, House. <u>Other Evocative Language</u>: Gazing Grain

In the first poem the poet uses alternate rhymes, followed by a couplet at the end of the stanza. All the A rhymes are masculine but the B rhymes are feminine. This gives a sense of competition or struggle which fits the subject well. We expect the second poem to rhyme, because the first stanza rhymes 'me' with 'Immortality'. Even though this is not a perfect rhyme our expectations of a pattern are aroused. When they are not fulfilled we find it disturbing and unsettling. Once again this is appropriate to the subject: a journey with death.

The tone of the first poem is one of warning against danger, though the struggle against death seems exciting. Finally the poet is defiant. The tone of the second poem is one of acceptance of Death's supremacy, although the poet appears regretful.

Both poets personify death but they give him a different character. In the first poem he is to be feared and hated. He is the enemy of Earth, who is spoken of as the mother of the living. In the second poem he is a courteous companion, accompanied by Immortality, which is also personified.

Have you explained the metaphors and related them to the mood and meaning of the poem?

The first poet uses many metaphors to create the picture of the pond at night and the skaters' sense of danger and excitement. The comparison of the hop-poles to church steeples suggests the height of the stars and the stars' grandeur is suggested by calling them 'thrones'. The magnificent immensity of the heavens is evoked by the phrase 'sound gulfs of wonder'. These are contrasted with the unfathomable depths of the secret waters under the ice where death lurks. Words like 'secret' and 'lurks' create the sense of danger which is intensified by the images of death waiting like a medieval invader with his siege engines. The ice becomes a parapet set up to protect the children. The thinness of the ice is conveyed by comparing it to the fragility of crystal. In the final stanza the imagery changes. To show the vitality of youth, their blood is imagined to be shouting. The ice becomes a dance floor and the movements of the skaters become a dance in which they taunt death by flirting with him but escaping.

In the second poem an extended metaphor depicts life as a ride with Death. This is introduced in the first stanza with the image of Death kindly stopping his carriage for the speaker. The journey continues throughout the poem. A series of images stand for the various aspects of life: the School represents childhood, the Fields everything round us in the world, the Setting Sun shows life drawing to an end. The fear of what the end will bring is evoked by the cold Dews and the frailty of the human body by a comparison with a thin gossamer dress. The metaphor of the house with its roof almost buried in the ground is a vivid image for the graveyard but it is not the end for the journey goes on through the centuries. At the end of the poem the original metaphor is reinforced by the mention of the horses which are still pulling the carriage through eternity.

This is a very full answer and shows how much there is to say. The same advice as given in the previous chapter also applies here. Get down the main points, leave a space, come back if you have time. Never leave yourself with too little time to do the required number of questions.

SUGGESTIONS FOR COURSEWORK

1. Use the question above as a model for a coursework unit. You could compare 'The Midnight Skaters' with Wordsworth's description of skating in **The Prelude** (Book 1, lines 433-446). It begins: 'All shod with steel/ We hissed along the polished ice', and it is often included in anthologies.

   Emily Dickenson's poem could be compared with Robert Frost's 'Stopping by Woods on a Snowy Evening', Robert Graves' 'The Twin of Sleep' or W. B. Yeats' 'Death'.

   In fact the question above can be used for any two poems with a similar subject or theme.

2. Choose several poems by one poet, which have different rhyme schemes. Write about the similarities and differences between the poems and include comments on rhyme.

3. Make a study of a number of poems which use different kinds of rhyme, or no rhyme.

4. Compare two or more sonnets, or two or more ballads.

STUDENT'S ANSWER – EXAMINER'S COMMENT

Question

The question asked the student to discuss rhyme, along with other aspects of Robert Graves' poem 'The Leveller'.

"This account is far too brief and lacking in detail"

"Good. Identifies the rhyme scheme and states its effect."

"Good. Notices the change in the rhyme and gives a reason for it."

"Good. Relates the rhyme scheme to the meaning of the poem."

This poem tells of how two men were struck by the same shell and died together. One was only an eighteen year old boy. He died cursing. The other was a man who had been in many battles. He was a hardened soldier but he called for his master as he died. The sergeant has the difficult job of writing to the men's relatives to give them the news. He has a standard letter which he writes every time this happens, praising the heroism of the soldiers.

The poem has a regular rhyme scheme (AABB) all the way through. It is so simple that it seems almost like a nursery rhyme. All the rhymes are perfect, like hell and shell, until we get to the final stanza

> 'He died a hero's death: and we
> His comrades of 'A' company
> Deeply regret his death: we shall
> All deeply miss so true a pal.'

The imperfect rhyme of 'we' and company is a shock after the ones that have come before. It is jarring and breaks the smooth harmony. This makes the sergeant's letter seems insincere. All the other stanzas seem so direct and straightforward that we believe what they say and feel it is true. We know that the sergeant's letter is false because the men did not die like heroes. The poet uses the change in rhyme to make us feel the falseness. The stanza ends with the word 'pal' to rhyme with 'shall' which also makes us feel awkward because it does not seem the right word to use about someone who has been fighting alongside you. It is more the sort of word you would use about a friend at home.

The poet uses rhyme very cleverly in this poem. First of all in a simple and direct way which makes the feelings seem true and sincere. Then in a contrasting way to bring the feeling of awkwardness.

"The weakness of this answer is to do with the way it is expressed. All the points on rhyme are made. The answer would get higher marks if it were expressed more concisely and in more vivid language which showed the student's response to the poem."

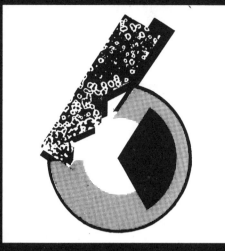

RHYTHM

GETTING STARTED

You may be specifically asked to say what contribution rhythm
makes to a poem. Sometimes you will be asked to comment on
the form of a poem. This means the rhythm, rhyme and the way
the poem is divided into lines and stanzas. All these aspects can
also be included in your coursework writing. Rhythm makes
such an enormous contribution to poetry that the more you can
understand about it the better you will be able to appreciate the
poems you are studying. Like Rhyme (see Ch.5) it is a technical
matter and so you need to become familiar with poetry that uses
it. Therefore if you are not used to reading poetry that has a
fixed rhythm, accustom your ear by reading as much rhythmic
poetry as possible.

There is a lot of technical vocabulary to do with rhythm.
But this vocabulary is only important and useful if it helps us to
recognize how a poem works. There is no merit in simply being
able to slap the right labels on in the right places. We learn the
technical words solely in order to show how the poet has used
rhythm to help in the poem's total effect, and say what is
interesting or exciting about it.

ESSENTIAL PRINCIPLES

1 ⟩ RHYTHM, METRE AND FREE VERSE

In poetry we use the word *rhythm* to mean the sense of movement in the verse. When this is strong and regular, like a beat, it is called *metre*. The line:

> *When the bell began to ring*

has a regular metre. Very few poems have an absolutely regular metre.

"Note the spelling of rhythm. Are you confusing rhyme and rhythm? This is a common mistake."

When we talk about the rhythm of a poem we mean the regular beat of the metre and the way this beat varies, as it does in speech. Some poems, especially modern ones, are not written with a regular metre at all. Poetry that has no metre and no rhyme is called *free verse*. Free verse has no fixed metre but it still has rhythm, like the beginning of this poem by T. S. Eliot.

> *The river's tent is broken: the last fingers of leaf*
> *Clutch and sink into the wet bank. The wind*
> *Crosses the brown land, unheard.*

2 ⟩ SYLLABLES

To understand and talk about rhythm you first need to know how to divide a word into syllables:

> *Caught* is a monosyllable. It cannot be divided.
> *Today* can be divided into two syllables – *to/day*.
> *Property* divides into three syllables – *pro/per/ty*.
> *Supersonic* has four syllables – *su/per/son/ic*.

If you have already had practice in dividing words into syllables, this will help your work on rhythm.

3 ⟩ STRESS

You will have noticed how when pronouncing words one syllable carries more weight than another. Thus we say 'toDAY' – putting more emphasis on the 'day' part of the word. We cannot say 'TOday'. It sounds wrong, as though we had a strange foreign accent. Similarly 'heavy' must have the emphasis on the first syllable. We call this emphasis *stress* and every word has a natural stress. In fact some words change their meaning depending on where the stress is placed:

> *DEfect* is a fault
> *deFECT* means to change sides

We mark the stress of a word by a line above the stressed syllable. An unstressed syllable is marked ∪ :

⏑ —   — ⏑   — ⏑ ⏑   — ⏑ — ⏑

today, heavy, property, supersonic.

4 ⟩ STRESS IN POETRY

Poets who write in metre use the natural stress of words to make the rhythmic pattern, or metre. They deliberately choose words to fit the stress pattern they want. In this poem the poet has chosen to work with seven syllables in each line, in a pattern of alternating stressed and unstressed syllables:

> — ⏑   — ⏑   — ⏑ —
> *Lay your sleeping head my love*
>
> — ⏑   — ⏑   — ⏑ —
> *Human on my faithless arm*
> (W. H. Auden 'Lullaby')

He keeps up this metre throughout the verse. Here is a more usual metre of ten syllables:

So long as men can breathe and eyes can see

(William Shakespeare)

A great deal of English poetry has been written in that particular metre.

It is more important to be able to recognize stress than to know all the names of the different metres. You can talk about rhythm in poetry very well by just looking at the way poets use stress in a line. Stressed syllables are sometimes called *heavy* and unstressed syllables *light*.

---

5 ▶	FEET AND METRES

If you are unhappy with technical details, ignore this section and go on to the next. However, make sure that you understand 'stress'

I have included this section for the sake of completeness and for those of you who enjoy technicalities. Sometimes having labels to put on things helps you to feel confident.

Read through this section. If you find it too detailed or confusing do not worry about it: *concentrate on stress*. The only term you really should know is *iambic pentameter,* which is the metre of the previous Shakespeare quotation; that is ten syllables to the line arranged in a regular pattern of unstressed and stressed:

Once we have worked out the stresses of each line we can divide the line up into smaller units, or *feet*, each with the same number of stressed and unstressed syllables. Because we are dealing with syllables and not words sometimes a word is cut in two by a foot. This line would be divided like this:

It seemed/that out/of ba/ttle I/escaped.

There are four basic feet and three supplementary ones. The four basic feet are as follows:

- (i)   ∪—   Iambic foot, or iamb.
- (ii) —∪   Trochaic foot, or trochee.
- (iii) ∪∪— Anapaestic foot, or anapest.
- (iv) —∪∪ Dactylic foot, or dactyl.

Here are some examples:

If I/ should die/ think on/ly this /of me, is Iambic.

Thou thy /worldly /task has /done, is Trochaic.

O the goose/ and the gan/der walked o/ver the green, is Anapaestic.

This is the/forest prim/aeval,the/murmuring/pines and the/hemlocks, is Dactylic.

You will see that in the second of these lines there seems to be a spare syllable at the end of the line. You can think of this as a missing unstressed syllable, because the poet wants to end on a good strong beat. On other occasions there will be an extra unstressed syllable, for the opposite reason. It all depends on the effect that the poet wants. Later on you will find more examples of variations in rhythm with some suggestions on what effect they have.

Sometimes poets combine two of these metres in one line. Here is a mixture of iambic and anapaestic:

The moth/er of months/ in mead/ow and plain

The three supplementary, or occasional, feet are:

- (i)   ——   Spondaic foot, or spondee.
- (ii) ∪∪   Pyrrhic foot, or pyrrhic.
- (iii) ∪—∪ Amphibrach.

These three feet can bring variety into the rhythm of a line, or shift the emphasis onto a certain word, but they are not used throughout a line.

Here is an amphibrach used in a line that is a mixture of iambs and anapests:

When the pre/sent has latched/its postern/behind/my trem/ulous stay.

The effect of the extra unstressed syllable that makes an iamb into an amphibrach on the words 'its postern' is to make a pause in the middle of the line.

Once you have worked out what kind of foot, or feet, the poet is using you can work out the number of feet in a line:

Monometer has one foot in a line;

Dimeter has two feet in a line;

Trimeter has three feet in a line;

Tetrameter has four feet in a line;

Pentameter has five feet in a line;

Hexameter, also called Alexandrine, has six feet in a line;

Heptameter has seven feet in a line;

Octameter has eight feet in a line;

The most usual rhythm is the pentameter, followed by the tetrameter and hexameter.

It is far less important to know all these terms than it is to be able to recognize stress and to say what effects it has. You will not get a good grade for just knowing the terms; you will get a good grade if you can point out something interesting about the rhythm of a poem. Simply writing 'this poem is written in iambic pentameter', is a waste of time and effort unless you can say **why** the poet might have used it or point to an interesting variation. The terminology is only a useful way of referring to the rhythm, and may give you the confidence to know what you are talking about.

MEANING

The first question to ask yourself is, 'Has the poet selected this particular metre because it is in some way appropriate to the **meaning** of the poem?' For instance, Robert Louis Stevenson's 'From a Railway Carriage' clearly intends to convey the rhythm of the train:

> *Faster than fairies, faster than witches,*
>
> *Bridges and houses, hedges and ditches;*

He uses a regular metre (of dactyls and trochees) for this purpose. When Kipling writes about men marching, his rhythm sounds like a march.

> *We're marchin' on relief over Injia's sunny plains*
>
> *A little front of Christmas-time an' just be'ind the Rains*

In the poem Thomas Hardy wrote about men marching away from their wives to go to war, which we looked at in the previous chapter, he uses a different but equally strong rhythm:

> *O it was sad enough, weak enough, mad enough,*
>
> *Light in their loving as soldiers can be,*
>
> *First to risk choosing them, leave alone losing them*
>
> *Now, in far battle beyond the South Sea.* ('The Going of the Battery')

He calls this poem 'The Wives Lament' and writes it from the point of view of the women, trudging along beside the company of soldiers as they go to board their ship. This gives us a clue to the choice of rhythm. It must be strong and regular, because they are marching. But the women are sad and reluctant for the men to go. There is a hesitancy in their step which is conveyed by the two unstressed syllables between the stresses:

> ‾ ‿ ‿   ‾ ‿ ‿   ‾   ‾ ‿ ‿   ‾ ‿ ‿
>
> *O it was sad enough, weak enough, mad enough,*

Look back at the comments on the rhymes of this stanza and you will see how well the rhymes and the rhythm work together to create the effect of the difference between the men and the women and the women's sadness at parting.

This is not to say that this kind of rhythm (dactylic) is always sad. 'Merrily, merrily, shall I live now' is the same rhythm. A rhythm can fit the mood of the words, can be appropriate to the meaning of the poem, but it cannot have a mood or meaning in itself. Every poem has to be looked at separately to see what effects the poet is creating in that particular case.

VARIATION

The second question to ask is, 'Can I hear any *variations* in the basic metre?' This takes practice. If there are variations then we have to try and say what effect they have.

This poem, by Dylan Thomas, is basically iambic, but it has several irregularities.

> *The force that through the green fuse drives the flower*
> *Drives my green age; that blasts the roots of trees*
> *Is my destroyer.*
> *And I am dumb to tell the crooked rose*
> *My youth is bent by the same wintry fever.*

If the metre were completely regular it should look like this

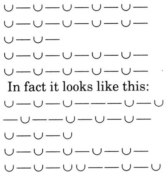

In fact it looks like this:

The irregularities come on 'green fuse drives' – there is a stress on 'fuse' where we do not expect one. This gives three stressed syllables in a row which makes the rhythm heavy and emphatic. At the beginning of the second line there is again a stress on 'Drives' where there is not one in the first line. Then there is an unexpected stress on 'green'. In both these lines, the stresses are used to emphasize the force that drives youth inexorably onwards, towards old age and death.

Finally the rhythm of the last line is jumbled. The line talks about youth being 'bent'. After the word 'bent' there is a pause and two unstressed syllables, which throws a lot of emphasis on to 'bent'. It is as if the line itself is bent out of shape to mirror the meaning.

---

7 ▷ PAUSE

Poetry uses punctuation just as prose does: to show *pause*. The rhythm and rhyme also lead us to expect pauses at the end of lines but the poet often defies our expectations by omitting the pause at the end of a line or by putting a pause in the middle of a line. The first of these effects is called the *run-on line*, or *enjambement*. The second is called *caesura*. Both are important because they affect the rhythm and flow of the verse.

THE RUN-ON LINE (ENJAMBEMENT)

When there is no punctuation at the end of a line the sense is carried on without a break into the next line. W. B. Yeats uses the run-on line three times in this stanza:

> *At the grey round of the hill*
> *Music of a lost kingdom*
> *Runs, runs, and is suddenly still.*
> *The winds out of Clare-Galway*
> *Carry it: suddenly it is still.*

Here the line ends have broken phrases in two. Because the pause we expect at the end of the line does not happen; we get a sense of being carried forward. This fits very well with Yeats' subject.

If the rhythm is heavy and ponderous, an unexpectedly long unpunctuated phrase may give us a sense of something long and drawn out, even tedious:

> *but evermore*
> *Most weary seemed the sea, weary the oar.*

Here Tennyson uses the run-on line, together with extra stress, long vowels (see Ch.7) and repetition to convey the sailors' utter inability to stir themselves into action.

There are no hard and fast rules. You cannot say what a run-on line is going to do *until* the poet has done it. It all depends upon the meaning of the poem. If you think about the words and the meaning of the poem you may be able to suggest why the the poet used a run-on rather than an end-stopped line.

CAESURA

Many lines of poetry have a definite pause somewhere in the middle of the line. This too breaks up the metre of the poem and brings variety:

> *The day is past, and yet I saw no sun;*
> *And now I live, and now my life is done.*

(Chidiock Tichborne,' Elegy for Himself')

Here the poet is using the caesura to point up a contrast and balance of ideas in each line. This kind of contrast is called antithesis. The pause is the point of balance.

You may find the caesura very near the beginning of the line to emphasize the opening word or phrase. Christina Rossetti emphasizes 'Yes' in this way:

> *Yes, to the very end*

and so does Matthew Arnold:

> *Yes! in the sea of life enisled.*

On another occasion Arnold puts the caesura near the end, just before the word 'we' which, as a result, is isolated at the end of the line and thus very prominent:

> *it brought*
> *Into his mind the turbid ebb and flow*
> *Of human misery; we*
> *Find also in the sound a thought*

Run on lines and caesurae often go hand in hand.

If, as we have seen, rhythm can contribute to the mood of the poem, the use of pause can bring some fine-tuning to the tone or the mood. Think of the occasions when you might use a pause in conversation – to bring attention to a particular word, or to make something dramatic. It might be difficult to say something sad, or even exciting, and so you pause before it. A poet can do all these things with caesurae.

Here is a rather obvious piece of drama by A. E. Housman. A young man is waiting to be hanged:

> *Strapped, noosed, nighing his hour,*
> *He stood and cursed his luck.*
> *And then the clock in the tower*
> *Gathered its strength – and struck.*

The heavy caesura in the last line gives a dramatic pause, a stillness, before the final words when the fatal hour arrives. Those words, 'and struck', fall heavily, like the man swinging on the end of the rope. The caesura is even more effective for coming so late in the line, after the run-on from the previous line. We are kept waiting. The poet never actually tells us that the man is dead. He tells us the clock struck the hour, and leaves the rhythm to imply the rest.

---

8 ▷ SUMMARY

➤ When we speak, some syllables of our words are stressed and some are not.

➤ Poets use the natural stress of words to give rhythm, sometimes but not always in a regular metre.

➤ Variations in the metre are often connected with meaning or mood.

➤ Pauses at the end of lines, or in the middle (caesura) also affects the rhythm and pace of the verse.

ADDITIONAL EXAMPLES

Use these examples to test your understanding of what you have read in this chapter. Work through them before looking at the Key below.

1. What can you say about this rhythm? Can you suggest why it is used for this poem?

    Before the Roman came to Rye or out to Severn strode
    The rolling English drunkard made the rolling English road.
    A reeling road, a rolling road, that rambles round the shire,
    And after him the parson ran, the sexton and the squire.

2. *The Frost performs its secret ministry*
    Unhelped by any wind. The owlet's cry
    Came loud – and hark again! loud as before.

    (i)   What is the basic rhythm of these lines?
    (ii) What is the effect of the long caesura, shown by a dash?
    (iii) Suggest a reason why this line is so broken by pause.
    (iv) Can you find an irregularity in the rhythm and suggest a reason for it?

1 KEY TO THE EXAMPLES

1. This is a good strong regular rhythm (iambic heptameter) to suggest movement. It pushes forward purposefully, as though we are setting off down the road. The length of the lines also helps give this effect. But then it becomes broken up by pauses as the road twists and turns in typical English country manner.

2. (i)   The basic rhythm is iambic pentameter
    (ii) The caesura imitates the action of listening, as though the poet is actually speaking to someone and pauses to listen to the owl before going on.
    (iii) The effect of the line being broken is to suggest disturbance. The quiet of the night is broken. The owlet's cry is strange, perhaps distressing.
    (iv) There is an unexpected stress on 'loud' in 'loud as before' (a trochee). Compare this line with the previous two lines and you will see the stress here is the opposite way round. This gives emphasis, showing the strength of the cry.

EXAM QUESTIONS

You can use your knowledge of rhythm to help you write the kind of general question on language which is frequently asked. Here is an example:

What do you find specially effective in the way this poem is written? What is the mood of the writer and how has he communicated his mood to the reader? (MEG)

This question could be asked about almost any poem. You would be expected to touch on all the aspects of poetic language covered in these chapters. You should look at:

➤ figurative language
➤ rhyme
➤ rhythm
➤ sound.

Say what the mood of the poem is, and what each aspect of the poem adds to the mood.

You may be asked a short question specifically on rhythm. One of these is answered below, together with a longer question.

QUESTIONS, NOTES AND TUTOR'S ANSWERS

1 ⟩ **QUESTIONS**

1. Comment on the rhythm of the following lines.
   (On the exam paper the whole poem would be quoted and you would be directed to look at certain lines. Here are just the lines in question.)

   The doctor put him in the dark of ether.
   He lay and puffed his lips out with his breath.
   And then – the watcher at his pulse took fright.
   No-one believed. They listened at his heart.
   Little – less – nothing! – and that ended it.

2. Read again 'Exposure', by Wilfred Owen. What do you feel about this poem? You may like to think about the following questions:

   What are the specially effective phrases that Owen uses here?
   How does Owen use sound effects and rhythm in this poem to make it more effective still if read aloud?
   What is the special importance of the last line of each stanza?
   What is Owen thinking about the involvement of God? (MEG)

   Our brains ache, in the merciless iced east winds that knive us. . .
   Wearied we keep awake because the night is silent. . .
   Low, drooping flares confuse our memory of the salient. . .
   Worried by silence, sentries whisper, curious, nervous,
   But nothing happens.

> **Use this poem as an unseen if you have not read it before.** "

   Watching, we hear the mad gusts tugging on the wire,
   Like twitching agonies of men among its brambles.
   Northward, incessantly, the flickering gunnery rumbles,
   Far off, like a dull rumour of some other war.
   What are we doing here?

   The poignant misery of dawn begins to grow. . .
   We only know war lasts, rain soaks, and clouds sag stormy.
   Dawn massing in the east her melancholy army
   Attacks once more in ranks on shivering ranks of gray,
   But nothing happens.

   Sudden successive flights of bullets streak the silence.
   Less deathly than the air that shudders black with snow,
   With sidelong flowing flakes that flock, pause , and renew;
   We watch them wandering up and down the wind's nonchalance,
   But nothing happens.

   Pale flakes with fingering stealth come feeling for our faces.
   We cringe in holes, back on forgotten dreams, and stare, snow- dazed,
   Deep into grassier ditches. So we drowse, sun-dozed,
   Littered with blossoms trickling where the blackbird fusses.
   Is it that we are dying.

   Slowly our ghosts drag home: glimpsing the sunk fires, glozed
   With crusted dark-red jewels; crickets jingle there;
   For hours the innocent mice rejoice: the house is theirs;
   Shutters and doors, all closed: on us the doors are closed,-
   We turn back to our dying.

Since we believe not otherwise can kind fires burn;
Nor ever suns smile true on child, or field, or fruit.
For God's invincible spring our love is made afraid;
Therefore, not loath, we lie out here; therefore were born,
For love of God seems dying.

Tonight, His frost will fasten on this mud and us,
Shrivelling many hands, puckering foreheads crisp.
The burying party, picks and shovels in their shaking grasp,
Pause over half-known faces. All their eyes are ice,
But nothing happens.

ON QUESTION 1

1. If you have practised reading poetry you will realize that the first two lines are regular and smooth but the next three broken. Before writing anything:
   (i) Quickly work out the rhythm of the first line to give you the basic metre.
   (ii) Look at the meaning and decide what it is about the subject which makes the poet break up the rhythm with dashes.
   (iii) Note any other variations and use of the caesura. When you have done these things, write your answer before reading the one below.

ON QUESTION 2

1. There is more in this poem than you can possibly hope to cover in an exam. The question suggests various things that you might like to look at besides rhythm. An exam answer would spend a paragraph on rhythm, one on sound, one on imagery, perhaps two on what Owen is thinking at the end. **My answer concentrates just on rhythm to show you how much there is to say about it, but you would not be expected to do so.**
2. This is from an open-book exam, therefore your first task is to read the poem carefully to remind yourself of the work you have done on it.
3. Mark on the exam paper those phrases you think worth commenting on. Mark the rhythm above the line in the usual way. Jot notes in the margin to remind yourself of the important points as you write.
4. Write a paragraph on rhythm before reading the answer below.

SUGGESTED ANSWERS

1. The poet is writing about a death. Even though the doctor has had to use ether no one appears to expect the boy to die. The poet writes in a regular rhythm, iambic pentameter, but this begins to break down as the crisis approaches. The dramatic pause in the third line, marked by a dash, increases the tension. No one can believe the boy will die. This is emphasized by the unexpected stress on 'No-one' at the beginning of the line, and the strong caesura in the middle of the line. Finally, as the boy dies the rhythm breaks down completely to imitate the stopping of his heart.
   (The most important points are the breaking down of the rhythm by the use of pause and the way this relates to the meaning by showing first the tension and anxiety and then the heart stopping. If you have got those points you have a good answer.)

2. Wilfred Owen's poem is an excellent example of the sound echoing the sense. He uses rhythm and sound to heighten awareness of the dreadful reality of the soldier's position, when silence is not peace but the prelude to another attack and the weather a more deadly enemy than the opposing army.
   The tense expectancy, the waiting in dread, is increased by the irregularity of the rhythm and the use of pause. The unstressed line endings, long pauses, indicated by dots and unexpected caesurae near the beginning of lines: all these give jumpiness, a terrible uneasiness. The long night of unexpected silence, which keeps the soldiers wakeful, is depicted by an unbroken line of almost regular iambic hexameter:

Wearied we keep awake because the night is silent. . .

In contrast the nervousness of the sentries on watch is depicted in a matching regular line, but broken and disjointed by three pauses:

Worried by silence, sentries whisper, curious, nervous,

The half-line which ends the stanza leaves us with a sense of something unfinished. More is expected. The breaking off of the line shows both the soldiers' sense that there is more horror to come and the reader's sense that there is more to say than the inadequate statement, 'All's quiet'.

The first stanza shows the way Owen uses rhythm to point the meaning. Gusts of wind and incessant gunfire in the distance are both conveyed by the rhythm. The blustery wind is imitated by grouping stressed syllables together, followed by light syllables, as if the strong gust has eased:

Watching we hear the mad gusts tugging on the wire,

The gunfire is conveyed in a pattern of almost regular stressed and unstressed syllables (anapests), rapid and light, giving the pattering distant noise and flashes:

the flickering gunnery rumbles,

When Owen describes the rain and the long misery of exposure in the trenches the rhythm becomes heavy with extra stressed syllables:

We only know war lasts, rain soaks and clouds sag stormy.

The massed clouds, marching the sky like the armies of another enemy are given a strong and regular beat and the line ends with a heavily stressed syllable. We read that Dawn:

Attacks once more in ranks on shivering ranks of gray,

In contrast is the haphazard fall of the snowflakes, which 'flock, pause and renew'. The snowflakes pause in their fall; the line is broken by pause to show it.

When the soldiers dream and their thoughts turn to home, the rhythm becomes lighter. Owen uses fewer stresses and chooses words in which the natural stress is not so heavy:

Littered with blossoms trickling where the blackbird fusses.

There is, though, a painful line depicting their return home in memory:

Slowly our ghosts drag home: glimpsing the sunk fires glozed
With crusted dark-red jewels;

Here the stress is combined with sound to give, not weight, but slowness.

Although it is never regular, the rhythm becomes calmer towards the end of the poem as Owen turns his thoughts to God and the meaning of the soldiers' suffering. But the mood is despairing; it is a calm caused only by exhaustion.

SUGGESTIONS FOR COURSEWORK

1. The question on 'Exposure' shows you the sort of work that can be done on a poem. Take two or three poems of this length and compare them, looking at effective phrases, sound effects and rhythm as this question suggests.
2. Take a group of poems around a theme, like War, and examine how different poets treat it.
3. Make a selection, as if for a radio programme, of poems that have strong rhythms. Write the script for the programme, introducing each poem to the listener.

STUDENT'S ANSWER – EXAMINER'S COMMENTS

Question

Comment on the rhythm of a Verse XLI of 'The Eve of St. Agnes'.

> **Good. States the basic rhythm and then makes careful observations of the variation. This continues throughout**

> **Good. Relates the variations in the rhythm to the meaning of the words in this, and the next, paragraph.**

> **There is no need to spend time pointing out a variation if there is nothing to say about its effect.**

> **Notices the use of the caesura and comments on the effect of the pause.**

The poem is basically written in Iambic Pentameter, with variations to relate rhythm to the meaning. In the first line, two stressed syllables on the words 'wide hall' evoke an image of a large spacious area, and the word 'Phantoms' indicates the lovers gliding swiftly through the empty hall. A sense of urgency is added when three hurried syllables 'to the iron porch' indicate a sense of urgency in the lovers flight. A slightly awkward three short beats in line three on the words 'uneasy sprawl', emphasize the porters awkward position. In the following line, the words 'huge' and 'empty' are stressed, to indicate the large quantity of wine that the porter has drunk.

The next two lines are written in regular Iambic Pentameter, without any particular rhythm inflections to highlight and add meaning. The next line begins with the words 'By one, and one' to emphasize slow, cautious pulling back of the bolts. 'full, easy slide' are emphasized to show the slowness of each bolt as it is drawn back. Three unstressed syllables in the penultimate line have no particular importance to the meaning of the poem. The last line is known as an Alexandrine line, and is two syllables longer than the rest of the lines in this verse. Keats often used Alexandrine lines. The pause after 'The key turns' is called a Caesura, and is pregnant with suspense, and the final word 'groans' is stressed to emphasize its drawn out sound in the silence.

> **A well written comment on the rhythm of the stanza. Variations in the basic rhythm noticed and related to the meaning of the words. On occasions the answer omits to say which words carry the extra stress and which would be stressed in any case by the metre.**

PATTERNS
OF
SOUND

ONOMATOPOEIA
INDIVIDUAL SOUNDS
ALLITERATION
ASSONANCE
THE PURPOSE OF
SOUND PATTERNS

G E T T I N G   S T A R T E D

In every examination question on poetry there is always an opportunity to comment on the way the poem is written. The question often takes the form of an invitation to write about words or phrases you find interesting. What the examiner is looking for is the ability to discuss the language and techniques of poetry. The candidate who can do this, as well as say what the poem is about, is the one who will get the highest marks.

One of the aspects of language to discuss is the poet's use of sound. Sound patterns are important in poetry because they give the poet an extra dimension to work with, an additional way of saying things. It is as if the poet has some of the resources of music at his disposal, as well as the power of words. The way to become sensitive to the sounds of poetry is to read aloud as much as possible, and certainly it is essential to read aloud all the poetry you intend to answer questions on, not just once but several times.

ESSENTIAL PRINCIPLES

The first task is to identify these patterns. This is easily done once you have learned to recognize the following techniques.

Onomatopoeia depends on the ability of sounds to echo the sense of a word, for example swish, or plop. Strict onomatopoeia is confined to those words whose meaning has something to do with sound,

> **Only a cock stood on the rooftree**
>
> **Co co rico co co rico**

You will find such words used occasionally by poets, as in this example, but much more frequently onomatopoeia is interpreted in a rather wider sense of mimicry or imitation as in this piece of children's verse,

> **The dove said 'Coo**
>
> **What shall I do**
>
> **I can hardly maintain my two.'**

The poet is clearly trying to imitate the sound made by a dove by using 'Coo' which echoes the dove's peculiar noise, and then repeating the sound in 'do' and 'two'. Neither of these words is onomatopoeic in itself, but because they repeat the dove's cooing sound in the same way that doves continually repeat their noise, they appear to be imitating the dove's call.

Here is another way poets can imitate sounds,

> **Faster than fairies, faster than witches**
>
> **Bridges and houses, hedges and ditches,**

If you read this aloud you can hear that the poet has organized the rhythm to give the sound of wheels going over a railway track.

Very rarely is onomatopoeia employed throughout a poem but the following poem by Thomas Hardy was deliberately built around the technique, and 'Onomatopoeic' is its sub-title.

> **Reticulations creep upon the slack stream's face**
>
> **When the wind skims irritably past,**
>
> **The current clucks smartly into each hollow place**
>
> **That years of flood have scrabbled in the pier's sodden base;**
>
> **The floating lily leaves rot fast.**

The onomatopoeic qualities are these:

➤ There are two words that echo sense, 'clucks' and 'scrabbled'.

➤ The rhythm, which is not smooth and regular, tries to imitate the flow of the water, sometimes rapid, in other places slower.

➤ Hardy uses a lot of consonants like 't', 'c', 'p', 'b' to give the sound of the water slapping against the bank and the bridge.

➤ The phrase 'When the wind skims' uses the sounds 'w' and 's' to help suggest the blowing of the wind.

Look at the poems you are studying and identify any occasions where the meaning is echoed in the sound.

2   INDIVIDUAL SOUNDS

Try to be alive to the individual sounds in words. These frequently assist the meaning of a word by reminding us of other words with similar meanings, or by the way in which the sound is formed.

There are two kinds of sounds, vowels and consonants. When we form a consonant we stop, or half-stop, the breath somewhere in the mouth, or throat. When we form a vowel the breath is not stopped.

Some consonants can be very forceful, because the sound is dammed up, behind the lips or teeth or in the throat, and then let out suddenly in a small explosion. These consonants, 'p' and 'b', 't' and 'd', 'k' and 'g' are often called 'hard'. When they occur in words and phrases with a strong, hard or forceful meaning they seem to intensify that meaning. The sounds of 'bitter' and 'batter' add to the harshness of their meaning. Lines like John Donne's, 'Batter my heart three person'd God', and 'Death thou shalt die' use this quality of hard consonants to increase the impact of the line.

Other consonants, like 'm', 'n', 's', 'l' and 'w' are much softer. These sounds have a lot of soft or quiet associations from words in which they are found: 'slumber', 'sleep', 'lullaby', 'slowly', 'mellow', 'wistful' – you will be able to think of a lot more. Consequently John Keats' line, 'Season of mists and mellow fruitfulness', which uses a lot of these sounds has a feeling of mellow softness. He has matched the sound to the meaning.

The particular quality of vowels is that they can be sustained like a held note in music, some more easily than others. So we talk about short vowels, like the sounds in 'pig', 'tap', 'hot' and 'met', or long vowels, like the sounds in 'stream', 'low', 'moon' and 'star'. The kind of vowels used can affect the pace of a line. The line from Keats that I have just quoted uses a number of long vowels which helps to make it slow and calm.

You must not think that vowels and consonants have meaning in themselves. You should, however, notice when they fit the meaning of the word or line in which they occur.

3 ▷ ALLITERATION

Alliteration is the repetition of **consonants** at the beginning of words or syllables. For instance in the following line,

In a coign of a cliff between lowland and highland

the poet uses two different sets of alliteration. First there is the use of 'c' in 'coign of a cliff'. Second there is the use of 'l' in 'lowland and highland'. Notice that the 'l' appears twice at the beginning of a syllable (land) rather than a word. It is also necessary to remember that it is the sound that is important, not the spelling, so whether the poet writes 'Kiss me Kate' or 'Kiss me Catherine' makes no difference. Both are alliteration because both 'c' and 'k' have the same **pronunciation**. This is one of the reasons why it is so essential to read poems **aloud**; reading with the eyes just does not have the same effect. One further point: the repetition must occur in words that are fairly close together, perhaps in the same line, perhaps near the end of one line and the beginning of another.

In the following poem the poet uses alliteration a number of times. I have underlined the instances in the first two lines; there are two more examples in the following two lines.

On _W_enlock Edge the _w_ood's in trouble;
His _f_orest _f_leece the Wrekin heaves;
The gale it plies the saplings double,
And thick on Severn snow the leaves.

4 ▷ ASSONANCE

Assonance works on the same principle as alliteration, but now we are looking for repeated **vowel** sounds. The rule about sound rather than spelling is even more important when considering vowels because of some of the extraordinary spellings that have come about in English, that look the same but are pronounced quite differently – so be warned. You are already familiar with assonance of a particular type: when it occurs at the end of a line we call it rhyme. Assonance, then, is rhyme anywhere else in the line. The poet uses two sets of assonance in the following line,

And the May month flaps its glad green leaves like wings

'Flaps' rhymes with 'glad' and 'green' with 'leaves'. You might perhaps have noticed that 'its' and 'wings' also have the same vowel sound, but I have not counted this as an instance of assonance, not because they are too far apart but because 'its' is not a sufficiently prominent word in this line. When we read it we glide over it without noticing because it is not a stressed syllable. Keats was very adept at using assonance, as you can hear in this stanza. Again I have marked the first few lines and left the rest for you.

> *Thou <u>still</u> unrav<u>i</u>shed <u>Bride</u> of <u>quietness</u>*
> *Thou foster <u>child</u> of <u>si</u>lence and slow <u>Time</u>,*
> *<u>Syl</u>van <u>his</u>torian, who canst thus express*
> *A flowery tale more <u>sweetly</u> than our rhyme:*
> *What <u>leaf</u>-fringed legend haunts about thy shape*
> *Of deities or mortals, or of both,*
> *In Tempe or the dales of Arkady?*
> *What men or gods are these? What maidens loath?*
> *What mad pursuit? What struggle to escape?*
> *What pipes and timbrels? What wild ecstasy?*

5 > THE PURPOSE OF SOUND PATTERNS

Collecting the evidence as we have been doing is relatively easy; deciding what to say about it is more difficult. To do that we have to decide what the poet achieves by using these effects. There is no point in listing them unless we can say why they are there.

ALLITERATION AND ASSONANCE

Alliteration and assonance are very good at **bringing words together** and making or emphasizing a connection between them. Among our examples we found 'green leaves'. We know, of course, the connection between green and leaves but the assonance makes it even firmer, as though greenness and leaves were interchangeable. Alliteration performs the same trick with 'green grass' and Dylan Thomas used this to marvellous effect in 'Fern Hill' when he wrote 'Fire green as grass'. Sometimes the bringing together is to show contrast, as in 'Bluish mid the burning water'. An interesting exercise is to jot down all the pairs of words which are often found together and which use alliteration or assonance like 'hearth and home' or 'high and dry'. It is not only poets who know how to use sounds to bind words together, it seems to be built into the language.

EFFECTS OF CONSONANTS AND VOWELS

The particular **kind of consonants and vowels used** give different effects. Ask yourself what there is in the **meaning** of the poem which makes the poet want to use hard or soft sounds. We have already seen how Keats uses a predominance of soft sounds to create the picture of an autumn day, with all the outlines of the landscape blurred by mist and the fruit ripened to softness. On the other hand Wilfred Owen, writing of the First World War, uses a high proportion of hard sounds to help create the noise of the guns:

> *Only the stuttering rifles rapid rattle*
> *Can patter out their hasty orisons.* ('Anthem for Doomed Youth')

In both cases the poets help the consonants by using appropriate vowel sounds: long, sustained vowels in Keats, like 'Season', 'mellow' and 'fruitfulness'; short abrupt ones in Owen, like 'rifle', 'rapid' 'rattle'.

SOUND PATTERNS

The least definite effect, but still an important one, is to give the poem a **beautiful** or an **interesting sound**, which gives pleasure for itself just as music does. Melodiousness is generally thought of as being created by long vowels like 'oo', 'ee' etc. and gentle consonants, as in this example from Tennyson's **Song of the Lotus Eaters.**

> *How sweet it were, hearing the downward stream,*
> *With half-shut eyes ever to seem*
> *Falling asleep in a half-dream!*

But there is also a more vigorous music, created by the use of harder consonants and fewer long vowels, which can be just as pleasing as in Browning's 'Home Thoughts from the Sea',

> *Nobly, nobly, Cape Saint Vincent to the North-west died away*
> *Sunset ran, one glorious blood-red, reeking into Cadiz Bay;*
> *Bluish 'mid the burning water, full in face Trafalgar lay;*
> *In the dimmest North-east distance dawned Gibraltar grand*
>   *and gray.*

6 ▷ SUMMARY

Individual sounds and patterns of sound (alliteration, assonance and onomatopoeia) have the following functions:

➤ To bring words together to emphasize a comparison or contrast in meaning.

➤ To imitate or enact the meaning by using onomatopoeia or a particular type of sound (i.e. hard or soft consonants, long or short vowels).

➤ To produce a 'melody' which is pleasing to the ear.

Remember that sounds support meaning. Very rarely do they mean anything in themselves.

ADDITIONAL EXAMPLES

Use these examples as exercises to test your understanding of what you have read in this chapter. What can you say about the way these poets are using sounds? Work out your answers before looking at the Key below.

1. *And the afternoon, the evening, sleeps so peacefully!* (T. S. Eliot)
2. *There was a whispering in my hearth*
   A sigh of coal, (Wilfred Owen)
3. *He does not die a death of shame*
   On a day of dark disgrace, (Oscar Wilde)

1 ▷ KEY TO THE EXAMPLES

1. T. S. Eliot is using the assonance of a long vowel in 'evening', 'sleeps' and 'peacefully'. This has the effect of slowing the line, emphasizing the connection between the three words and so intensifying its meaning.
2. Wilfred Owen uses two onomatopoeic words, 'whispering' and 'sigh', which imitate the sound of the coal burning. Only if you have listened to a coal fire burning can you know how accurate these words are for some of the little sounds a fire makes.
3. Oscar Wilde uses alliteration of hard consonants. This is appropriate to the harshness of his subject in these lines.

EXAM QUESTION

You can use what you have learnt in this chapter in response to any instruction to write about the language of a poem, remembering that you should also be writing about figurative language (see Ch. 4). The examiner may ask you to 'comment on the effectiveness of the language' or 'comment on the poetic qualities'. The following typical example is from an LEAG question.

A Child Half-Asleep – Tony Connor

Stealthily parting the small-hours silence,
a hardly-embodied figment of his brain
comes down to sit with me
as I work late.
Flat-footed as though his legs and feet
were still asleep.

On the stool,
staring into the fire,
his dummy dangling.

Fire ignites the small coals of his eyes;
it stares back through the holes
into his head, into the darkness.

I ask what woke him.

'A wolf dreamed me,' he says.

Write about the poem. You may wish to consider the following:
➤ any phrases, lines or ideas which you feel are interesting;
➤ how the ones that you select have helped to convey the feeling of the poem, or have helped you to understand what the poet is trying to explain.

> **Many students make the mistake of thinking every word echoes its sense. Think carefully before you say that the sound is appropriate for the meaning.**

NOTES AND TUTOR'S ANSWER

1 ▷ NOTES

You would have about 15 minutes to do this part of the question in the exam but do not attempt to limit your time yet. Take as much time as you need at first and gradually work towards the time limit.

1. Make a list of all the examples of alliteration, onomatopoeia and assonance. This is rough work but do it in the answer book and then put a single line through it.
2. Try to say something about the effect in the poem of each example on your list. You will get some marks for making good choices of words or phrases and more for your explanations. If you have difficulty doing this look back at the explanations in sections 1 to 5 above which should give you some ideas. Do not worry if it does not come easily. Keep re-reading.
3. Do not read the answer below until you've written your own.

2 ▷ SUGGESTED ANSWER

Alliteration:
stealthily small silence
Flat-footed
still asleep stool staring
dummy dangling
woke wolf

Assonance:
Fire ignites eyes
coals holes
dreamed me

Onomatopoeia:
Flat-footed.

The poet has used several words in the first line beginning with 's': 'Steal-thily. . . small-hours silence'. This alliteration of a soft consonant helps to establish the quietness of the house and the sleepiness of the child. Later examples of allite-ration of the same sound, 'still asleep' and 'stool staring' continue the same mood. The mood is created by the sound itself and by the association with many words to do with sleep and quietness which contain this sound.

> **Always say what the effect is. Only use the explanation 'musical' occasionally, otherwise it looks as if you don't really know what effect the sound has.**

'Flat-footed' has an onomatopoeic effect which suggests the slap of the child's feet on the floor as he patters downstairs.

The alliteration of 'dummy dangling' makes an interesting phrase which adds to the musical effect of the poem.

Several important words are brought together by assonance in the line 'Fire ignites the small coals of his eyes'. First, sound underlines the connection between fire and burning. Then, the sound also stresses the sense of his eyes burning like coals with the reflected firelight, because 'eyes' repeats the vowel in 'Fire ignites'. The metaphor which compares his eyes to coals is also supported by the assonance of 'coals' and 'holes'.

The very important connection between the idea of the wolf and waking up is made by the alliteration of 'wolf' and 'woke'.

Finally the unusual word order which shows the child's point of view is em-phasized by the assonance of 'dreamed me'.

This is a suggested answer to the question. There is no *right* answer and if you have made roughly the same points but expressed yourself differently in your attempt there is no need to worry.

SUGGESTIONS FOR COURSEWORK

1. Add work on sounds to your examination of a poem when you are writing a coursework unit.
2. Use the question above as a model for a coursework unit and look at the way sounds are used in several poems by the same poet. Or compare poems by different poets.
3. Choose a number of poems to read aloud and 'perform' these in a class group or to an audience. Write a record of this performance, examining how successful the choice of poems was and how well the poems went down with the audience.
4. Go to a public poetry reading, or listen to a poetry programme on the radio, and write a review. Make sure that you have a copy (or a tape) of at least some of the poems read.

STUDENT'S ANSWER – EXAMINER'S COMMENT

Question

These are extracts from student answers to questions that asked for comments on the use of sound.

66 **Good. Correctly identifies onomatopoeia and describes how the words used make their effect.** **99**

> Doomed Youth
>
> (a) ' Stuttering, rapid rattle, patter' these words create the effect of rat tat tat – the firing of machine guns. This effect is onomatopoeia where these words sound like actual noise made by the firing of machine guns. It is created by using words that sound like the actual noise of the object being described which get one to imagine one is actually in the place at the time being described.
> (b) 'Choirs of wailing shells' (line 7)
> The noise of shells (bombs) or bullets tearing through the air created a series of high pitched noises sounding like high notes. The different timing of when the shells were dropped created an effect of a series of notes which sounded like a group of people singing, therefore a choir of wailing shells.

66 **Good. Does not fall into the trap of thinking this line sounds like a choir. Correctly identifies its effect as being due to the simile.** **99**

Question

Write about the poem, 'To Autumn'. What is the poet saying about the season? How does he create a picture of the season and it's atmosphere? Does the atmosphere change during the poem?

> To Autumn
>
> The poet is saying that one season is happening now, it is all warm and the bees have made their honey, and it is over flowing, but soon one season will change and another one will come. The season was very hot, and lots of flowers came into trees, which bend with the weight of the heavy apples. Also all the fruit is ripe, and the sun is ripening all the time; to become hotter and hotter. A picture of the season and its atmosphere is created by, lots of descriptive words, and on long words, there are long ending letters, a bit like (ness), (ow), (sts) and (bosom). Most of the words have a lot of vowels in, which helps to bring the word, sound much more smooth. The poem is very slow, but also sounds very lazy, with all the descriptive words in it.

 In this comment on the poem 'To Autumn' there are a number of strengths and weaknesses.

Strengths:
1. Notices that the descriptive words are important
2. Points out that the vowels give the effect of slowness and laziness

Weaknesses:
1. Does not choose particular words or sounds to comment on, so that the writing is too vague to gain many marks.
2. Although the student makes a great effort to say precisely what he/she means, the student does not have the vocabulary to talk about what is happening in the poem **99**

READING
TO
UNDERSTAND:
DRAMA

GETTING STARTED

Without a doubt, the greatest help in studying drama is seeing plays acted on the stage. The experience of watching a play in the theatre is very different from reading it, or of seeing it on TV or video. Nowhere except in the theatre can you experience the relationship between the audience and live performers acting out the drama for you. Every performance is a unique occasion, an interplay between that particular set of people on that particular night. Actors wait apprehensively to see how responsive the 'house' will be, and come offstage at their first break with encouragement for their colleagues, 'good audience tonight' or warnings, 'rotten house, absolutely dead'.

You put yourself at a disadvantage if you have no idea of what goes on in a theatre. Ideally you should have paid several visits so that you are familiar with theatre techniques, and then go to see the play you are studying, after reading it first. You may be lucky enough to find a performance of your chosen play but, if not, any experience of theatre will be helpful in enabling you to bring the play to life as you read it.

BRINGING A PLAY TO LIFE
STAGE DIRECTIONS
STAGE DESIGN
SETTING
COSTUME
PLAYING THE PARTS
MOVEMENT
OTHER EFFECTS
LIGHTING EFFECTS
SOUND EFFECTS
RADIO AND TELEVISION

ESSENTIAL PRINCIPLES

1 > LIFTING THE PLAY OFF THE PAGE

A playscript is only a blueprint. Like a builder faced with an architect's drawing, or a conductor with a musical score, when you read a play you have to fill in all the details in your mind from the outline that the dramatist gives you. You have far more work to do in your *imagination* than you do when reading a novel. There, the author gives you descriptions of the places, the characters, their actions, their dress, their feelings. In a play text you have only the dialogue and the stage directions.

In fact, in reading the text you are being asked to do what the director in the theatre has to do: that is, to lift the words off the page and envisage the play as it would be when performed in the theatre. To do that you need to be able to imagine the stage, the setting, the costumes, the lighting, the actors and their voices and movements. You begin to do some of these things as soon as you begin to read. When the text says:

GREGSON: *(menacingly)* I shouldn't do that if I were you!

you imagine the line being spoken in a menacing way, as the bracketed stage direction instructs. As you go on reading you will gradually build up a more complete picture.

Your first task in studying a play is **to read it right through to the end**. Ideally you should try to do this in one sitting with a short break in the middle. In this way you imitate the experience of seeing the play in the theatre, in one stretch of time. Try to do your first reading on your own before any reading you are going to do in class. Do not worry too much about detail at this stage; just try to get a general impression.

The following paragraphs should help you with the imaginative work you should try to do when you go through the play for the second time.

2 > STAGE DIRECTIONS

In a play text you only have two sources of information: the dialogue, that is the words the characters say, and the stage directions. The *stage directions* are vitally important because they tell you how the dramatist wants the characters to look and sound, where the action takes place, what the time is, what the weather is like – anything that the dramatist thinks is important for you to know. Some playwrights give very brief stage directions. Some, like Bernard Shaw make them so long that we might be reading a novel. They are frequently found in the following places:

(i) At the beginning of the scene, to tell us where the action is to take place.

(ii) When a new character enters, to tell us some thing about the appearance, voice, personality, dress, position of the character.

(iii) At the beginning of a speech, to tell the actor how it should be spoken.

These instructions must be read with at least the same attention as the dialogue. Often you will have to read them very slowly and carefully to work out exactly what a room or a character should look like.

3 > THE STAGE

When we think of a stage we most probably think of it as being at one end of a hall, with rows of seats facing it and perhaps with a curtain to draw across to hide the 'picture'. This kind of stage, called an *end-stage*, for obvious reasons, is, however, not the only kind. At different periods of history plays have been written to be shown on different kinds of stage.

A *thrust stage* juts or thrusts out into the audience. The audience sits round three sides which brings them into much closer contact with the actors. This was the kind of stage for which Shakespeare wrote.

An *arena*, or theatre-in-the-round, has the audience sitting all round the stage. The actors enter and exit down gangways through the audience. This kind of stage has become quite popular in recent years. When you see a play staged in this way you feel very close to the action. Clearly some plays are more suited to one kind of stage than others. For instance it is not possible to have a curtain around a thrust or an arena, which makes some scenes rather difficult to do. Large pieces of furniture are also impossible in an arena, because part of the stage would then be hidden for some of the audience.

End-stages are best for those plays that are written for big fixed sets, such as rooms full of furniture. **Hobson's Choice**, which is set in a boot and shoe shop, is an example. This kind of set takes a lot of time and effort to move, so the curtain is usually dropped and the audience has an interval while the stage hands dash around heaving the furniture about. Since the audience will only want one or two intervals this means you can only have a big set change once or twice. If the dramatist wants more set changes they have to be done differently, and this is something the dramatist has to think about when writing the play.

Thrust stages and arenas can easily accommodate those plays which have a succession of scenes in different places where the setting is simply suggested, perhaps by something which the actors can bring on and take off with them, or perhaps by the audience being told in the words of the play. When a character strolls on and says:

How sweet the moonlight sleeps upon this bank,

then the audience knows that it must imagine the character sitting on a bank in the moonlight, even though the stage may be completely bare. Because Shakespeare was writing for this kind of stage (with no lighting effects either) he had to use extremely vivid language to arouse the imagination of his audience.

When reading a play you would do well to decide what kind of theatre it could best be performed in and imagine yourself sitting in that theatre. Usually the opening stage directions will give you an idea.

4 ▷ THE SETTING

Once you have decided what kind of stage you are going to work on in your imagination you can then get on with setting the scene. This is really the work of the designer, but in this production which takes place in your head you are director, designer, actor, lighting technician and everything else. Once again you go back to the stage directions to see what the dramatist wants the set to be like. The instructions may be very precise:

It is Mrs Higgins at home day. Nobody has yet arrived. Her drawing room, in a flat on the Chelsea embankment, has three windows looking on the river; and the ceiling is not so lofty as it would be in an older house of the same pretensions. The windows are open, giving access to a balcony with flowers in pots. If you stand with your face to the windows you have the fireplace on your left and the door in the right hand wall close to the corner nearest the windows. Mrs Higgins was brought up on Morris and Burne-Jones; and her room, which is very unlike her son's room in Wimpole Street, is not crowded with knicknacks. In the middle of the room there is a big ottoman; and this, with the carpet, the Morris wallpapers, and the Morris chintz window curtains and brocade covers of the ottoman and its cushions, supply all the ornament, and are much too handsome to be hidden by odds and ends of useless things. A few good oil paintings from the exhibitions in the Grosvenor Gallery thirty years ago are on the walls. The only landscape is a Cecil Lawson on the scale of a Rubens. There is a portrait of Mrs Higgins as she was when she defied fashion in her youth in one of the beautiful Rossettian costumes. . . In the corner diagonally opposite the door Mrs Higgins, now over sixty and long past the age of taking the trouble to dress out of fashion, sits writing at an elegantly simple writing table with a bell-button within reach of her hand. There is a Chippendale chair further back in the room between her and the window nearest her side. At the other side of the room, further forward, is an Elizabethan chair roughly carved in the taste of Inigo Jones. On the same side a piano in a decorated case. The corner between the fireplace and the windows is occupied by a divan cushioned in Morris chintz. (**Pygmalion**)

Or they may be quite vague:

Thunder and lightning. Enter three Witches.

This opening stage direction from **Macbeth** makes deciding on the setting easy. The scene obviously has to be played on an empty stage, deserted except for the three figures. All we have to decide is whether to dress the stage at all, or just let Shakespeare's words do the work. We might decide to have something on the floor to suggest the roughness of the heath. But then again, remembering the later scenes in a palace we might reject such a notion. Possibly we could have some large stones jutting up near the back of the thrust stage for the witches conveniently to disappear behind. These could later be moved slightly and used as the palace gate, or battlements, or whatever. Shakespeare's stage would have been completely bare and the witches would probably have emerged on to it through a trap door.

Pygmalion is much more complicated. Shaw specifies some very elaborate furniture, in an elegant room, with a particular pattern of wallpaper and curtains and pictures by named artists. Shaw knew perfectly well that in practice such a set would not be possible, even in the most lavish of professional productions. What is interesting is the detail with which he imagined his character's surroundings. He was trying to give the designer and director an idea of the elegant kind of drawing room Mrs Higgins would have. Every production does not need to have a Chippendale chair and an Elizabethan chair carved in the taste of Inigo Jones, a painting by Cecil Lawson and so on. But the stage set must create the impression of a finely decorated and furnished room and we must try to create this in our imagination when reading.

The set is usually the first thing the audience sees and it should make a strong impression. It must not only give a sense of place but also suggest something of the mood or atmosphere of what is to come. When reading a play it is a good idea to have in our minds a setting as complete as the one Shaw imagined for his characters.

5 ▷ COSTUME

Now on to our set walks a character. Or perhaps he or she is sitting there already. The way the character is *dressed* also contributes to the atmosphere of the play. The elegant ladies in evening dress waiting in the rain at the opening of *Pygmalion* give us certain expectations. So does the untidy old tramp who enters the room at the beginning of *The Caretaker*. More specifically a costume tells us something about the person who is wearing it. Although in real life we should never judge a man by his clothes, in drama the impressions the costumes make on us adds to our other impressions. Costume may, for example, tell us the period in which the drama is taking place, or the social class of the character, whether rich or poor, and something of the personality. Everything put on stage is there for the purpose of showing us something, giving information. Lady Bracknell appears in frills and furbelows, draped in furs and jewellery, with a huge decorated hat. She is richly and fussily overdressed because she is rich, fussy and overbearing. In *A Man for All Seasons* Sir Thomas More's plain, monk-like gown reflects the honest integrity of his nature.

In a similar way, dramatists may be very precise in their descriptions of characters' appearances. In practice they know that it may not be possible to dress the character exactly according to the instructions, to say nothing of finding actors who look the same as the descriptions. What matters is fulfilling the spirit of the dramatist's instructions, and having the actor give the correct impression.

As long as we are working in imagination, though, these difficulties do not arise. We can create the character in our mind's eye exactly as the dramatist would wish. A little research in a costume book or an illustrated history will enable us to imagine the correct dress.

6 ▷ PLAYING THE PART

It sometimes helps you to 'see' the characters and 'hear' the words they say in your mind if you **imagine** the play being performed by actors you have seen on stage, film, or television. You can choose your cast from international stars, expense no object. Alternatively you can see and hear yourself playing all the different parts, becoming appropriately older or younger, thinner or fatter, taller or shorter, as the part dictates. As with costume, looks are important because the audience must receive the right impression. In *Hobson's Choice* Maggie Hobson must look older than her sisters, otherwise we will not believe she is in danger of becoming an old maid. In **Romeo and Juliet** Juliet must look very young because the Nurse says she is not yet fourteen.

Once again the stage directions often provide the character details the dramatist wants to give. Even so, we are sometimes given very little to go on especially in older plays. For example, in **She Stoops to Conquer** it is the text of the play which provides our information about the heroine. Her father tells us at the beginning that she is decked out in silks as usual, and a little later notes that she has changed into a plainer dress to please him. Not until Act 3 do we find any further clues to her appearance, when her suitor says, 'I vow, child, you are vastly handsome. . . Never saw a more sprightly malicious eye.' In cases like this, when the stage directions are little help and there is very little in the text, we begin to form our idea of appearance from the character's behaviour, which shows how closely the two are connected in drama.

Even more important is the actor's voice. First, it has to be suitable for the character: it is no use having Billy Liar's father ranting and raving in a thin little wheeze, or Juliet booming like a foghorn. Secondly, every change in the character's feeling has to be expressed in the way the dialogue is spoken. When we are reading the dialogue we have to hear these changes in our minds so that the feeling becomes real for us. When Macbeth's mind is filled with horrible imaginings his voice shakes with fear. When Beatie Bryant, at the end of **Roots**, finds herself speaking her own mind instead of parroting her boyfriend's thoughts, she shouts for joy, her voice full of wonder at her own achievement.

When we are in the theatre we hear all these things; when we are reading at home we only have lifeless words in front of us until we lift them off the page through the strength of our imaginations and hear them in our inward ear.

7 › MOVEMENT

Everything that has just been said about the need for an appropriate voice also applies to the way each character **moves**. We should **see** Harold Pinter's tramp, Davies, moving with the uncertain clumsiness of an unsure old man: he shuffles or lurches across the stage in **The Caretaker**. Rita, in **Educating Rita**, might begin by slouching and lolling around in an ungainly fashion, but by the end of the play when she is more aware of herself her posture will have changed and she will be more restrained.

There is also the movement, or positioning of characters in relation to each other, to consider. What we see onstage are moving pictures which tell us about relationships. The king enters at the head of a procession. He takes his seat on a raised throne. The court stands humbly round at a respectful distance, all facing him attentively. We know he is an important man before he speaks, even if he has no crown on his head. Bernard Shaw illustrates this idea in **St Joan** when the Dauphin hides in the crowd and an imposter is placed on the throne to fool Joan. Her ability to see through what she is first presented with is taken as a mark of God's hand upon her.

When we are presented with pictures in the theatre we respond without having to think. A crowd on one side of the stage, and a solitary man on the other, means this character is in some way special – a stranger or an outsider, a rebel or an enemy, someone different from the others. In **An Enemy of the People** when Dr Stockman confronts a crowd of his fellow townspeople alone we see what they think of him even before we hear them call him 'an enemy of the people'. The difficulty that Romeo has in reaching Juliet on her balcony is a visual parallel to the difficulty of their relationship because of the feud between their two families.

Every movement and every grouping onstage has a message in this way, though not always as clearly as in these examples. If we are simply reading the play we are robbed of these pictures and have to do our best to provide them for ourselves.

8 › OTHER EFFECTS

LIGHTING

Another important tool in the theatre is **lighting**. The director can use it realistically, for instance to show night falling, or the red glow in the sky produced by burning buildings. Or it can be used to produce atmosphere. The murder of Thomas Becket in Canterbury cathedral might be accompanied by a red light flooding the stage, not because the cathedral is on fire, but to symbolize the blood that has been spilt. Sometimes such effects are written into the play, particularly in Shakespeare. The language of **Macbeth** is full of references to darkness, blackness and night, to create the atmosphere of evil and the guilt-tormented mind of Macbeth, as he pursues his murderous course. Shakespeare's theatre had no lighting and his plays were performed in daylight. Therefore it was the imagery of his poetry alone which had to work on the imagination of his audience, exactly what it has to do for a reader today.

SOUND EFFECTS

These are almost always used realistically. We *hear* the clank of chains offstage as Elizabeth Proctor is arrested in **The Crucible**; we *hear* Willy Loman's son knocking and knocking on the door of his father's hotel room while Willy frantically tries to get rid of the woman he has there (**Death of a Salesman**). Like seeing things happen, hearing them as you read, brings the events of the play vividly to life. There is no reason why sound effects should not also be used atmospherically. If you have imagined thunder rumbling in the distance while the murderer stalks his victim, or lovers plighting their troth to the song of skylarks, you may have had a directorial stroke of genius that no-one has thought of yet.

---

9 ⟩ RADIO AND TELEVISION

Most, but not all, of the plays we read have been written for the theatre. Some very fine plays have been written for radio, for example those by Giles Cooper and Dylan Thomas, and an increasing number of good plays are being written for television. When writing for these media the dramatist both knows the limitations of the form he has chosen, and makes the fullest use of its advantages. The advantage for us is that we can see and hear these plays on tape just as they were intended to be experienced.

A radio dramatist has to take into account the fact that all the information he wants to convey has to be through sound. Sound has to create the whole environment. The actors have to do much more work with their voices because their actions and feelings cannot be seen. If a character is called on to lift something heavy the audience has to hear it through the strain in his voice. If a character is sad it is no good weeping silently: the emotion has to be heard. Knowing this, the dramatist tries to make everything clear through the dialogue.

These limitations might be thought of as disadvantages when compared to the theatre. On the other hand, a radio play is not restricted to a particular space represented by the stage. Radio drama can jump from place to place at will. It can happen in the most strange and extraordinary locations. Fantasy is no difficulty when the listeners are providing their own visual imaginings. It can travel through time with ease. And it is particularly good at exploring characters' thoughts.

Television shares some of this freedom with radio. It too can easily move from place to place and even contrive to allow the audience to see two places at once. Because we see things on TV in clear photographic detail and close-up it is a medium where realistic drama can be done very well. Because the camera can play visual tricks television is also a medium which can explore fantasy.

---

10 ⟩ SUMMARY

➤ Whenever possible go and see the play you are studying.

➤ The script is only an outline; you must fill in all the details when reading.

➤ The stage directions are an important source of information for everything you would see in a performance.

➤ Imagining the stage performance (stage, costume, sets, lighting) gives atmosphere and brings to life the situation and the characters.

➤ Imagining the actors' appearances, voices and movements helps us to understand the characters' feelings and relationships.

ADDITIONAL EXAMPLES

Use the following examples as exercises to test your understanding of what you have read in this chapter. This kind of work will help you to visualize the plays you are studying. It will also give you good material for revision or for writing a course-work unit. Work through the examples and then read the key at the end.

1. Read the following stage directions and opening lines of **A Taste of Honey** Then describe how you might set the stage and how you imagine the looks and dress of the characters. The play was written in 1957 but could equally well take place in 1987.

The stage represents a comfortless flat in Manchester and the street outside. Jazz music. Enter Helen, a semi-whore and her daughter Jo. They are loaded with baggage.

HELEN: Well! This is the place.

JO: And I don't like it.

HELEN: When I find somewhere for us to live I have to consider something much more important than your feelings . . . the rent. It's all I can afford.

JO: You can afford something better than this old ruin.

HELEN: When you start earning you can start moaning.

JO: Can't be soon enough for me. I'm cold and my shoes let water . . . what a place . . . and we're supposed to be living off her immoral earnings.

HELEN: I'm careful. Anyway what's wrong with this place? Everything in it's falling apart it's true, and we've no heating – but there's a lovely view of the gasworks, we share a bathroom with the community and this wallpaper's contemporary. What more do you want? Anyway it'll do for us. Pass me a glass Jo.

> 66 **You can do the exercise on the first passage even if you have not read the play, because it comes from the opening. You will find the second passage difficult if you have not read Romeo and Juliet or some other plays by Shakespeare** 99

2. Read the following short scene from **Romeo and Juliet** (III. i. 34-89). Describe how you see the characters: their dress, their actions and how they stand and move on stage. What kind of lighting or other effects could be used in this scene?

BENVOLIO: By my head, here comes the Capulets.

MERCUTIO: By my heel, I care not.

TYBALT: (*to Petruccio and the others*) Follow me close, for I will speak with them. (*To the Montagues*) Gentlemen, good e'en. A word with one of you.

MERCUTIO: An but one word with one of us? Couple it with something. Make it a word and a blow.

TYBALT: You shall find me apt enough to that, sir, an you will give me occasion.

MERCUTIO: Could you not take some occasion without the giving?

TYBALT: Mercutio, thou consort'st with Romeo.

MERCUTIO: 'Consort'? What dost thou make us minstrels? An thou make minstrels of us, look to hear nothing but discords. (*touching his rapier*) Here's my fiddlestick; here's that shall make you dance. Zounds – 'Consort'!

BENVOLIO: We talk here in the public haunt of men.

Either withdraw unto some private place,

Or reason coldly of your grievances,

Or else depart. Here all eyes gaze on us.

MERCUTIO: Men's eyes were made to look, and let them gaze.

I will not budge for no man's pleasure, I.

Enter Romeo

TYBALT: Well peace be with you, sir. Here comes my man.

MERCUTIO: But I'll be hanged, sir, if he wear your livery.

Marry, go before to field, he'll be your follower.

Your worship in that sense may call him 'man'.

TYBALT: Romeo, the love I bear thee can afford

No better term than this: thou art a villain.

ROMEO: Tybalt, the reason that I have to love thee

Doth much excuse the appertaining rage

To such a greeting. Villain am I none.

Therefore, farewell. I see thou knowest me not.

TYBALT: Boy, this shall not excuse the injuries

That thou hast done me. Therefore turn and draw.
ROMEO: I do protest I never injured thee,
But love thee better than thou can'st devise
Till thou shalt know the reason of my love.
And so, good Capulet – which name I tender
As dearly as my own – be satisfied.
MERCUTIO: *(drawing)* O calm, dishonourable, vile submission!
Alla stoccado carries it away.
Tybalt, you ratcatcher, come, will you walk?
TYBALT: What would'st thou have with me?
MERCUTIO: Good King of Cats, nothing but one of your nine lives. That I mean to make bold withal, and, as you shall use me hereafter, dry-beat the rest of the eight. Will you pluck your sword out of his pilcher by the ears? Make haste, lest mine be about your ears ere it be out.
TYBALT: *(drawing)* I am for you.
ROMEO: Gentle Mercutio, put thy rapier up.
MERCUTIO: *(to Mercutio)* Come sir, your *passado*.
They fight
ROMEO:(drawing) Draw Benvolio. Beat down their weapons.
Gentlemen for shame, forbear this outrage.
Tybalt, Mercutio, the Prince expressly hath
Forbid this bandying in Verona streets.
Hold Tybalt, good Mercutio.
(Romeo beats down their points and rushes between them. Tybalt under Mercutio's arm thrusts Mercutio in)
PETRUCCIO: Away Tybalt!
(Exeunt Tybalt, Petruccio and followers)

1. ***A Taste Of Honey***. The following suggestions are only *one* way of setting the stage and dressing the characters. What is important is to convey the depressing atmosphere of squalor in the surroundings and the lack of care that Helen takes of her daughter, even though she spends time and money decking herself up. I see the play taking place on an end or thrust stage. Your ideas may be quite different: what is important is that you should create a definite visual impression of your own.

The stage directions give us two important indications as to how the stage must look. The first is the word 'comfortless'. The second is that part of the stage represents the street outside. The front strip of the stage could represent the street. The rest of the stage could be at a slightly higher level with a few steps leading up to an imaginary front door. The way the characters talk about the flat shows how dreary and broken down it is.

The wallpaper is garishly bright and modern but is streaked with damp and peeling in places. The furniture is the kind you see on the pavement outside junk shops: a square table painted with dark brown varnish, two straight chairs in a similar colour, their seat bottoms hastily covered in cheap plastic; an ancient sofa in an indeterminate dirty green material with a large stain across the back. It has been split along the seat, a long cut, probably made by a knife, so that the stuffing and springs are bursting out. Against one wall stands an old sideboard, its doors hanging crookedly from wrenched hinges. Papers, plastic bags and a couple of empty jars have been left littering the floor in front of it. The curtains are torn and in one corner a scattered pile of mouldy garments might be forgotten dirty washing. A bare electric light bulb hangs from the ceiling.

Helen, a short woman, is plumper than she likes to admit. Her bright yellow coat is too tight for her. She wears black lacy stockings and very high heels. Her hair is dyed bright auburn and her make-up is far too thick. Jo seems to be in a sort of school uniform, the only clothes she has: a dark navy skirt, rather stained and creased, a whitish blouse, button missing at the neck and a threadbare blazer, the sleeves far too short. Her shoes are clearly worn out.

2. ***Romeo and Juliet***. These characters should be dressed in Elizabethan costume of bright colours. The stage is bare so the costume needs to provide visual interest and also give a sense of the Italian heat – reds, yellows and oranges will do this. The scene takes place in a street on a hot afternoon. Mercutio strolls lazily across and leans on a pillar, followed reluctantly by Benvolio who wants to go indoors. But he suddenly jerks to attention when he sees Tybalt coming. Mercutio ostentatiously ignores Tybalt and his friends. The animosity between the two groups is apparent: They cluster on opposite sides of the stage until Tybalt marches stiffly across and challenges Mercutio. The derision Mercutio feels is shown by his lazy, unhurried response. When Tybalt persists, Mercutio's attitude changes: he leaps up, his hand going for his sword. At this Benvolio, who has been hanging back, comes towards them and tries to calm them down or at least agree to go to a more private place, but Mercutio stands firm.

The arrival of Romeo causes Tybalt to bow stiffly to Mercutio and turn his attention to Romeo. As Tybalt walks across to challenge Romeo, Mercutio calls tauntingly after him. Everyone now expects a fight; they stand back watching, very quiet and still. Contrary to expectations Romeo listens quietly to Tybalt's insults and then gently puts out his hand. Mercutio cannot stand this. He draws his rapier. Tybalt swings round and Mercutio circles him, taunting him with little thrusts of his extended sword. When Tybalt also draws his sword Romeo holds Mercutio's arm, trying to prevent the fight. Mercutio only shakes him off, his eyes concentrating on Tybalt. They lunge furiously from side to side of the stage.

Tybalt fights very properly and precisely but Mercutio has the superior skill and teases Tybalt. Romeo, who has been hovering around shouting in vain for them to stop, finally rushes between them. Tybalt, taking advantage of the fact that Mercutio can no longer fully see him, thrusts his rapier under Romeo's arm into Mercutio's body, and quickly rushes out with his followers.

The lights should give a bright golden glow, as if it were a sunny afternoon, at the beginning of the scene. Little peaceable domestic noises could accompany the opening: someone softly whistling, a child calling in the distance. All sounds would cease as the men started to quarrel.

Do not think that you have to write about each scene in this amount of detail, but you should imagine them in detail. Writing everything down for a few key scenes helps to get the imagination working on the rest of the play.

E X A M   Q U E S T I O N S

This chapter describes very important techniques of reading a play. These techniques which will enable you to answer well the kind of questions which ask you to select a scene from the play and write about it. Some questions will specifically ask about stage directions.

1. How do the stage directions help you to understand what is happening in this extract? (***City Sugar***; NEA)
2. How do the stage directions in this passage influence the ways we are meant to regard the characters and the events taking place? (***Look Back in Anger***; NISEC)

If you have studied the stage directions as suggested in this chapter you will have no difficulty in answering such questions.

3. We see a lot of people eating in the play. Give an account of some of these occasions, and try to say why you think Dylan Thomas wanted to include them. (***Under Milk Wood***; WJEC)
4. Sally says of herself, "Ah'm one for plain speaking". Write about two scenes where you find her showing this particular quality, and say what effect her plain speaking has, both on other characters and on you. (***Love on the Dole***; MEG)

NOTE: Your answers will be much more vivid and will give evidence of the personal response that examiners are looking for if you can include lively descriptions of the characters' behaviour and reactions.

QUESTIONS, NOTES AND TUTOR'S ANSWER

5. ***The Long and the Short and the Tall***. Read the following passage and answer the questions printed beneath it. (SEG)

WHITAKER: *(Notices the radio which is still standing on the table)* Sarge! The set!

MITCHEM: Oh God, lad! Get it! Quick! *(WHITAKER moves as if to cross to table, but changes his mind and hugs wall in terror.)* Get the set! *(WHITAKER is still afraid to move. SMITH is about to fetch the radio when we hear the sound of feet on the wooden veranda.)*

Too late! *The members of the patrol squeeze up against the wall as* MITCHEM *edges away from the window out of sight.   JOHNSTONE tenses himself. The* JAPANESE SOLDIER *can be heard clattering on the veranda for several seconds before he appears at the left hand window. He peers into the room but fails to see the patrol and is just about to turn away when he notices the radio on the table. He stares at it for a short while and then moves out of sight as he crosses along the veranda towards the door. A further short pause,* JOHNSTONE *raises his hands in readiness. The door opens and the* JAPANESE SOLDIER *enters. As he steps into the room* JOHNSTONE *lunges forward and grabs the* JAPANESE, *putting an arm round his throat and his free hand over the soldier's mouth. MITCHEM, holding the sten at his hip, darts out of the door and covers the jungle from the veranda.* JOHNSTONE *and* THE PRISONER *struggle in the room.*

JOHNSTONE:Come on then, one of you! Get him! Quick!. . . Evans! Do for him! *(EVANS crosses and raises his rifle, releasing the safety catch.)*No you burk! You want to do for me as well? Come on lad! Use your bayonet! In his guts! You'll have to give it hump. *(EVANS unsheathes his bayonet and approaches the struggling figures.)*Sharp then lad! Come on! Come on! You want it in between his ribs. *(EVANS raises the bayonet to stab* THE PRISONER *who squirms in terror.)* Not that way lad! You'll only bust a bone. Feel for it first, then ram it in. Now, come on, quick! *(EVANS places his bayonet point on the chest of* THE PRISONER, *who has now stopped struggling and is cringing in the grip of* JOHNSTONE. *)* Come on! Come on! I can't hold on to him forever! Will you ram it in!

EVANS:*(steps back)* I. . . I can't do it, Corp.

JOHNSTONE: Stick it in! Don't stand there tossing up the odds! Just close your eyes and whoof it in!

EVANS: I can't! I can't! Corp, I can't.

MACLEISH: Not me!

JOHNSTONE: Smith! Take the bayonet! Don't stand there gawping. Do the job!

SMITH: For God's sake do it Taff. Put the poor bastard out of his misery.

EVANS: *(proffering the bayonet to* SMITH*)* You!

BAMFORTH: *(crossing and snatching the bayonet from* EVANS*)* Here. Give me hold. It's only the same as carving up a pig. Hold him still.

BAMFORTH *raises the bayonet and is about to thrust it into the chest of the prisoner as* MITCHEM *enters, closing the door behind him.*

MITCHEM: Bamforth! Hold it!

BAMFORTH:*(hesitates, then moves away)* I'm only doing what I'm told.

   (i)   What does this passage tell you of Johnstone's character? (4 marks)

  (ii)   What do you learn from this passage about all the other members of the patrol who appear in it? (8 marks)

1 > NOTES

1. In this passage the characters emerge as much from the stage directions which describe the action as from the words. Therefore when you are reading through the passage you must envisage the characters in action.
2. Go through the stage directions underlining all Johnstone's actions.
3. Read Johnstone's speeches again and jot down a few adjectives to describe this behaviour here (e.g. experienced, brutal)

4. Write a paragraph about Johnstone's character as shown by his behaviour here. Note how many marks there are for this part of the question.
5. Make a list of all the other members of the patrol. Go through the passage identifying what each one does and jotting down adjectives alongside their names.
6. Write a second, longer paragraph about the others. Notice there are twice as many marks to be gained here.

2 ➤ SUGGESTED ANSWER

❝Have you supported all your character points with evidence from the passage?❞

(i) Johnstone is an experienced and hardened soldier. The stage directions show he has positioned himself ready to attack the Japanese soldier if he enters the room and he waits, tense, ready for action, when the door opens. He knows how to capture and silence the man effectively by 'putting an arm round his throat and his free hand over the soldier's mouth'.

He has no hesitation in ordering his subordinates to kill the Japanese. He realizes the method necessary in this situation is bayoneting, a most brutal and vicious way of killing a man. While the other soldiers quail at the act, he has no qualms. His only concern seems to be that they should do it in the right place and make a good job of it. He even appears to relish it, urging them on with vigour:

'In his guts. You'll have to give it hump'.

He shows no sympathy for the Japanese and no humanity.

(ii) Whitaker has sufficient wits about him to realize that the radio set will give their presence away but is too frightened to move away from the wall and pull it out of sight.

Smith has the courage to risk moving to fetch the set but he is too late. Later Smith shows some pity for the prisoner by wanting to get the horrible performance with the bayonet over as quickly as possible, though he will not contradict his superior officer.

Both Evans and Macleish also show their revulsion for killing the Japanese. Evans does try to respond to the order from Johnstone but the sight of the helpless man, reduced to immobile terror, arouses his sympathy. Macleish refuses point blank.

Only Bamforth equals Johnstone in ruthlessness. He deliberately hardens himself against the Japanese by speaking of him as an animal rather than a human being. His response is unthinking, that of a man who is unused to using his imagination to put himself in another man's shoes. Later he will react equally unthinkingly in defence of the Japanese.

Mitchem's authoritative command saves the man. He has the stature to command his men. He thinks clearly and acts decisively in an emotional situation.

SUGGESTIONS FOR COURSEWORK

1. All the exam questions above are suitable for coursework units. You can adapt them to the plays you are studying. Notice that questions 3 and 4 are similar to the kind of work done on the passages of 'Additional Examples'.
2. In their suggestions for possible coursework units, SEG includes: Suggestions for producing a play. Take a play that you have studied. Write about how you would direct it showing the kind of stage you would use, the set, costumes, lighting and sound effects, and the instructions you would give to the actors on their characters
3. Write a review of a play you have seen.
4. Rewrite a scene from a play as a short story, or an episode from a novel as a scene from a play. Give full stage directions.

STUDENT'S ANSWER – EXAMINER'S COMMENT

Question

Although *The Merchant of Venice* takes its title from Antonio, Shylock is the central character. Can you think of a better title? If so, justify it.

> 66 **Good. Shows an understanding of how all the parts of the play contribute to the central idea** 99

> 66 **Good. Shows how different characters relate to this central idea.** 99

> 66 **A central theme of the play is that appearances are deceptive. Discussion of this theme needs to be taken further.** 99

> 66 **Good. Relates the chosen title to important events in the play.** 99

> 66 **These scenes with Shylock primarily show his love of money. It is straining a point too far to say that he thinks of his daughter first. The fact that Shylock is presented as a figure of fun in these scenes is also not mentioned.** 99

I feel that the title, 'All that glisters, is not gold', is a better title than 'The Merchant of Venice', and is more suited to the play. I feel this way, because it plays a major part in the courting of Portia, as to which casket; gold, silver or lead; must be chosen in order for her hand in marriage to be won. My chosen title can also portray its meaning through other minor parts.

The actual words of the title turn up when Morocco makes his choice of casket, that being the gold, and having made the wrong choice, finds concealed in the casket a scroll upon which the following words were imprinted:

'All that glisters is not gold;
Often have you heard that told:..'

Morocco had thus fallen into the trap that many men fall into, being led by their unending greed for wealth. The words of the title, relevant at this point in the play, corresponds to a well known phrase of this day, that being,

'Beauty is only skin deep'.

However, Bassanio is careful not to fall into this trap, and so disregards the gold chest with the words:

'So may the outwards shows be least themselves:
The world is still deceiv'd with ornament...'

Bassanio knows how gold still misleads many men, and this knowledge leads him to choose the right casket. Thus an important step is taken in the play, as Bassanio takes Portia's hand in marriage.

From the way Portia's father organized the procedure of courting it can be seen that he was a very wise man, and realized how wealth deceived and blinded many men. He wanted only the best for his daughter, and he knew that the suitor who was not overcome by the greed for wealth, would have the time and love for Portia. So, as a test, he placed Portia's portrait into the lead casket, along with the words,

'You that choose not by the view,
Chance as fair, and choose as true!...'

Thus meaning that he who did not judge by what he could see, would succeed in winning Portia's hand.

Although the choosing of the caskets is the main justification of my choice of title, there are also other small points that can be perceived from the play, to justify it.

One of these points is Shylock's initial reaction to the news that his daughter had run away. It can be understood from his words that for one split portion of time he could see that money and wealth were not the only important aspects of life, and that his daughter was of greater importance, and thus realized that, because she did not 'glister' as his gold, he had taken her for granted. This view could be obtained from the way he is said to have firstly cried.

'My daughter!'
and then, more typical of his character, continued to add,

'O my ducats!'
The fact that his first thought was for his daughter, implies
that he is humane, and does look further than wealth, but all
his humanity is overwhelmed by his miserly ways, and he cries
out once more for his money.

CONVENTIONS OF DRAMA

ACTS AND SCENES

TIME

CHORUS

DISGUISE

THE SOLILOQUY

THE ASIDE

THE SUPERNATURAL

BATTLES

RADIO CONVENTIONS

FILM AND TV CONVENTIONS

G E T T I N G   S T A R T E D

When we go to the theatre or watch a play on television, listen to the radio or go to the cinema we have to accept that things are going to be presented to us in a particular way. Often this way is not realistic but the audience accepts what happens because they are used to seeing it done in this way. Such methods or techniques of presentation are called *conventions*. For instance it used to be the convention in films always to have music in the background at moments of high drama or emotion. The audience did not imagine there was a full orchestra playing behind the sitting room curtains when the hero took the heroine in his arms. The soaring violins were accepted as mood music, showing the strength of the characters' feelings. More recent films are much less likely to use music in quite so obvious a way. If we are used to watching plays frequently we do not think of the conventions any more.

To understand and appreciate what the dramatist is doing we should be able to recognize these conventions and know what effects they have. This chapter helps you to do that and shows you how to use your knowledge.

ESSENTIAL PRINCIPLES

1 ⟩ ACTS AND SCENES

The first convention we notice when reading, rather than watching, a play is that it is divided into acts and scenes which break up the action in the same way that chapters do in a novel. The practice in Shakespeare's time was to divide the play into five *acts*. Later on it became three acts. Modern plays are often divided into only two acts and some do not have acts at all, simply a succession of scenes.

A *scene* generally marks off a piece of action which happens in one place, in one continuous stretch of time. When the action moves to another place, or the dramatist wants a gap in time, then the scene ends and another one begins. The first four scenes of *Macbeth* take place on a heath in Scotland. We first see the witches, then the king and his nobles. We go back to the witches, and then move once again to the king's camp. With each move we start a new scene to denote a change of place. Shakespeare could use short scenes and move the action freely from place to place like this because he had no scenery to move.

Bernard Shaw writes in a different style. *The Devil's Disciple* opens with Mrs. Dudgeon sitting up in the kitchen in the middle of the night with Essie. Characters come and go, but the whole of the action takes place continuously in the kitchen until the end of Act 1. Therefore, the act is not divided into scenes.

Another play written in this century, *Journey's End* (R.C. Sheriff), all takes place in a dug-out in the British trenches in the First World War. The divisions are these:

Act I: Evening on Monday 18. March 1918.
Act II: Scene 1 – Tuesday morning
               Scene 2 – Tuesday afternoon
Act III: Scene 1 – Wednesday afternoon
               Scene 2 – Wednesday night
               Scene 3 – Thursday, towards dawn.

The location never changes, but the advancing time is important. The gaps in time represented by these scene divisions are often shown on stage by dimming the lights.

There is a dramatic purpose to scene divisions. The way in which the dramatist divides the action into scenes affects the pace and tension of a play. A series of short scenes gives the sense of rapidly advancing action, perhaps of events becoming beyond the control of a character. Shakespeare's battles are often constructed of a series of very short scenes. Long scenes are needed to give cohesion and the development of relationships, feelings and ideas. Trial scenes, like those in *The Crucible* (Arthur Miller) and *St Joan*,(Bernard Shaw) are long for this reason. Notice the act and scene divisions in the plays you are studying and ask yourself what is achieved by them and what effect they have on stage.

2 ⟩ TIME

As well as having to show gaps in the passage of **time** by scene changes, the dramatist has to manipulate time in other ways. Shakespeare talks about 'the two hours traffic of our stage'. But during the time that the play takes to perform we understand that we may see days, even years, passing. The dramatist has to concentrate all the important events of the story into two or three hours.

Most of these events will have to be telescoped into a far shorter time than they would take in reality. In Thornton Wilder's short play *A Happy Journey to Trenton and Camden* a family travels 70 miles by car in 20 minutes of stage time. Love scenes or quarrels come to a head much faster on stage than they would in real life. Algernon and John Worthing would have to gobble their muffins and teacakes to get through them in the time allowed for tea in *The Importance of Being Earnest* (Oscar Wilde).

Another favourite dramatic trick with time is the *flashback*. Arthur Miller uses this convention in *Death of a Salesman*. Willy Loman is approaching the crisis of his life which leads to his suicide. In a series of flashbacks we are shown how the events of his life have led him to this. Each scene from the past gives us a deeper understanding of his character and relationships with his family and we slowly learn how his long-standing inability to see things as they really are has led him to despair. The value of seeing the ageing Willy enacting the scenes from earlier, happier times in flashback is that it makes his failure all the more poignant and the happy scenes all the more painful.

In ***The Skin of Our Teeth*** Thornton Wilder uses time in yet another way. The audience sees two eras at once. The Antrobus family lives both in prehistoric times and in modern America. The dramatist here is trying to set the daily events of his play in a greater perspective.

Whenever a dramatist uses time differently from actual time we must consider what the dramatic purpose is.

3 > CHORUS

Generally we learn of events from what characters say or what we see them do. Occasionally, however, when the dramatist wants to give the audience a lot of information in a hurry, a ***Chorus*** can be used.

Originally, in Greek drama, a Chorus was a group of people who watched the actions of the main characters and then commented on them and gave their reactions. They could not affect the actions of the play, only voice their hopes and fears. This kind of group Chorus has been little used since the Greeks, but there is one modern play, T. S. Eliot's ***Murder in the Cathedral***, where it is used very successfully. A group of the women of Canterbury wait for Thomas, the Archbishop, to return to his cathedral. They are filled with an awful sense of doom. Their speeches express fear and helplessness and, after Thomas' murder, horror, guilt and finally submission to the will of God. Their role is to stand for the ordinary people.

It is much more usual to have a single person as Chorus, but the function can remain the same. In ***A Man for All Seasons*** Robert Bolt uses a character called the Common Man: his name states clearly whom he represents. He slips in and out of the scenes, sometimes commenting on them, sometimes taking part as a boatman or steward, or whatever is needed.

Shakespeare occasionally uses a Chorus figure. In ***Henry V*** his purpose is to introduce each act and to set the scene. He rouses the imagination with descriptions of the horses 'printing their proud hooves in the receiving earth' and reminds the audience of details of who is treacherous and who is true. In ***The Winter's Tale*** his purpose is to describe the lapse of sixteen years between Acts III and IV.

A Chorus acts as a kind of intermediary between the audience and the play. Because he speaks directly to the audience as commentator or narrator, he forcefully reminds us we are sitting in a theatre listening to an actor. We cannot get carried away by the spell of a story and begin to believe the characters are real people with lives that continue beyond the end of the play. Some dramatists, like Bertolt Brecht, very deliberately use chorus and narrator figures to prevent the audience being carried away on a wave of sympathy for the characters. In ***The Caucasian Chalk Circle*** Brecht uses the Singer to break up the action with songs and snatches of narrative. He does not want the audience simply to feel for Grusha and the child she has rescued; he wants them to think about what their story means for society as a whole.

If there is a Chorus in a play, try to determine what function it fulfils.

4 > DISGUISE

Disguise is used a great deal in drama. This sometimes worries those who are not used to this convention because it does not seem believable. In ***Twelfth Night*** a pair of twins, separated in a shipwreck, are both washed up in Illyria. The girl dresses up as a boy and we are asked to believe firstly that no one notices she is not a man – so much so that a woman falls in love with her – and secondly no one can tell her apart from her brother. Of course, Shakespeare had a particular reason for wanting to get his heroines disguised as young men, as quickly as possible, because they were all acted by boys. There were no actresses. But this does not help our sense of the reality of the action. The answer is not to worry about realism, any more then we would with ***ET*** or ***Superman***

Disguise allows a dramatist to construct extraordinary situations, to confront the characters with situations which they might never otherwise see and know of. In *Twelfth Night* Olivia is made to fall in love with a disguised woman so that she can learn something about her own nature and the nature of love.

When a character assumes a disguise ask yourself what it allows the dramatist to do with him or her that could not otherwise be done.

5 ▶ THE SOLILOQUY

The *soliloquy* is a way of letting the audience know what a character is thinking. Almost everyone knows Hamlet's famous words 'To be or not to be'. It is the beginning of a speech in which he debates with himself about suicide. We are to suppose that these are the thoughts going round in his brain. The convention allows us to get inside his head. Another, perhaps equally famous soliloquy is Macbeth's 'Is this a dagger that I see before me'. Very frequently the character is alone on stage with his thoughts, but not always. The fact that we, the audience, can hear, but the rest of the characters on-stage cannot, is not a problem because the soliloquy is not intended to represent someone talking to himself, but his unspoken thoughts.

There is a second kind of soliloquy, not of unspoken thoughts but of the character very directly addressing the audience and telling them what he is up to. When Launcelot Gobbo has a tussle with his conscience about leaving the Jew, his master, in *The Merchant of Venice*, he discusses all the pros and cons with the audience and confidentially makes them a party to his decision to run away.

6 ▶ THE ASIDE

Another means of communicating directly with the audience is the *aside*. A character turns aside from the action onstage and speaks to the audience. The difference between this and the soliloquy is that the aside is usually very short and, although there are other people onstage, the convention is that they do not hear what the audience is told.

> ABSOLUTE: [*Aside*] So much thought bodes me no good. – [*to her*] So grave Lydia!
> LYDIA: Sir!
> ABSOLUTE: [*Aside*] So! egad I thought as much! – that damned monosyllable has froze me! – [*to her*] What Lydia, now that we are happy in our friends' consent, as in our mutual vows –
> LYDIA: Friends' consent indeed!
> (*The Rivals; Richard Sheridan*)

Absolute, commenting to the audience on his mistress' silence, and then her monosyllabic reply, makes the audience feel like a friend and confidante. An aside can give the audience more knowledge than characters onstage. It is often used for comic effect.

7 ▶ THE SUPER-NATURAL

Witches, ghosts and spirits are frequently portrayed on the stage. They can be given knowledge that ordinary mortals do not possess. We have to remember that in previous centuries many people believed in the *supernatural* much more literally than we do now. The spirits that were thought of as agents of the devil, as many were, were usually given a hideous appearance. The witches in *Macbeth* are called 'secret, black and midnight hags' to show that they are evil creatures. The devil's henchman, Mephistopheles, is so ugly on his first appearance in *Doctor Faustus* (Marlowe) that he is sent away to assume a more acceptable shape. Ghosts are dangerous beings whose credentials have to be established. They, too, may come from the devil and so must not be immediately trusted.

There are also good and benevolent spirits. Shakespeare brings on the god of marriage, Hymen, to bless the couples at the end of *As You Like It*, and a trio of goddesses appear to sing and dance in *The Tempest*.

The theatre Shakespeare worked in had special winching gear by which actors playing gods and good spirits could be lowered from the roof on to the stage, as though descending from the heavens. Evil spirits rose through a trapdoor in the stage as though coming up from the bowels of the earth. In modern productions they are more likely to appear and disappear in a cloud of dry ice.

In more modern plays ghosts can be treated comically because the audience is no longer very frightened by the thought of them. In **Blithe Spirit** Noel Coward allows a man to be plagued by the ghost of his dead wife because she is jealous of his second wife. The pranks she gets up to are mischievous rather than frightening and create comic situations.

When ghosts, gods or spirits appear in a play you are reading consider what use the dramatist is making of them. Think too of what their appearance should be and how they can be got on and off the stage.

8 ▷ BATTLES

Many of Shakespeare's plays, notably the history plays, include **battles**. Film has many advantages over the stage in the representation of battles. The film of **Richard III** can use hundreds of extras carrying spears and dozens of horses. The armies confronting each other look like real armies. Looked at objectively, battles on stage are often quite farcical. All the male members of the cast run on and off stage several times pausing only to shout instructions or give a brief report of somebody's friend or son dying bravely; several people have duels; a lot of trumpets are blown, usually offstage. Finally somebody staggers to the front, declares that he has won, and everybody cheers.

We accept the convention that the noise and confusion represents the real battle, and the duels stand for all the fighting. If we insist on seeing these realistically we destroy the play. We have to accept the convention for the drama to work.

9 ▷ RADIO CONVENTIONS

Radio has a set of conventions quite different from the stage, which have to be understood in order to grasp what is going on. Since everything had to be conveyed through sound, the silences are very important. Through silence the dramatist shows the passing of time, or a change of place: the sound of birds fades, then after a short silence we hear a lot of traffic, so we know that we have moved from the country to the town.

When radio wishes to convey a character's thoughts it, too, can use soliloquy. A quiet voice close to the microphone can show that this is the character thinking; the same voice, louder and more distant, is the character speaking aloud. One of the advantages of radio is that it can switch instantly from one to the other, or even have both thought and voice speaking at the same time. Dylan Thomas does this in **Under Milk Wood**. Blind Captain Cat hears Polly Garter with her bucket and mop. His thoughts about her are spoken quietly, then he calls to her, 'Hello Polly'. This is said loudly. Her reply is distant from the microphone to show that she is down in the street outside his window.

10 ▷ FILM AND TELEVISION CONVENTIONS

Yet another set of conventions apply to films or plays on television. Change of time or place is conveyed by the picture fading or being cut. As with radio techniques, this means that moving from scene to scene can be very quick. Inner thoughts can be conveyed by a technique called the voice over. The picture on the screen may show the view from a window, while the character talks about her feelings, or her past life, or what she is going to do next. Like radio, television can travel in time with enormous ease: flashbacks are a common technique. It can also 'crosscut' to show things going on at the same time in different places. The screen picture moves rapidly back and forth between the two places. The screen can also be split in two, for instance to show the reactions of both speakers in a telephone conversation. We are so familiar with these conventions, which are used all the time in soap operas or sitcoms like **Dallas** or **Yes, Minister**, that we forget that these are things which the medium of film can do which other media cannot do.

One of the best TV dramatists, who uses the medium creatively, is Dennis Potter. **The Singing Detective** is about a man lying in hospital recovering from a skin disease and thinking about his life and about a detective story he once wrote.

We see what happens to him in the hospital, are shown his thoughts and fears about his past life and relationships, and we are told the detective story as well. The scenes flash between the present and his memories and the fictional thriller in the same way that ideas flit in and out of our minds, especially when we are feeling ill. The conventions of the TV drama allows the action to progress on all three levels at once.

11 ❯ SUMMARY

➤ Conventions are accepted ways of presenting action, often non-realistically as with battle scenes or the use of the supernatural.

➤ Act and scene divisions are used to denote changes in time and place.

➤ Time in plays is usually compressed. It can also move from present to past in flashback, or show the future.

➤ A Chorus is an accepted way of narrating or commenting on events.

➤ Disguise is often used as a way of developing situations.

➤ The soliloquy and the aside are ways of letting the audience know what the character is thinking, without the other characters knowing.

➤ Radio and Television have their own conventions. They enable the action to move quickly in time and from place to place.

ADDITIONAL EXAMPLES

The following passages illustrate some of the techniques discussed in this chapter. You can test your understanding of what you have read by answering the questions on them. Write down your own ideas before reading what I have written in the Key below.

1. For what purpose does the dramatist use the character of the Stage Manager in the following extract?

STAGE MANAGER: In our town we like to know the facts about everybody. There's Mrs. Webb, coming downstairs to get her breakfast, too. – That's Doc. Gibbs. Got that call at half past one this morning. And there comes Joe Crowell Junior, delivering Mr. Webb's *Sentinel*.

[DR. GIBBS *has been coming along Main Street from the left. At the point where he would turn to approach his house he sets down his – imaginary – black bag, takes off his hat, and rubs his face with fatigue, using an enormous handkerchief.* MRS. WEBB, *a thin, serious, crisp woman, has entered her kitchen, left, tying on her apron. She goes through the motions of putting wood on the stove, lighting it and preparing breakfast. Suddenly,* JOE CROWELL, *eleven, starts down Main Street from the right, hurling imaginary newspapers into the doorways.*]

JOE CROWELL: Morning, Doc Gibbs.

DR. GIBBS: Morning, Joe.

JOE CROWELL: Somebody been sick, Doc?

DR. GIBBS: No. Just some twins born over in Polish town.

JOE CROWELL: Do you want your paper now?

DR. GIBBS: Yes I'll take it – Anything serious goin' on in the world since Wednesday?

JOE CROWELL: Yessir. My schoolteacher, Miss Foster's, getting married to a fella over in Concord.

DR. GIBBS: I declare – How do you boys feel about that?

JOE CROWELL: Well, of course, it's none of my business – but I think if a person starts out a teacher, she ought to stay one.

DR. GIBBS: How's your knee, Joe?

JOE CROWELL: Fine, Doc. I never think about it at all. Only like you said, it always tells me when it's going to rain.

DR. GIBBS: What's it telling you today? Goin' to rain?

JOE CROWELL: No sir.

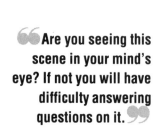

❝Are you seeing this scene in your mind's eye? If not you will have difficulty answering questions on it. ❞

DR. GIBBS: Sure?

JOE CROWELL: Yessir:

DR. GIBBS: Knee ever made a mistake?

JOE CROWELL: No sir. [JOE *goes off*. DR. GIBBS *stands reading his paper*.]

STAGE MANAGER: Want to tell you something about that boy Joe Crowell there. Joe was awful bright – graduated from high school here, head of his class. So he got a scholarship to Massachusetts Tech. Graduated head of his class there, too. It was all wrote up in the Boston paper at the time. Goin' to be a great engineer Joe was. But the war broke out and he died in France – All that education for nothing.

(**Our Town**; Thornton Wilder)

2.What is achieved by the use of asides in the following scene? This scene is the first meeting between the hero and the heroine. She already knows that he has a reputation for being forward, but only with lower class women.

MARLOW: It's a disease of the mind madam. In the variety of tastes there must be some who, wanting a relish for um- a - um -

MISS HARDCASTLE: I understand you sir. There must be some who, wanting a relish for refined pleasures , pretend to despise what they are incapable of tasting.

MARLOW: My meaning madam, but infinitely better expressed. And I can't help observing – a –

MISS HARDCASTLE (*Aside*) Who could ever suppose this fellow impudent upon some occasions. (*to him*) You were going to observe, sir –

MARLOW: I was observing Madam, - I protest, madam, I forget what I was going to observe.

MISS HARDCASTLE (*Aside*) I vow and so do I. (*to him*) You were observing, sir, that in this age of hypocrisy – something about hypocrisy, sir.

MARLOW: Yes, madam. In this age of hypocrisy, there are few who upon strict inquiry do not -a – a – a-

MISS HARDCASTLE: I understand you perfectly, sir.

MARLOW: (*Aside*) Egad! and that's more than I do myself!

(**She Stoops to Conquer**; Oliver Goldsmith.)

3. In the following scene the audience knows that Sebastian is Viola's twin brother but because Viola has disguised herself as a man and taken a man's name, Cesario, the characters onstage think Sebastian is Cesario. Olivia has fallen in love with Cesario, and Sir Andrew has challenged him to a duel in the sure belief he is a coward who cannot use a sword. Now read on!

SIR ANDREW: (*to Sebastian*) Now, sir, have I met you again? (*striking him*) There's for you.

SEBASTIAN: (*striking Sir Andrew with his dagger*) Why there's for thee, and there, and there. Are all the people mad?

SIR TOBY: (*to Sebastian, holding him back*) Hold sir, or I'll throw your dagger o'er the house.

FESTE: This I will tell my lady straight, I would not be in some of your coats for twopence. (*Exit*)

SIR TOBY: Come on, sir, hold.

SIR ANDREW: Nay, let him alone, I'll go another way to work with him. I'll have an action of battery against him if there be any law in Illyria. Though I struck him first, yet it's no matter for that.

SEBASTIAN: Let go thy hand.

SIR TOBY: Come sir, I will not let you go. Come my young soldier, put up your iron. You are well fleshed. Come on.

SEBASTIAN: (*freeing himself*)

I will be free from thee. What would'st thou now?

If thou dar'st tempt me further, dray thy sword.

SIR TOBY: What, what? Nay then I must have an ounce or two of this malapert blood from you.

Sir Toby and Sebastian draw their swords. Enter Olivia.

OLIVIA: Hold, Toby, on thy life I charge thee hold.

SIR TOBY: Madam.

OLIVIA: Will it be ever thus? Ungracious wretch,

Fit for the mountains and the barbarous caves,

Where manners ne'er were preached – out of my sight!
Be not offended, dear Cesario.
(*to Sir Toby*) Rudesby, be gone. (*Exeunt Sir Toby and Sir Andrew*)
Let thy fair wisdom, not thy passion sway
In this uncivil and unjust extent
Against thy peace. Go with me to my house,
And hear thou there how many fruitless pranks
This ruffian hath botched up, that thou thereby
May'st smile at this. Thou shalt not choose but go.
Do not deny. Beshrew his soul for me,
He started one poor heart of mine in thee.
SEBASTIAN: What relish is in this? How runs this stream?
Or am I mad, or else is this a dream?
Let fancy still my sense in Lethe steep
If it be thus to dream, still let me sleep.
OLIVIA: Nay come, I prithee, would thou'dst be ruled by me.
SEBASTIAN: Madam, I will.
OLIVIA: O, say so, and so be.
(*Twelfth Night*: IV i. 23-64)
What does Shakespeare achieve through the use of disguise in this scene?

4. How would you expect the following scene to look onstage? It was written by Christopher Marlowe in about 1592 and is usually, but not always, acted in Elizabethan or medieval costume. Doctor Faustus has sold his soul to the devil, but is now regretting and repenting of it.
FAUSTUS: Ay go, accursed spirit, to ugly hell!
Tis thou hast damned distressed Faustus soul
Is't not too late?
Re-enter the GOOD ANGEL *and* EVIL ANGEL
EVIL ANGEL: Too late
GOOD ANGEL: Never too late if Faustus can repent.
EVIL ANGEL: If thou repent, devils shall tear thee in pieces.
GOOD ANGEL: Repent, and they shall never raze thy skin (*Exeunt Angels.*)
FAUSTUS: Ah, Christ, my Saviour,
Seek to save distressed Faustus' soul!
(*Enter* LUCIFER, BELZEBUB AND MEPHISTOPHELES.)
LUCIFER: Christ cannot save thy soul, for he is just:
There's none but I have interest in the same.
FAUSTUS: Oh who art thou that lookst so terrible?
LUCIFER: I am Lucifer,
And this is my companion prince in hell.
FAUSTUS: O, Faustus, they are come to fetch away thy soul!
LUCIFER: We come to tell thee thou dost injure us;
Thou talkst of Christ, contrary to thy promise:
Thou should not think of God, think of the devil,
And of his dam too.
FAUSTUS: Nor will I henceforth: pardon me in this
And Faustus vows never to look to heaven,
Never to name God, or to pray to him,
To burn his Scriptures, slay his ministers,
And make my spirits pull his churches down.
LUCIFER: Do so, and we will highly gratify thee.
Faustus we are come from hell to show thee some pastime: sit down and thou shalt see all the Seven Deadly Sins appear in their proper shapes.
FAUSTUS: That sight will be as pleasing unto me,
As Paradise was to Adam the first day
Of his creation.
LUCIFER: Talk not of Paradise nor creation; but mark this show: talk of the devil, and nothing else. – Come away!
(*Enter the Seven Deadly Sins.*)
Now Faustus, examine them of their several names and dispositions.
FAUSTUS: What art thou, the first?

PRIDE: I am Pride. I disdain to have any parents. I am like to Ovid's flea; I can creep into every corner of a wench; sometimes like a periwig I sit upon her brow; or, like a fan of feathers, I kiss her lips; indeed I do – what do I not? But fie, what a scent is here! I'll not speak another word, except the ground were perfumed and covered with a cloth of arras.
FAUSTUS: What art thou the second?
COVETOUSNESS: I am Covetousness. . .
(*The rest of the Seven Deadly Sins follow in a procession –* WRATH, ENVY, GLUT-TONY, SLOTH *and* LECHERY. *They describe the sin they represent to Faustus as they pass.*)

1.   *.Our Town*: The dramatist uses the Stage Manager as a Chorus and narrator. He introduces the characters to the audience and tells us a little of their background. In this way the audience gets a lot of information that couldn't be shown onstage in this scene. His manner of speaking to the audience is the chatty, gossipy way in which people talk to each other in the street, which helps to give the small town atmosphere and make the audience feel part of it. When Joe goes off, the Stage Manager tells his story up to his death (that is, he moves us into the future). Joe is only a very minor character. Knowing what eventually happens to him gives a sense of a community all leading their lives around the main characters which the play concentrates on. When the Stage Manager concludes 'All that education for nothing' it is a moral comment on the waste of war in the traditional manner of a Chorus. The Stage Manager acts as a guide around the town and a commentator. His presence, along with other techniques such as having only an imaginary black bag and newspapers rather than real ones, means that the audience is continually reminded that they are watching a play. They are not expected to be carried away by the illusion or imagine that the scene on the stage is real.

2.   *She Stoops to Conquer*: Marlow is incredibly shy. Miss Hardcastle's asides express her astonishment because she has been told that he can be impudent, yet he seems absolutely tongue-tied and she has to finish his sentences for him. She has to keep up a polite, smiling conversation with him but she is really wondering what sort of person he could possibly be. He speaks in a very formal, stilted way and doesn't seem to be able to keep an idea in his head. The asides allow her to show her perplexity and amusement to the audience, while keeping up her polite facade to Marlow.
Marlow's aside shows that he knows he is making a fool of himself by being so incapable of conversation. He is able to talk quite normally and naturally to the audience, but not to Miss Hardcastle.

3.   *Twelfth Night*: Sebastian is mistaken for Cesario by Sir Andrew, who strikes him. Instead of the weakling that he expected he finds a vigorous young swordsman, more than ready to defend himself. In this case the disguise is used to create a humorous situation. The tables are turned. Sir Andrew retreats in alarm and bewilderment at the change and Sir Toby has to defend his friend's honour by taking up the fight. Part of the humour is created by Sebastian not knowing why on earth this person, who seems to think he knows him, should suddenly come up and strike him.
Olivia also mistakes Sebastian for Cesario. On previous occasions Cesario would not respond at all to Olivia (naturally, since Cesario is really Viola, and a woman). Sebastian behaves quite differently. He can't believe his luck when a beautiful young, and apparently rich, woman throws herself at him. He responds with enthusiasm, although he wonders if it is himself or everybody else who has suddenly gone mad. Now it is Olivia's turn to be astonished and delighted. The humour is still in the reactions of the characters to the situation which the disguise has created.
There is another more serious purpose in the use of these disguises. Olivia does not really know what love means. At the beginning of the play she declares that she will mourn for her brother for seven years because she loved him so much, but she falls in love simply with the appearance of

Cesario. She has to wait until Sebastian appears for the reality of love. Viola, through her disguise, is able to teach Olivia and other characters in the play the difference between appearance and reality. Disguise is a very convenient technique for the dramatist to use to make this point.

This kind of comedy of situation depends on the audience knowing more than the characters do themselves. This is called dramatic irony.

4.   *Doctor Faustus*. The Good Angel and the Evil Angel should be dressed to show their opposing characters – white and black are the obvious colours. They should enter from opposite sides of the stage – the Elizabethans would have put the good one one the right and the bad one on the left (or sinister) side. When Lucifer appears Faustus is terrified, therefore Lucifer must look terrifying, perhaps wearing a mask, or painting his face in lurid colours. He could wear built-up shoes, a high headdress and hugely padded shoulders, with a long swirling black cloak, to make him seem bigger and taller. He should really come up from below the stage in an explosion of fireworks or smoke. This is how the Elizabethans would have done it: modern productions could use lights and dry ice to get the effect of coming up out of hell. Lucifer and Belzebub are representations of evil and are intended to arouse fear in the audience so that they understand and appreciate Faustus' plight.

The Seven Deadly Sins are conjured up to entertain Faustus. They are agents of the devil and so have to appear exotic and strange but also corrupted and dangerous. They too would have appeared through the trapdoor in a procession, moved around the stage and disappeared again through the trap. Each character passing in front of Faustus should appear repugnant in an appropriate way. Pride might not be disgusting to look at, indeed might be quite dazzlingly dressed, but must be so haughty and arrogant in his manner that the audience despises him. Gluttony, who comes later, could be incredibly fat and all the time he is onstage be stuffing food into his mouth and spilling it down his clothes. Marlowe expected his audience to be fascinated and disgusted. The purpose of showing the spirits of the Seven Deadly Sins was to teach a moral lesson. They are the embodiment of evil, sin personified, to teach the audience to shun evil ways.

EXAM QUESTIONS

You may be asked to comment on the use of a particular convention in a short question about an extract. For example:

What is the purpose of Macbeth's Asides in this scene (Act 1 Scene 3)?

Why does Puck speak in an Aside in lines 71 and 81 (*A Midsummer Night's Dream*, Act 3, Scene 1)?

If a particular convention is used in a significant way by the dramatist it may be the subject of an essay:

1.   Describe the part played by the Common Man. How does Robert Bolt use this character in the play (*A Man for All Seasons*). This question could be asked of any chorus or narrator.

2.   Describe the part played by the Witches in *Macbeth*. Do you find them effective? This question could be asked of any use of the supernatural.

In both these questions you are being asked about the function of the characters. As well as giving an account of what the characters do in the scenes in which they appear you should also say how the dramatists use the characters to perform certain tasks. For instance the function of the Common Man is to act as Chorus. The function of the witches in *Macbeth* is to show the evil hidden in Macbeth's mind, to create an atmosphere of doom and tragedy, and to draw Macbeth towards his fate.

3.   ***Under Milk Wood*** was written as a play for radio. What effect does this
have on the way Dylan Thomas presents the characters and the town of
Llaregyb?

QUESTION, NOTES AND TUTOR'S ANSWER

The following question is about Arthur Miller's use of flashback in ***Death of a
Salesman*** The extract is a long one, about the length of extract you would be expected to read in an open book exam. The extra fifteen minutes allowed in this type
of exam is to give you time to find and read such extracts. The present-day scene is
taking place in a restaurant, where Biff and Happy have gone with their father,
Willy, but scenes from the past continually keep interrupting. The first character
to speak is someone from the past.

1 ▷ QUESTION

> **When you have
> read the passage go
> back and underline or
> highlight those
> speeches which are
> 'flashbacks'.**

Miller often uses flashback in this play for dramatic effect. How well does it work
here for you? Support your viewpoint in detail from the passage. (MEG)
(*The light of green leaves stains the house, which holds the air of night and a
dream*. YOUNG BERNARD *enters and knocks on the door of the house.*)
YOUNG BERNARD [*frantically*] Mrs Loman, Mrs Loman!
HAPPY: Tell him what happened!
BIFF (*to* HAPPY) Shut up and leave me alone.
WILLY: No, no! You had to go and flunk math!
BIFF: What math? What are you talking about?
YOUNG BERNARD: Mrs Loman, Mrs Loman! (LINDA *appears in the house, as of
old*)
WILLY (*wildly*) Math, math, math!
BIFF: Take it easy, Pop!
YOUNG BERNARD: Mrs Loman!
WILLY: [*furiously*] If you hadn't flunked you'd've been set by now!
BIFF: Now, look, I'm gonna tell you what happened and you're going to listen to
me.
YOUNG BERNARD: Mrs Loman!
BIFF: I waited six hours –
HAPPY: What the hell are you saying?
BIFF: I kept sending in my name but he wouldn't see me, So finally he. . . (*He con-
tinues as the light fades low on the restaurant.*)
YOUNG BERNARD: Biff flunked math!
LINDA: No!
YOUNG BERNARD: Birnbaum flunked him! They won't graduate him!
LINDA: But they have to. He's gotta go to university. Where is he? Biff! Biff!
YOUNG BERNARD: No, he left. He went to Grand Central.
LINDA: Grand – You mean he went to Boston!
YOUNG BERNARD: Is Uncle Willy in Boston?
LINDA: Maybe Willy can talk to the teacher. Oh the poor, poor boy! (*Light on
house area snaps out*)
BIFF (*at the table, now audible, holding up a gold fountain pen*) . . . so I'm washed
up with Oliver, you understand? Are you listening to me?
WILLY (*at a loss*) Yeah, sure. If you hadn't flunked –
BIFF: Flunked what? What are you talking about?
WILLY: Don't blame everything on me! I didn't flunk math – you did! What pen?
HAPPY: That was awful dumb, Biff, a pen like that is worth –
WILLY (*seeing the pen for the first time*): You took Oliver's pen?
BIFF: (*weakening*): Dad I just explained it to you.
WILLY: You stole Bill Oliver's fountain pen!

BIFF: I didn't exactly steal it! That's just what I've been explaining to you!

HAPPY: He had it in his hand and just then Oliver walked in, so he got nervous and stuck it in his pocket!

WILLY: My God, Biff!

BIFF: I never intended to do it, Dad!

OPERATOR'S VOICE: Standish Arms, good evening!

WILLY (*shouting*) I'm not in my room!

BIFF (*frightened*) Dad what's the matter? (*He and* HAPPY *stand up.*)

OPERATOR: Ringing Mr. Loman for you!

WILLY: I'm not there, stop it!

BIFF [*horrified, gets down on one knee before* WILLY]: Dad I'll make good, I'll make good. [WILLY *tries to get to his feet.* BIFF *holds him down*] Sit down now

WILLY: No, you're no good, you're no good for anything.

BIFF: I am Dad, I'll find something else you understand? Now don't you worry about anything. [*He holds up* WILLY's *face*] Talk to me Dad.

OPERATOR: Mr Loman does not answer. Shall I page him?

WILLY [*attempting to stand, as though to rush and silence the operator*]: No, no, no!

HAPPY: He'll strike something Pop.

WILLY: No, no. . .

BIFF: (*desperately, standing over* WILLY): Pop, listen! Listen to me! I'm telling you something good. Oliver talked to his partner about the Florida idea. You listening? He – he talked to his partner, and he came to me . . . I'm going to be all right, you hear? Dad, listen to me, he said it was just a question of the amount.

WILLY: Then you . . . got it?

HAPPY: He's gonna be terrific, Pop!

WILLY: [*trying to stand*]: Then you got it haven't you? You got it! You got it!

BIFF [*agonized*] No, no. Look, Pop. I'm supposed to have lunch with them tomorrow. I'm just telling you this so you know that I can still make an impression, Pop. And I'll make good somewhere, but I can't go tomorrow, see?

WILLY: Why not? You simply –

BIFF: But the pen, Pop.

WILLY: You give it to him and tell him it was an oversight!

HAPPY: Sure, have lunch tomorrow!

BIFF: I can't say that –

WILLY: You were doing a crossword puzzle and accidentally used his pen!

BIFF: Listen, kid, I took those balls years ago, now I walk in with his fountain pen? That clinches it, don't you see? I can't face him like that! I'll try elsewhere.

PAGE'S VOICE: Paging Mr Loman!

WILLY: Don't you want to be anything?

BIFF: Pop, how can I go back?

WILLY: You don't want to be anything, is that what's behind it?

BIFF [*now angry at* WILLY *for not crediting his sympathy*]: Don't take it that way! You think it was easy walking into that office after what I'd done to him? A team of horses couldn't have dragged me back to Bill Oliver!

WILLY: Then why'd you go?

BIFF: Why did I go? Why did I go? Look at you. Look at what's become of you! [*off left* THE WOMAN *laughs*]

WILLY: Biff, you're going to that lunch tomorrow, or –

BIFF: I can't go. I've no appointment!

HAPPY: Biff for. . . !

WILLY: Are you spiting me?

BIFF: Don't take it that way! Goddammit!

WILLY [*strikes* BIFF *and falters away from the table*]: You rotten little louse! Are you spiting me?

THE WOMAN: Someone's at the door, Willy!

BIFF: I'm no good, can't you see what I am?

HAPPY [*separating them*] Hey, you're in a restaurant! Now cut it out both of you! [*The girls enter*] Hello girls, sit down. [THE WOMAN *laughs, off left*]

MISS FORSYTHE: I guess we might as well. This is Letta.

THE WOMAN: Willy, are you going to wake up?

BIFF [*ignoring* WILLY]: How're ya, miss, sit down. What do you drink?

MISS FORSYTHE: Letta might not be able to stay long.

LETTA: I gotta get up very early tomorrow. I got jury duty. I'm so excited! Were you fellows ever on a jury?

BIFF: No, but I been in front of them! [*the girls laugh*] This is my father.

LETTA: Isn't he cute? Sit down with us, Pop.

HAPPY: Sit him down, Biff!

BIFF [*going to him*]: Come on, slugger, drink us under the table. To hell with it! Come on, sit down, pal. [*On* BIFF'S *insistence* WILLY *is about to sit.*]

THE WOMAN [*now urgently*]: Willy are you going to answer the door! [THE WOMAN's *call pulls* WILLY *back. He starts right, befuddled.*]

BIFF: Hey, where are you going?

WILLY: Open the door.

BIFF: The door?

WILLY: The washroom. . . the door. . . where's the door?

BIFF [*leading* WILLY *to the left*]: Just go straight down. [WILLY *moves left*]

THE WOMAN: Willy, Willy, are you going to get up, get up, get up, get up? [WILLY *exits left*]

LETTA: I think its sweet you bring your Daddy along.

MISS FORSYTHE: Oh, he isn't really your father!

BIFF: [*at left, turning to her resentfully*] Miss Forsythe, you've just seen a prince walk by. A fine and troubled prince. A hard-working unappreciated prince. A pal, you understand? A good companion. Always for his boys.

LETTA: That's so sweet.

HAPPY: Well, girls, what's the programme? We're wasting time. Come on Biff. Gather round. Where would you like to go?

BIFF: Why don't you do something for him?

HAPPY: Me!

BIFF: Don't you give a damn for him Hap?

HAPPY: What're talking about? I'm the one who –

BIFF: I sense it, you don't give a good goddam about him. [*He takes the rolled up hose from his pocket and puts it on the table in front of* HAPPY] Look what I found in the cellar, for Christ's sake. How can you bear to let it go on?

HAPPY: Me? Who goes away? Who runs off and–

BIFF: Yeah, but he doesn't mean anything to you. You could help him – I can't. Don't you understand what I'm talking about? He's going to kill himself, don't you know that?

HAPPY: Don't I know it! Me!

BIFF: Hap, help him! Jesus. . . . help him. . . Help me, help me, I can't bear to look at his face! [*Ready to weep, he hurries out, up right.*]

HAPPY [*staring after him*]: Where are you going?

MISS FORSYTHE: What's he so mad about?

HAPPY: Come on, girls, we'll catch up with him.

MISS FORSYTHE: Say, I don't like that temper of his!

HAPPY: He's just a little overstrung, he'll be all right!

WILLY: [*off left, as* THE WOMAN *laughs*]: Don't answer! Don't answer

LETTA: Don't you want to tell your father –

HAPPY: No, that's not my father, He's just a guy. Come on, we'll catch Biff, and, honey, we're going to paint this town! Stanley, where's the check! Hey Stanley! [*They exit.* STANLEY *looks toward left*]

STANLEY [*calling to* HAPPY *indignantly*]: Mr Loman! Mr Loman! [STANLEY *picks up a chair and follows them off. Knocking is heard off left.* THE WOMAN *enters laughing.* WILLY *follows her. She is in a black slip; he is buttoning his shirt. Raw, sensuous music accompanies their speech.*]

---

2 ▷ NOTES

1. Read the passage through carefully.
2. Make a list of the different people and events in the flashbacks.
3. Notice the way the past and present events are organized on stage.
4. Make a note of any relationships you can see between past and present events.
5. Decide what the effect of this technique is on the way we see Willy.

3 ▷ SUGGESTED ANSWER

In **Death of a Salesman** Arthur Miller uses the technique of flashback as far more than a means of providing the audience with information about the past. It becomes a device for exploring a character's mind and demonstrating how the past is always a part of the present. In this scene the past and the present are inextricably mixed. The effect is a confusion which shows the confusion in Willy's mind. The purpose is to show some of the causes of Willy and Biff's present relationship and show how their situation is influenced by past events. These events in themselves demonstrate the life-long traits in Willy's personality which have led him to this crisis.

The scene is set in a restaurant where Willy has gone to meet his boys. Their outing is supposed to be a special treat but it is spoiled by Biff's difficulties with Bill Oliver. Willy feels guilty about Biff's failure to make his proper mark in the world. Scenes from the past arise in Willy's mind. Alongside the scene in the restaurant we see, bathed in green light as though in a dream, the young Bernard trying to tell Linda of Biff's failure in his maths exam. Willy's mind is taken over by these figures from the past who play out the news of the event that caused the division between Willy and Biff. The voices from the past intrude on the present, cutting across Biff's story of his attempt to see Oliver, as though Willy can no longer concentrate on reality. As Biff insists on telling of his failure with Oliver the past overwhelms the present in Willy's mind, and the figures of Linda and young Bernard take over the stage. Biff's past failure is equated with his present one, If he had not flunked maths everything would have been different.

As Willy struggles back into the present, the lights go out on Linda and Bernard. He has hardly heard what Biff has been saying but for a moment he concentrates on the awful fact that Biff has walked out with, stolen, Oliver's gold pen. His mind cannot hold on to it. As though every dire event in the present forces him deeper into the trauma of past events he now answers aloud the voice of the operator in his head. The progression in Willy's reaction is important in increasing the tension. His sudden inexplicable shout, 'I'm not in my room', forces a reaction from his startled sons, who think he is either ill or mad. Worried for his father Biff backs off from the truth and starts inventing the kind of lying, soothing story they have always told. As Willy becomes calmer in response to this new tale, the past recedes and Willy begins to talk coherently, deceiving himself into hope for Biff's future.

Miller is using the flashback to make a clear connection between Willy's need for present optimism and his memory of past failure. The past can only be pushed aside if it seems as though Biff will succeed. Willy is prepared to go on lying to maintain the fiction necessary to keep himself going. Biff is not. When Biff insists on the truth, on reality, the voices return. As Biff turns on Willy the most painful visions begin to take over his mind. The woman's laugh signals the onset of his most dreadful, shameful, memories. Her voice is so insistent in his head that it pulls him to his feet and he goes to answer her instruction to open the door. He leaves the stage to Biff, Happy and the visiting girls. The juxtaposition of the arrival of the girls in the present with the woman from the past points to another parallel. Happy too is a failure, a womanizer with no sense of direction. Happy's weakness is also a reflection of Willy's past misdeeds, exaggerated as if in a distorting mirror.

Willy does not hear Biff calling him 'a prince, a fine troubled prince', does not see Biff's concern and love for him. He remains locked in the belief that Biff has thrown away his life for spite. The flashbacks enable Miller to display that troubled mind to us. They indicate that for Willy the past is painfully ever present. He has lived these scenes over and over again; he can no longer push them aside and his grip on reality is slipping. When he finally commits suicide we understand the process that has led him there.

> 66 **Have you written an introduction explaining the purpose of the flashback technique? If not, it should be in your conclusion.** 99

SUGGESTIONS FOR COURSEWORK

1. The exam questions above are all suitable as a basis for coursework units.
2. Make a study of a particular convention, as used in different plays or by different dramatists. For instance: disguise, the supernatural, the use of time, the use of Chorus.
3. Compare different versions of a play, on stage and on television or film.
4. Write a review of a radio play or a television play. Write about
   the characters;
   the setting;
   the dramatist's ideas;
   the actors' portrayal of their roles;
   any effects you found outstanding;
   your opinion of the whole production.

STUDENT'S ANSWER – EXAMINER'S COMMENT

This essay discusses how a character who is not 'real' can be presented on stage. It is based on J.B. Priestley's play *An Inspector Calls*.

Question

Who is Inspector Goole?

> At the beginning of the play Mr Birling is saying that a man should just take care of himself and his family and not other people:
>
>   'A man has to look after himself and he won't come to any harm...community and all that nonsense.'
>
> This is the first time we see what is wrong with these people. The inspector arrives then so stopping him in the middle of this speech, this is significant – as if he just came to set that attitude right and teach them a lesson, this suggests that he wasn't a Police Inspector but had another, special purpose. Mr. Birling had just been talking about 'the way these cranks talk', the Inspector could have been a 'crank' – at least in their eyes. Police Inspector Goole then involves the Birlings and Gerald in the murder of Eva Smith. From what we know of Priestley's plays, they all have a message to the whole of society, they criticise the social system, through Inspector Goole his message is effectively portrayed to us all. Priestley cleverly makes him different by what he says and how he acts; we cannot put a class to the Inspector, he acts in a way that creates an impression; he has a way of looking hard at people before he talks to them. Even in the lighting directions it says 'the lighting should be pink and intimate until the inspector arrives and then it should be brighter and harder' this shows the Inspector shatters their homely complacent lives.

Good. Points out the significance of the exact moment the Inspector appears and how this points to him being a non-naturalistic figure.

Good. Notices how everything onstage contributes to the effects, from the character's words to the lighting.

Throughout the whole play he creates an atmosphere of strangeness and doubts; he has a cool way of talking and manages to get everything out of the person by not saying very much. They get annoyed with him because he asks questions which they would rather not answer and puts them on their guard with cutting replies. Birling says 'we were having a nice little family celebration tonight...and a nasty mess you've made of it now!'

The Inspector replies 'that's more or less what I was thinking at the Infirmary...A nice little promising life there, I thought, and a nasty mess someone has made of it.' So how do we answer exactly, the question, 'Who is Inspector Goole?' He doesn't act like a Police Inspector; they don't make moral speeches to the people they are inspecting. They actually found out in the end that he wasn't a real police inspector, but the older ones think of realistic alternatives like – he was a practical joker – trying to frame them and just pretending to be a police officer, a hoax, but the younger generation Eric and Sheila are more impressionable and susceptible to change, they sense that he may be something supernatural, they don't know where he comes from but are influenced by what he said. The others try to let themselves out of their responsibility – but there is still a girl dead.

I think we all know that Inspector Goole is not human, but just because of what the Birlings and Gerald did, it's still the same. As Eric said, 'Whoever that chap was, the fact remains that I did what I did...it's still the same rotten story whether it's been told to a police inspector or to someone else.' The young realise this and have been taught something by the Inspector. This shows the difference between young and old attitudes. Even when they find out that Eva Smith was not dead she could have been, they did the same things to her. The younger ones have learnt to care for everyone and they have responded to Priestley's message, they feel their conscience and guilt. Sheila said 'I behaved badly too. I knew I did. I'm ashamed of it. But now you're beginning all over again to pretend that nothing much has happened.'

❝Good. Correctly identifies the dramatist's use of the supernatural connection to make a moral point.❞

❝This goes back to discussing the reactions of the various characters. It is better to group all points on one issue together, and discuss them in one place.❞

GETTING STARTED

Plot is a good word because it suggests a plan, something carefully worked out, and this is exactly what the dramatist does. You have to remember that in a play nothing happens by accident. Everything is the result of deliberate choice by the dramatist. In the world of the play the dramatist has the power of life and death, success or failure, over the characters. Every development, every turn of the plot, could have gone another way if the dramatist had chosen to make it do so. So every action has its function in the whole. Your job is to work out the dramatic interest and significance of the actions.

This chapter will help you to understand plots and show you how to look for their significant features so that when you give an account of what happens you will be able to say why it is the way it is.

THE
PLOTS
OF
PLAYS

DRAMA
SUSPENSE
CONFLICT
TENSION
PACE
OPENING THE ACTION
CONSTRUCTING THE
ACTION
GUESSING RIGHT AND
WRONG
SUBPLOTS
HUMOUR
CLIMAX
ENDINGS
THEMES

ESSENTIAL PRINCIPLES

1 > DRAMA Think about the word 'drama' and the way we use it in ordinary speech. A man is standing on a ledge high up on a cathedral and threatening to jump. A priest is trying to talk him out of it. The cameras down in the street are trained on the man and a reporter describes the scene for the television news. We would call this a drama. The greatest all-round cricketer in the world comes on to bowl after a two months' suspension. He needs two wickets for the world record. Can he prove his critics wrong? He gets a wicket with his first ball. This too is called drama. Both these incidents, from real life, have the essential ingredients of ***suspense, conflict and tension***. When studying a scene try to identify these elements so that you can then describe and explain them.

SUSPENSE

The dramatist creates ***suspense*** by getting us involved and then keeping us waiting. At its mildest, suspense is wanting to know what happens next. The dramatist must create this level of interest or the audience will just stop watching, stop reading, or not go to see his next play. At its most acute, suspense brings the audience to the edge of their seats hoping that something will or will not happen. Most plays move between a low level of suspense for the greater part of the scenes and a high level at important moments.

Try to decide while you are reading or watching just what it is that the dramatist is doing that keeps the suspense going. One thing may be interest in the characters: this will be dealt with in the next chapter. Another is the situation. When Tony Lumpkin in ***She Stoops to Conquer*** pretends that his father's house is an inn and directs Marlow there, we know that an interesting situation will develop. We expect Marlow to behave in a quite inappropriate manner towards his future father-in-law because Tony has made him believe he is the landlord of this supposed inn. As expected Marlow behaves quite rudely. The situation creates suspense, in this case humorously, because we wait to see how it will develop and be resolved. Such suspense is not extreme or acute, so it cannot be expected to hold the audience's attention for long. New twists and complications have to be introduced to keep the interest going.

Acute suspense is created when the outcome is very serious and we are kept waiting, not knowing what will happen. Such a situation occurs at the end of ***The Devil's Disciple***. Dick Dudgeon, the roguish hero, awaits execution. The rope is around his neck. The hour has begun to strike when his rescuer arrives. The dramatist, Bernard Shaw, has kept his audience waiting until the very last moment, with no clue as to where the rescue will come from.

Acute suspense must be used sparingly. An audience quickly gets tired of such tension. The screw has to be loosened before it can be tightened again, to be effective.

Work out the kind of suspense that the dramatist is using in the plays you are studying. Ask yourself these questions:

➤ Does the situation develop through a whole series of events which create some suspense, but not too much?

➤ Is the suspense acute. If so how long does the dramatist take to build it up?

CONFLICT

Every drama includes ***conflict*** of some sort. Sometimes it is of the literal, physical sort: duels are fought; families feud; battles are waged. Often these battles are expressions of strains or differences between characters which are the subject of the whole play. The subject of ***Romeo and Juliet*** is the destructive enmity between two clans which is only changed by the death of their children. The enmity is depicted in street brawls, arguments and duels, which are all signs of the conflict. The subject of conflict is so universal that it has been adapted to all sorts of environments. ***Look Back in Anger*** is about class conflict, but there is no fighting. The conflict takes the form of bitter rows between a husband and wife who come from different social classes.

The conflict need not be so obvious as an argument. Some struggles are silent. Some are so unequal that they seem over before they are begun. In ***Hobson's Choice***, when Maggie Hobson decides she wants Will as her husband she sends Will's girlfriend packing in three or four sentences. Poor little Ada Figgins does not stand a chance. Nevertheless there has been a conflict. Some are internal struggles of the mind like John Proctor's in ***The Crucible***. His fight is with his own conscience when faced with the choice between death with honour, or signing a false confession of witchcraft.

Whenever a difference of interest occurs between characters, a conflict follows. In ***comedy***, conflicts are resolved and there is a happy ending. In ***tragedy*** the conflicts are more difficult and serious and are frequently only resolved by death.

Look for the points of conflict in the plays you are studying, not just the obvious ones but all the subtle and minor ones too. Try to trace how they came about and what they show about the differences of interest between the characters. Ask yourself too if they represent ideas that the dramatist is trying to explore in the play.

TENSION

Both suspense and conflict create ***tension***. Tension mounts as we wait to see if Eliza Doolittle will manage to speak properly on her first outing in polite society. Professor Higgins has taught her the correct pronunciation; can she say the right things? It is not a serious scene and nothing vital depends on Eliza getting it right so the tension is not acute. Laughter relieves it at the end of the scene when Eliza sweeps out saying, 'Walk? Not bloody likely!'.

Tension of a quite different quality is built up as Macbeth prepares to kill the king, Duncan. We see his reluctance and watch Lady Macbeth urging him on, overcoming his objections, making the plan. We see him again struggling with his conscience. Finally a bell rings, the signal for the murder, and he goes to do the deed. The suspense generated is intense because of the horror of the deed about to be committed. Even those who have never seen or read the play before realize the probable outcome, because of the Witches' prophecy, but the enormity of the crime still creates great tension.

PACE

Another aid to tension is ***pace***, or the speed at which things happen.

A series of events in swift succession gives a sense of excitement or one of things getting out of control. When Richard III is losing his grip on the country he is given no time to digest one piece of bad news before another messenger arrives telling of a second disaster. A third messenger of doom follows almost immediately

The pace changes during a play according to the importance of the events, what kind of atmosphere is required, or perhaps what the dramatist wants to show us about the characters involved. A death or a marriage can happen quickly or slowly. Maggie Hobson courts and marries Will in ***Hobson's Choice*** and Kate is married to Petruchio in ***The Taming of the Shrew***, both with relative speed. In neither case is the wedding the important event. After getting married the couples have to sort out their relationship. Kate is gradually tamed and Will is painstakingly taught a sense of his own worth. The pace of these events is much slower than the whirlwind courtships.

On the whole the pace of comedy is faster than that of tragedy. The grave events of tragedy have to be prepared for in long serious scenes which convey the terrible importance of the events they record. If one dreadful event follows another too quickly we lose the sense of horror and may even begin to laugh.

When you are studying a play look at the way events are spaced out in individual scenes and throughout the play as a whole. Are they coming thick and fast at some points and at other times does it seem that not much is happening? Why is this? What is the effect of the pace on the atmosphere of the play? What does it tell you about the characters and themes of the play?

2 OPENING THE ACTION

The dramatist has a lot to do in the opening scene. This is the scene which has to catch the audience's attention and arouse interest in the characters and situation, and it has to set things moving so the audience has an idea of what is going to be important in the play.

Shakespeare often opens his plays with a couple of less important characters discussing something which we later realize is important to the theme of the play. *A Midsummer Night's Dream* begins with Theseus and Hippolyta talking about their forthcoming marriage. Very quickly other characters enter and the conflict between Demetrius and Lysander for Hermia's hand in marriage is introduced. Clearly marriage, and the proper basis for love, is going to be a theme.

Occasionally Shakespeare opens with a piece of really strong dramatic action, like the Witches appearing amid thunder and lightning in *Macbeth*, or the storm and shipwreck at the beginning of *The Tempest*. No trouble about catching the attention there.

Look at the opening scene of any play you are studying.
➤ How does it arouse your interest?
➤ Does it introduce major characters?
➤ What major themes does it introduce?

3 CONSTRUCTING THE ACTION

> **If you have made summaries of each scene as you read the play, your own reactions will help you assess the development of the plot, the use of suspense and the characters' consistency.**

Having set the situation in motion the dramatist now has to find ways of portraying his ideas through action. The more that can be shown in action rather than simply talked about in words, the more essentially dramatic it will be. Every action on stage is a sign of something.

One scene must follow another logically so that the audience can see links with what has gone before. The more characters of importance that are involved the more difficult it is. The dramatist has to keep the audience up to date with what everybody is doing, thinking and feeling. Even when there are only two characters the dramatist has to construct his scenes carefully. *Educating Rita* plots the developing relationship between a girl and her Open University tutor. The scenes have to be organized to show the pair's changing behaviour and feelings in a believable and understandable way so that the audience does not lose sympathy with the characters. By the end of the play the girl has changed enormously, but we have seen her changing gradually, each scene charting the progress of her course, so that we understand how the change has come about.

When you are studying a play ask yourself these questions:
➤ Are there strong links between scenes?
➤ How do the links work?
➤ Are the scenes connected by events following on from the previous scene or by developments in feelings or relationships?

4 GUESSING RIGHT AND GUESSING WRONG

Suspense keeps an audience guessing. Will it happen or won't it? We feel a sense of satisfaction when we have guessed rightly, and our expectations are confirmed. The dramatist can also keep our interest by failing to fulfil expectations. If we guess wrongly we are surprised and we want to know why we were wrong. We must be given good reasons when this happens or we will feel it is just a cheap trick. When Pastor Anderson rides in to rescue Dick Dudgeon from the gallows at the end of *The Devil's Disciple* it is not what we expect. He is a preacher and earlier in the play he had disappeared, apparently in fear of his life. But when we learn that he went to join the rebels and defeat the British at Springtown it seems consistent with what we know of his character and so we can accept the surprise.

Think about the plays you are studying. Has the dramatist ever surprised you with a development in the plot you didn't expect? If so did you feel it was justified when you thought about it?

5 SUBPLOTS

Some plays tell more than one story. Once the main story is under way a second one will be introduced. This is often related thematically to the first. We saw, above, how **A Midsummer Night's Dream** opens with two sets of characters. There is also a third set, Oberon and Titania, who also contribute to the main plot. But then a quite different group appears. These are a group of uneducated workmen who plan to produce a play for the Duke's wedding. All the other characters are involved in the main story of the lovers: these characters are not, so their story forms a **subplot**. A great deal of comedy arises from their efforts to rehearse and perform their play which provides a comic commentary on love, although they intend to present it seriously. They are also joined to the main plot through the exploits of Bottom, their leader, when Titania, under a spell, falls in love with him. In this way, every thread of the story contributes to the central theme.

This degree of unity is unusual, however. Very few modern plays have subplots.

Look carefully at the plays you are studying. Do they have subplots? If so how are they related to the main plot? And how are they linked to the theme of the play?

6 HUMOUR

Humour is just as much a product of a developing situation in a play as it is of the words. Some humour is purely verbal but some of the best comedy comes from action. Farce is built completely on the humour of action: characters are discovered where they should not be and escape in the nick of time with their trousers round their ankles, and so on. The humour of Titania and Bottom relies on the situation of a beautiful fairy ridiculously in love with an ass. When you are asked to explain or describe the humour in a scene look for the things which are out of place, the mistakes, the accidents in a situation as well as the characters and the language.

7 CLIMAX

The **climax** is the point towards which all the action moves. There can be several climaxes in a play, but one is usually more important than the others. It does not necessarily have to come at the end, though it frequently does. There is a sense in which the climax of **Macbeth** is the murder of Duncan and the rest of the play a consequence of that act. If you have read **Macbeth** try to decide whether you think Duncan's murder or the defeat and death of Macbeth is the greater climax, and why.

Bernard Shaw is particularly good at ending each Act with a resounding dramatic climax. In **Caesar and Cleopatra** Act 1 ends with a terrified Cleopatra being forced to face Caesar for the first time, alone; Act 2 with Caesar rushing off to win a battle; Act 3 with Cleopatra being thrown into the sea; Act 4 with the murder of Cleopatra's nurse and Act 5 with the final parting of Caesar and Cleopatra. Each of these is a very decisive moment and three of them highly exciting and visually striking.

We tend to think of climax as always being of this nature – a very strong dramatic moment - but it is not always so. At the end of Tom Stoppard's **Rosencrantz and Guildenstern Are Dead** the two main characters stand talking about what has happened to them and the lights quietly go out, on first one and then the other. Yet this is the climax of the action because it is the point towards which everything has been moving, the culmination of the theme of the play – their 'deaths'.

A climax should show how the situation or conflicts have been, or are going to be resolved. In a comedy the conflicts will be resolved happily. The characters will sort out their problems, the future will look rosy. In a tragedy the only way out of a situation is through suffering, and often death.

Where are the climaxes in the plays you are studying? What kind of climaxes are they?

8 > ENDINGS

When the climax comes at the end of a play it makes a good, neat finish. When it comes before the end, though, what is the rest of the action supposed to do? Often it is used to show how the events of the play have changed those who witnessed them. **Romeo and Juliet** ends like this. The climax is the death of the lovers. The **ending** shows how the families are brought together by the lovers' deaths and how they repent of their previous foolish antagonisms.

At other times endings show how, despite everything that has happened, life is essentially the same. At the end of **A Taste of Honey** Helen comes back to her daughter's flat, kicks Jo's friend out and takes over again just as if she had not left. All that Jo has been through in the intervening months, and the fact that Helen left her to fend for herself, is just pushed aside. Often this point is made by the setting – it is just as it was at the start, showing that nothing has changed.

9 > THEMES

The **theme** of a play can be brought out very strongly by the ending. But everything throughout the play can express the dramatist's ideas. The way the plot is shaped, and the way the characters are drawn, reveals the theme. Sometimes those views are so strong that the play gives a definite message. For instance Bertolt Brecht was a Marxist and his plays are intended to change the audience's ideas about how society should be run. Many exam questions which ask you about what happens in a play will also ask about ideas. As you read, try to think about what ideas the dramatist is trying to convey. If this seems a little difficult now, do not worry; Chapter 17 on themes and ideas in novels looks at this more closely.

10 > SUMMARY

➤ To hold the interest of the audience the dramatist uses suspense, conflict and tension.

➤ The opening scene should:

> catch the attention of the audience;
> introduce the characters;
> introduce the major themes of the play.

➤ As the action progresses the audience's attention is held by developing relationships or situations which express the underlying ideas.

➤ The pace at which events happen is important for atmosphere and theme.

➤ If a play contains a subplot, or second story, it usually contributes to the main theme of the play.

➤ Humour is a product of situation as much as of character or language.

➤ The climax is the critical point towards which the action moves.

➤ Endings show how things have changed or how they must remain the same.

ADDITIONAL EXAMPLES

You can test your understanding of the ideas in this chapter by reading the passages below and answering the questions on them. This work will help you to answer exam questions. Write down your own ideas first then read the key below which tells you what my thoughts on the passages are.

1. Why is this an effective opening scene?

As the curtain rises REVEREND PARRIS *is kneeling beside a bed in prayer. His daughter,* BETTY PARRIS *aged 10 is lying on the bed, inert. . . . The door opens, and his Negro slave enters.*

TITUBA: My Betty be hearty soon?

PARRIS: Out of here!

TITUBA: My Betty not goin' die. . .

PARRIS [*scrambling to his feet in a fury*]: Out of my sight! [*She is gone*] Out of my– [*He is overcome with sobs. He clamps his teeth against them and closes the door and leans against it exhausted.*] Oh my God! God help me! [*Quaking with fear, mumbling to himself through his sobs, he goes to the bed and gently takes* BETTY's *hand.*] Betty child, dear child. Will you wake, will you open your eyes! Betty, little one . . .

[*He is bending to kneel again when his niece,* ABIGAIL WILLIAMS, *17, enters–a strikingly beautiful girl, an orphan with an endless capacity for dissembling. Now she is all worry and apprehension and propriety.*]

ABIGAIL: Uncle? [*He looks at her*] Susanna Walcott's here from Dr. Griggs.

PARRIS: Oh? Let her come, let her come.

ABIGAIL [*leaning out the door to call to* SUSANNA, *who is down the hall a few steps*]: Come in Susanna. [SUSANNA WALCOTT, *a little younger than* ABIGAIL, *a nervous, hurried girl, enters*]

PARRIS [*eagerly*]: What does the doctor say, child?

SUSANNA [*craning round* PARRIS *to get a look at* BETTY]: He bid me come and tell you, reverend sir, that he cannot discover no medicine for it in his books.

PARRIS: Then he must search on.

SUSANNA: Aye, sir, he have been searchin' his books since he left you, sir. But he bid me tell you, that you might look to unnatural things for the cause of it.

PARRIS [*his eyes going wide*]: No – no. There be no unnatural cause here. Tell him I have sent for Reverend Hale of Beverly, and Mr. Hale will surely confirm that. Let him look to medicine and put out all thought of unnatural causes here. There be none.

SUSANNA: Aye, sir. He bid me tell you. [*She turns to go.*]

ABIGAIL: Speak nothin' of it in the village, Susanna.

PARRIS: Go directly home and speak nothing of unnatural causes.

SUSANNA: Aye, sir. I pray for her. [*She goes out.*]

ABIGAIL: Uncle, the rumour of witchcraft is all about; I think you'd best go down and deny it yourself. The parlour's packed with people, sir. I'll sit with her.

PARRIS [*pressed, turns on her*]: And what shall I say to them? That my daughter and my niece I discovered dancing like heathen in the forest?

ABIGAIL: Uncle, we did dance; let you tell them I confessed it – and I'll be whipped if I must be. But they're speakin' of witchcraft. Betty's not witched.

PARRIS: Abigail, I cannot go before the congregation when I know you have not opened with me. What did you do with her in the forest?

ABIGAIL: We did dance, uncle, and when you leaped out of the bush so suddenly, Betty was frightened and then she fainted. And there's the whole of it.

PARRIS: Child, sit you down.

ABIGAIL [*quavering as she sits*]: I would never hurt Betty. I love her dearly.

PARRIS: Now look you, child, your punishment will come in its time. But if you trafficked with spirits in the forest I must know it now, fir surely my enemies will, and they will ruin me with it.

ABIGAIL: But we never conjured spirits.

PARRIS: Then why can she not move herself since midnight? This child is desperate!

(***The Crucible***; Arthur Miller)

When asked about 'dramatic interest' look for conflict, suspense, tension, climax and interesting points about character.

2.   What would you say is the dramatic interest in the following scene?

GRUSHA: I won't give him away. I've brought him up and he knows me.

[*Enter* SHAUVA *with the child*]

THE GOVERNOR'S WIFE: It's in rags!

GRUSHA: That's not true. I wasn't given the time to put on his good shirt.

THE GOVERNOR'S WIFE: It's been in a pig-sty.

GRUSHA [*furious*]: I'm no pig, but there are others who are. Where did you leave your child.

THE GOVERNOR'S WIFE: I'll let you have it, you vulgar person. [*She is about to throw herself on* GRUSHA, *but is restrained by her lawyers.*] She's a criminal! She must be whipped!

THE SECOND LAWYER [*holding his hand over her mouth*]: Most gracious Natella Abashvili, you promised. . . Your worship, the plaintiff's nerves. . .

AZDAK: Plaintiff and defendant! The court has listened to your case, and has come to no decision as to who the real mother of the child is. I as judge have the duty of choosing a mother for the child. I'll make a test. Shauva get a piece of chalk and draw a circle on the floor. [SHAUVA *does so*] Now place the child in the centre. [SHAUVA *puts* MICHAEL, *who smiles at* GRUSHA, *in the centre of the circle.*] Stand near the circle, both of you. [*The* GOVERNOR'S WIFE *and* GRUSHA *step up to the circle.*] Now each of you take the child by the hand. The true mother is she who has the strength to pull the child out of the circle, towards herself.

THE SECOND LAWYER [*quickly*]: High court of justice, I protest! I object that the fate of the Abashvili estates, which are bound up with the child as the heir, should be made dependent on such a doubtful wrestling match. Moreover my client does not command the same physical strength as this person, who is accustomed to physical work.

AZDAK: She looks pretty well fed to me. Pull! [*The* GOVERNOR'S WIFE *pulls the child out of the circle to her side.* GRUSHA *has let it go and stands aghast.*]

THE FIRST LAWYER [*congratulating the* GOVERNOR'S WIFE]: What did I say! The bonds of blood!

AZDAK [*to* GRUSHA]: What's the matter with you? You didn't pull!

GRUSHA: I didn't hold on to him. [*She runs to* AZDAK] Your worship, I take back everything I said against you. I ask your forgiveness. If I could just keep him until he can speak properly. He only knows a few words.

AZDAK: Don't influence the court! I bet you only know twenty yourself. All right I'll do the test once more, to make certain.

[*The two women take up positions again*]

AZDAK: Pull!

[*Again* GRUSHA *lets go the child.*]

GRUSHA [*in despair*]: I've brought him up. Am I to tear him to pieces? I can't do it.

AZDAK: [*rising*] And in this manner the court has established the true mother. [*to* GRUSHA] Take your child and be off with it. I advise you not to stay in town with him.

(***The Caucasian Chalk Circle***; Bertolt Brecht)

1. ***The Crucible***: The first task of an opening scene is to arouse interest. This scene does that by showing Betty motionless on the bed, with Parris and Tituba afraid that she might die. This raises one question in our minds but an even stronger question is posed by the reaction of the other characters to the nature of Betty's illness. They do not seem merely to be grieving but are in a panic. There is tremendous tension in Parris' fear: he calls on God, pleads with Betty to wake and almost strikes Tituba in his fury. What has happened to make him like this? When Susanna Walcott comes to say the doctor can discover no medicine for it in his books, some explanation for their fear is given, but further questions are raised when Susanna says they might have to look for unnatural causes. This seems to be the root of Parris' fear as he immediately denies the possibility of such a thing and Susanna is sworn to silence. Abigail makes clear that she is frightened of being accused of witchcraft and, when we learn that she and Betty have been discovered dancing in the forest, we begin to wonder what they have been up to and what the consequences will be.

   This is a very effective opening scene because it immediately creates suspense through the condition of Betty and the fear of Parris and Abigail. The mention of witchcraft, which excites our curiosity, introduces an issue of major importance in the play. It also introduces two major characters, Parris and Abigail, and shows us from the beginning Parris' fearful and intolerant nature. The scene is tense with the characters' strong emotions.

2.   The Caucasian Chalk Circle: The dramatic interest in this scene lies chiefly in the conflict between the Governor's Wife and Grusha over the child. There is suspense as we wait to see the way the judge's decision will go. The test shows us the contrasting characters of the two sides, and this relates to the theme of the play.

Any trial is a conflict, and here we see Grusha is determined to fight to keep the child. The battle is not just a legal one because the Governor's Wife insults Grusha and is about to attack her until she is restrained by her lawyer. When Azdak announces the test of the chalk circle – a surprising way of deciding the case – this seems to favour Grusha, but to our amazement she simply lets the child go and does not pull. Even with a second chance she cannot do it. It seems her case is lost. In another twist, Azdak declares that this has determined her to be the true mother, the one who cares most for the child. The Governor's wife is rich, supercilious, surrounded by attendant lawyers who pamper her. They are clearly unscrupulous about how she secures her right to benefit from the great Abashvili estates that the child is heir to. Grusha, on the other hand, is poor but caring and straightforward. Our sympathy is with Grusha and our interest is maintained by the desire to see her win.

The characters represent two classes of society and, in making Grusha the winner, the playwright brings the argument of his play to a conclusion and demonstrates the principle he believes in. Grusha gains the child because she is a properly caring person. This illustrates the theme that things must belong to those who are most fitted for them.

EXAM QUESTIONS

You may be asked a question about
➤ an opening or closing scene;
➤ dramatic tension or climax;
➤ or simply what makes a scene interesting or enjoyable.

You should always try to say how the actions of a scene bring out ideas important to the whole play. Here are some examples of questions:

1.   Right from the beginning there are ideas and issues which become important later in the play. Write about what expectations these early pages set up for you and show how details included here are developed later in the play.
     (Based on an extract from ***Death of a Salesman*** - NEA)

This question could be applied to a great many plays. Look back at the sections on suspense, opening the action, and the first of the additional examples in Section C to help you answer.

2.   You have probably noticed that many scenes in Macbeth take place at night, in darkness. By referring to two scenes that have impressed you, explore how this feature has made the scenes effective for you. (MEG)

Here you are being asked about how atmosphere and tension are achieved through the use of a particular dramatic effect. You should first examine your two chosen scenes, looking at how the language stresses the darkness, and how the tension is created through the language and the action. A good answer would relate the use of darkness to Macbeth's situation and go on to discuss character and themes.

The same kind of question, mentioning other dramatic features can be asked about other plays.

3.   How does Galsworthy create tension and drama in this extract? (Based on an extract from ***Strife*** - WJEC)

The following question asks for explanation and comment on the surprise created by the entrance of a character. His appearance is not expected either by the other characters or by the audience.

4. Account as fully as you can for the change that comes over the scene when Old Mahon rushes in. (Based on an extract from ***The Playboy of the Western World*** - NI)

QUESTION, NOTES AND TUTOR'S ANSWER

The following question on *A Man for All Seasons* is answered below.

1 ⟩ QUESTION

Several scenes show Sir Thomas More with his family. Choose one of these scenes and say what it adds to your enjoyment of the play.

2 ⟩ NOTES

1. I have chosen to answer this question using the scene in which More's family visit him in jail.
2. There are numerous things which can make a scene enjoyable. Different people are likely to make different choices. The answer below is based on my own response to the scene. What is important is that you base your opinion firmly on what is happening in the text.
3. Jot down the important aspects of the scene which seem to you to make it enjoyable. Here are my notes:

> contrast of characters;
> argument with Meg – resolved;
> uprightness of More;
> conflict with Alice – resolved;
> family affection.

In an exam your notes would have to be made from memory.
4. As you write your answer use details from the scene to illustrate the enjoyable aspects you have chosen.

3 ⟩ SUGGESTED ANSWER

❝Have you clearly stated in your introduction what it is that adds to your enjoyment? If not, it should be in your conclusion.❞

The enjoyment of the scene in which More's family visit him in jail comes from the contrast in the characters of More, Meg and Alice, contrasts which cause tensions and conflict. Much of our pleasure derives from the interplay of the characters and the resolution of the conflicts, which represent the choices that More has to make.

Thomas is overjoyed to see his family, especially Meg, though briefly alarmed that she might have been imprisoned too. This is what he fears: that his family may suffer harm because of the stand he has taken. The conflict that we see in this scene is over the place of his family in his scale of values. First, however, he has to combat Meg's arguments.

Meg, who is under oath to try to persuade More to swear to the Act of Succession, is constrained as she unpacks the basket of food they have brought him. Her father is a formidable opponent in argument and she knows that she is setting herself against his most deeply held convictions. Nevertheless she feels bound to try to alter his mind: his life depends on it. It is the vital consequences that give this conversation between More and his daughter its dramatic tension. As she seeks to persuade him to speak the words of the oath but believe otherwise in his heart we sympathize with both his position and hers. She loves her father and desires him to live above all. He knows he cannot live with a bad conscience about a deed which would rob him of his self-respect. He must do what is right even at the risk of making himself a martyr or a hero.

Even in this most dire of circumstances, More enjoys wrestling intellectually with his daughter and is proud of her ability to advance compelling arguments. We share his enjoyment of this intellectual battle, and we derive satisfaction from

More's victory. Meg concedes out of love for her father and admiration for the honour and truth of his position. If More had departed from that position we, the audience, would have been shocked and disappointed. Part of our pleasure is in the spectacle of a man who can stand out for what he believes is good and right against all the odds. We are ennobled by his nobility.

More's conflict with his wife, Alice, is of a different nature. She is stiff and hostile, refusing to understand why he leaves his family alone when a mere signature would return him to them. When More begins to compliment her on her cooking and her dress she bursts out in anger. She feels that he belittles her in thinking such things are important to her at such a time. More begs for her understanding of his refusal to sign but she refuses to lie about what she feels. Where Meg's appeal was through reason, Alice's is through feeling. More is heart-rent but will not yield. Having failed to move him Alice repents and goes to comfort her husband. The intricacies of argument are beyond her, and do not interest her, but she knows that More is the best man she has ever met or is ever likely to. Her forgiveness means that More can go to his death, if necessary, more easily, assured of his family's love. The coming together of Alice and More is a very touching moment, especially because their affection has so far been hidden.

When the jailor comes to remove them the family is united. They have accepted More's instruction to flee the country – Alice with her usual truculence – and we are left with a sense of strong family affection and an increased admiration for the uprightness of Sir Thomas.

SUGGESTIONS FOR COURSEWORK

1. Any of the exam questions above can be used as a question for a coursework unit.
2. The kind of work done on the passages in 'Additional Examples' could be used as the basis for writing a coursework unit. You could write about the effectiveness of any opening scene, or the dramatic effect of any scene you chose.
3. Compare two plays with subplots and discuss how these relate to the main plot.
4. Make a study of conflict in drama.
5. Write a new scene or an alternative ending for a play.

STUDENT'S ANSWER – EXAMINER'S COMMENT

This question asks the student to look carefully at the progress of the plot of the play in order to discuss reaction to one character.

Question

'In our feelings about Shylock we swing as the play progresses between sympathy and disgust; between dislike and admiration.' Drawing your evidence from as many occasions as possible, show clearly why and for what reasons your own feelings for Shylock vary.

It is indeed true that as I progress through the play, 'The Merchant of Venice', my feelings for Shylock vary tremendously. In parts it is portrayed he is, in fact, a humane man, like any other; whereas in other parts, one is forced to wonder how such a man could be classed as 'human'. Shylock's opening speech in the play, immediately causes me to dislike him, for he deliberates purposely, on consenting to Bassanio's request, and he leads Bassanio to the point of begging for a loan of money. The word, 'well', uttered several times in his speech emphasizes his deliberate hesitation:

'Three thousand ducats; well.'

He seemingly delights in seeing his enemy plead for his help. Then Antonio, the one who wishes to borrow some money, enters, and Shylock talks spitefully of him to himself; thus succeeding in increasing my dislike of him. He says:

'I hate him for he is a Christian.'

However, this dislike gradually changes to an understanding of him, and then sympathy, as the reason for Shylock's spitefulness becomes clear. It is apparent that Antonio, as well as being unneccesarily unkind to Shylock, lends out money free of charge, and so destroys Shylock's business as a money lender. He also destroys Shylock's pride, when insulting his Jewish religion, so it is no wonder that Shylock bears a grudge against him. He says of Antonio:

'You call me misbeliever, cut-throat dog.
And spet upon my Jewish gaberdine.'

The sympathy therefore, arises when it can be understood that Shylock has a job to do that he cannot help but do, in order to earn a living; and he also has a religion which he takes great pride in, and I admire him for that. So it sees unjust that Antonio should destroy this and so treat him.

However, this sympathy does not last long, for it can be perceived that Shylock is cunningly planning revenge towards the end of their meeting. Only Bassanio notices this, and says:

'I like not fair terms and a villain's mind.'

When Launcelot comes on the scene, he comically talks of leaving Shylock. Once again I feel sympathetic, that nobody likes Shylock. However, this feeling is almost immediately contrasted with dislike, for Launcelot then goes on to tell his father of how ill-treated he as in Shylock's service. He says:

'I am famished in his services;
You may tell every finger I have with my ribs.'

Good. Looks carefully at words used in the beginning of the play and states their effect on the audience. This begins to answer the question set.

Good. Notes how Shakespeare shifts our sympathy, by giving Shylock's own point of view.

Points to a second shift of sympathy, i.e. the essay is moving carefully through the plot, just as the question requires.

This is a major part of the action, but it is only mentioned briefly.

The discussion of Launcelot is confused. The question is leading the student to strain after points that are not really there.

CHARACTER IN PLAYS

GETTING STARTED

More questions are asked about characters and their relationships than almost any other drama topic in the exam. A great deal of the material of the previous chapters is useful in helping you to understand character. This chapter will help you specifically to look for character points in what characters say and do and how they relate to each other. Always remember, though, that characters are not real people, although a good dramatist may make them seem so. They are inventions and our knowledge of them is strictly limited to their words and actions in a few scenes. You should make notes on each major character as you read. If you do this from the beginning you will be able to record how your impressions of a character develop as the play progresses.

ESSENTIAL PRINCIPLES

1 > ACTIONS
Just as with real people, we know and understand characters through their actions. When we go to see a play we see how the characters behave. When we read the same play we have to imagine that behaviour from the stage directions. This is one of the reasons why it is so important to learn to read a play effectively, as Chapter 8 explained. A great deal of the character of Billy Fisher is portrayed in the action described in these stage directions from **_Billy Liar_**:

> BILLY *hums to himself and then turns on the seat and takes up a garden cane. He toys with the cane for a moment, attempting to balance it on his fingers. His humming grows louder and he stands and conducts an imaginary orchestra using the cane as a baton. He is humming a military march and he suddenly breaks off as the garden cane becomes, in his imagination, a rifle. He shoulders the cane and marches briskly down the garden path .*
> BILLY [*marching*]: Lef', ri', lef', ri', lef'-ri'-lef'! Halt! [*He halts*] Order arms! [*He brings the cane down to the 'Order' position.*]
> *He pauses for a moment and the garden cane becomes, in his imagination, an officer's baton which he tucks under his arm and then he marches smartly off to an imaginary saluting base a few paces away. He has become, in his imagination, a major-general.*

We know from this that Billy is a dreamy, imaginative person who can easily lose himself in his thoughts. The world inside his head is often more real than the world outside, so much so that he often confuses imagination with reality. We can see how this might lead to trouble for him. In his imaginary world he sees himself in important positions – a conductor or a major-general – so we understand how he would like to be important and not just a very ordinary young man in a humdrum job in a small town. What we learn here is strengthened throughout the play by other actions and by words.

Some actions which display character can be suggested by the dialogue, as in this scene at a critical moment when Macbeth faces the prospect of battle with the English army.

> MACBETH: Throw physic to the dogs; I'll none of it.
> [*to an attendant*] Come put mine armour on. Give me my staff.
> Seyton, send out. Doctor, the thanes fly from me.
> [*to an attendant*] Come. sir, dispatch. – If you could'st, Doctor, cast
> The water of my land, find her disease,
> And purge it to a sound and pristine health,
> I would applaud thee to the very echo,
> That should applaud again. [*to an attendant*] Pull't off, I say.
> [*to the doctor*] What rhubarb, senna, or what purgative drug
> Would scour these English hence? Hear'st thou of them?
> DOCTOR: Ay, my good lord. Your royal preparation
> Makes us hear something.
> MACBETH [*to an attendant*]: Bring it after me.
> I will not be afraid of death and bane
> Till Birnam forest come to Dunsinane.

Macbeth instructs his servant to put on his armour. He is impatient, telling the servant to hurry when he says, 'Come, sir, dispatch'. A moment later he contradicts himself and tells the servant to pull it off. However he needs to be armed because as he goes out he tells the servant to bring the armour after him. All during these actions he is talking to the Doctor, half about his wife's illness and half about the English. He is clearly in a turmoil, abusing the Doctor, 'Throw physic to the dogs', speaking roughly to the servant and deciding first one thing and then another. His physical actions mirror his state of mind, unable to concentrate on one subject and prepare for the coming battle. It is a complete contrast to the picture we had of him at the beginning of the play.

Macbeth's actions, at this point in the play, add to the knowledge we have of him from other actions at other times. We build up our awareness of a character from his or her actions throughout the play.

When you have read a scene summarize the characters' actions. Then say what they tell you about the characters.

There are three ways in which we learn about characters from the dialogue of the play.

(i) What they say about themselves
(ii) What other characters say about them
(iii) The kind of language they use.

TRUE AND FALSE SELF-DESCRIPTIONS

What characters say about themselves need not necessarily be true. Just as with people we have to judge the characters' words alongside other evidence. When Owen Glendower says, in **Henry IV Part 1**:

I can call up spirits from the vasty deep

it shows that he believes himself to be a man endowed with unusual, mysterious powers. What he claims may not be true, in fact Hotspur obviously thinks it isn't because he answers:

Ay, so can I and so can any man, but will they come when you call them?

Hotspur's speech also tells us something about himself: that he doesn't believe in spirits and he thinks that Glendower is talking pretentious poppycock.

Let us look at two occasions when Lady Macbeth speaks about herself. In the first, when she is persuading Macbeth to murder Duncan she says, about a baby at her breast:

I would, when it was smiling in my face
Have plucked my nipple from its boneless gums
And dashed its brains out

She is characterizing herself as a most cruel and heartless woman. Are we to believe this? She certainly does organize a cruel and heartless deed – Duncan's murder. Later, however, she says:

Had he not resembled
My father as he slept, I had done it.

She could batter a baby in her imagination, but could not in reality kill a man because he looked like her father. This suggests she cannot be quite as cruel as she at first described herself, not quite as heartless as it was necessary to be. It is not surprising that she later breaks down.

REMARKS ON EACH OTHER

Characters make many remarks about each other. Again we have to decide whether to believe them on the basis of other evidence in the play.

In Bill Naughton's **Spring and Port Wine** Arthur turns on his future father-in-law:

ARTHUR: But you want to crush the spirit out of everybody who doesn't agree with you. You know what you are, Mr Crompton?
FLORENCE: Be quiet, Arthur.
ARTHUR: You're a bully.

We know this is true because we have just seen Mr Crompton bullying the son to the point where it brings on one of his fits, and the whole play grows out of his attempts to bully his daughter into eating a herring when she didn't want to. Arthur only puts into words what we already know.

In **A Taste of Honey** Jo says this about her mother:

JO: I won't set eyes on her for a week now. I know her when she's in the mood. What are you going to do about me, Peter? The snotty-nosed daughter? Don't you think I'm a bit young to be left on my own while you flit off with my old woman?

We have already seen enough of Helen's behaviour to believe that she is quite capable of neglecting her daughter to this extent. Jo's words tell us that Helen is a feckless and irresponsible person 'when she's in the mood'. We are not surprised when she goes off and leaves Jo to fend for herself and we are ready to believe that this has been a regular occurrence throughout Jo's life.

THE TRUTH BUT NOT THE WHOLE TRUTH

Characters may tell the truth about each other but they cannot tell the whole truth. When Hamlet kills Polonius by mistake he calls him a 'wretched, rash, intruding fool'. Polonius is all those things, and Hamlet is particularly justified in saying them because Polonius was hiding behind a curtain, eavesdropping, in the bedroom of Hamlet's mother. Yet this judgement misses out other, better aspects of Polonius' character. For instance he is an affectionate father, loved by his children. We have to weigh up *all* the evidence.

CONFLICTING OPINIONS

Sometimes a dramatist deliberately allows opinions about a character to conflict. Maggie Hobson's sisters think Will Mossop a poor specimen of a man. From what we see of him in the first act we would agree with them. Maggie disagrees: she sees Will's potential and by the end of the play it is her opinion which is shown to be right.

LIES

Characters may also lie about each other. This may be for their own devious reasons. In *Twelfth Night* Sir Toby lies to Viola when he tells her Sir Andrew is an excellent swordsman. He does it to goad Viola into a fight, not knowing she's really a woman in disguise and this is just the thing to put her off. The audience knows the truth about both characters. When characters lie the audience is usually told quite clearly: to mislead the audience is disorientating.

What have you learnt about the characters from their own and others' words?

USE OF LANGUAGE

Every time characters speak, no matter what the subject, we are told something about them by the kind of language they use. A very simple example is Cliff in *Look Back in Anger*. The playwright makes him say 'boyo' from time to time, so we know he is a Welshman. What we find out about Cliff's friend Jimmy Porter from the way he talks is much more complicated. He boasts of his working-class origins but his language is anything but that of an ordinary working man. It is full of images and flights of imagination. Even the length of the sentences show the extent of his education and the subtlety of his mind.

> JIMMY: There is no limit to what the middle-aged mummy will do in the holy crusade against ruffians like me. Mummy and I took one quick look at each other, and, from then on, the age of chivalry was dead. I knew that to protect her innocent young, she wouldn't hesitate to cheat, lie, bully and blackmail.
> Threatened with me, a young man without money, background or even looks, she'd bellow like a rhinoceros in labour – enough to make every male rhino for miles turn white, and pledge himself to celibacy. But even I under-estimated her strength. Mummy may look over-fed and a bit flabby on the outside, but don't let that well-bred guzzler fool you. Underneath all that, she's armour plated–

If we had no other information to go on we could tell from this speech that Jimmy was an aggressive young man, with a grievance against the middle-class. This language is witty, sarcastic, colourful and deliberately vulgar. Jimmy uses it as a weapon.

The extent to which we judge character from speech is the whole basis of *Pygmalion*. Eliza Doolittle will remain a common flower-girl as long as she talks like this:

> *Ow, eez ye-ooa san, is e? Wal, fewd dan y' dooty bawmz a mather should, eed now bettern to spawl a pore gel's flahrzn than ran awy athaht pyin.*

This is Bernard Shaw's way of representing Eliza's dialect. In other words: 'Oh, he's your son, is he? Well if you'd done your duty by him as a mother should, he'd know better than to spoil a poor girl's flowers and then run away without paying.' With Professor Higgins help she learns to speak differently and becomes a lady. As her speech changes people begin to see her differently and treat her differently. It seems that it is not just her speech but her whole character that changes so that by the end of the play she is unable to return to her former life.

What is distinctive about the way the characters speak in the plays you are studying?

3 ⟩ CHARACTER CONSISTENCY

Despite the fact that we see characters in only a few situations in a play we often come to feel we know them as real people. We forget they are inventions and begin to imagine what they would do in other situations. A good dramatist can do this because what the character is given to say and to do, as well as the manner of speech, all chime together as a believable whole. Everything Joan does and says in **St. Joan**, for example, is consistent with her country origins and her simple, sincere courage. Her manner of speech is that of a blunt, country girl:

Coom, Bluebeard! Thou canst not fool me. Where be Dauphin?

she says on her arrival at court. Everything else she says and does, however extraordinary, has the mark of a plain, uneducated girl applying her common sense to the situation. Therefore we believe in her.

This does not mean that characters do not surprise us with their words and actions. They do. Yet even as we are being surprised we must understand why the dramatist has made them do it and see clues to their behaviour in earlier scenes. At the end of **Spring and Port Wine** Mr. Crompton suddenly stops bullying his family and starts letting them behave more as they please. However we are shown that he was far more aware of his family's feelings and desires all the time, and that it was elements of his own experience which prevented him from being softer on them.

When we cannot see the reasons behind a character's change of behaviour it seems unreal, a dramatist's failure or trick and we criticize the playwright for not drawing consistent characters.

4 ⟩ CHARACTERS OF CONVENIENCE

Even great dramatists do not draw all their characters in depth. Some characters have different functions, within the scheme of the play. Some characters merely provide the right sense of place, situation or atmosphere. These can range from the spear-carriers in battle scenes to the townsfolk occupying the graveyard alongside Emily in **Our Town**, or those shouting abuse at Stockman in **An Enemy of the People**. Some are there simply to help the plot along, like messengers. Some have a single characteristic because they have only one function in the plot. Lady Macduff is characterised well but simply as a mother. She appears in the play just to be killed by Macbeth, to give us an example of Macbeth's cruelty and to give Macduff a personal motive for revenge.

If you remember that the dramatist brings in each character to do a job you will have fewer difficulties with characterisation. Even major characters who have been skilfully drawn sometimes have to drop out of character and speak in a purely functional way because the dramatist has a piece of the plot that has to be got across to the audience.

5 ⟩ SYMBOLIC CHARACTERS

Some characters are never intended to be seen as realistic representations of people. They stand for ideas. The Seven Deadly Sins in **Doctor Faustus** are this kind of character. Few characters are so obviously symbolic as that, but they have a symbolic aspect. The Inspector in J. B. Priestley's **An Inspector Calls** is such a character. He is not a real police inspector, as the other characters realize by the end of the play; he has come to show them what their moral responsibilities are. He is a modern representation of conscience.

6 ▷ CHARACTERS' NAMES

The names given to characters sometimes show their dominant characteristic, or what they stand for. Here are a few examples of characters whose names give them away: Justice Shallow, Joseph Surface, Lydia Languish, Sir Antony Absolute, Tony Lumpkin. In modern plays such names are thought inappropriate. Nevertheless some names can be very apt, like Willy Loman in **Death of a Salesman**. He is just an ordinary, little man. This is what he finds so difficult to accept. He dreams of big success – the American dream. (His brother, Ben, is another symbolic figure representing the fulfilment of those dreams.) Willy Loman is a very real, well-developed character but he has a symbolic aspect too, signalled by his name. He stands for every ordinary man.

Have you come across any symbolic characters or characters with significant names?

7 ▷ CONTRASTING CHARACTERS

Quite often you will find two characters in a play who form a deliberate contrast. Take Maggie and her sisters in **Hobson's Choice** or Kate and Bianca in **The Taming of the Shrew**. Bianca is lady-like, sweet-tempered and pliant, making Kate's tempestuous and uncontrollable nature seem worse by comparison. Maggie Hobson's firm, mature and decisive behaviour appears particularly outstanding beside her two rather ineffectual and conventional sisters. In both these cases the playwright has used contrast to highlight the character of his heroine. Shakespeare puts contrast to further use by turning the tables at the end: Kate becomes the contented wife, comparing favourably with her sister.

Contrasts need not last for the whole play. Similar characters can be shown reacting differently to certain situations. Macbeth and Banquo are initially shown as very similar in position and courage. The King praises them both for their bravery and loyalty. After the meeting with the witches they are seen to diverge. Banquo remains loyal; Macbeth becomes enmeshed in the evil consequences of his ambitions. Banquo is used first as a comparison and then a contrast to Macbeth, to show how he could and should have reacted to the Witches' prophecies.

Character contrasts are usually made for a purpose: ask yourself what that purpose is. Usually they tell you something about the themes and ideas of the play.

8 ▷ SUMMARY

➤ We learn about characters from:
  what they do;
  the way they speak;
  what they say about themselves;
  what others say about them.
➤ Well drawn characters are consistent: their behaviour can be understood and explained.
➤ Some characters are not drawn in depth. They are there to do a specific job in the plot.
➤ Some characters are symbolic, either wholly or in part, and represent ideas.
➤ Dramatists use contrasting characters to portray themes and ideas.

ADDITIONAL EXAMPLES

Use the passages below to test your understanding of what you have read in this chapter. Write down your own ideas before reading the key below.

What do we learn about the characters in the following extracts?

1. From **An Inspector Calls**.
  BIRLING: We shall be along in a minute now. Just finishing.
  INSPECTOR: I'm afraid not.

BIRLING: [*abruptly*]: There's nothing else y' know. I've just told you that.

SHEILA: What's all this about?

BIRLING: Nothing to do with you, Sheila. Run along.

INSPECTOR: No, wait a minute, Miss Birling.

BIRLING [*angrily*]: Look here, Inspector, I consider this uncalled for and officious. I've half a mind to report you. I've told you all I know–and it doesn't seem to me very important– and now there isn't the slightest reason why my daughter should be dragged into this unpleasant business.

SHEILA [*coming in further*]: What business? What's happening?

INSPECTOR [*impressively*]: I'm a police inspector, Miss Birling. This afternoon a young woman drank some disinfectant, and died, after several hours of agony, tonight in the Infirmary.

SHEILA: Oh–how horrible! Was it an accident?

INSPECTOR: No. She wanted to end her life. She felt she couldn't go on any longer.

BIRLING: Well, don't tell me that's because I discharged her from my employment nearly two years ago.

ERIC: That might have started it.

SHEILA: Did you, Dad?

BIRLING: Yes. The girl had been causing trouble at the Works. I was quite justified.

GERALD: Yes, I think you were. I know we'd have done the same thing. Don't look like that, Sheila.

SHEILA [*rather distressed*]: Sorry! I just can't help thinking about this girl–destroying herself so horribly– and I've been so happy tonight. Oh I wish you hadn't told me. What was she like? Quite young?

2. From *The Importance of Being Earnest*.

JACK [*Astounded*]: Well. . . surely. You know that I love you, and you led me to believe, Miss Fairfax, that you were not absolutely indifferent to me.

GWENDOLEN: I adore you. But you haven't proposed to me yet. Nothing has been said at all about marriage. The subject has not even been touched on.

JACK: Well. . . may I propose now?

GWENDOLEN: I think it would be an admirable opportunity. And to spare you any possible disappointment, Mr. Worthing, I think it only fair to tell you quite frankly beforehand that I am fully determined to accept you.

JACK: Gwendolen!

GWENDOLEN: Yes, Mr. Worthing, what have you got to say to me?

JACK: You know what I have got to say to you.

GWENDOLEN: Yes, but you don't say it.

JACK: Gwendolen, will you marry me? [*Goes on his knees*]

GWENDOLEN: Of course I will, darling. How long you have been about it! I'm afraid you have had very little experience in how to propose.

JACK: My own one, I have never loved anyone in the world but you.

GWENDOLEN: Yes, but men often propose for practice. I know my brother Gerald does. All my girl-friends tell me so. What wonderfully blue eyes you have, Ernest! They are quite, quite, blue. I hope you will always look at me just like that, especially when there are other people present.

Enter Lady Bracknell.

LADY BRACKNELL: Mr. Worthing! Rise, sir, from this semi-recumbemt posture. It is most indecorous.

GWENDOLEN: Mamma! [*He tries to rise; she restrains him.*] I must beg you to retire. This is no place for you. Besides Mr. Worthing has not quite finished yet?

LADY BRACKNELL: Finished what, may I ask?

GWENDOLEN: I am engaged to Mr. Worthing, mamma. [*They rise together*]

LADY BRACKNELL: Pardon me, you are not engaged to anyone. When you do become engaged to some one, I, or your father should his health permit him, will inform you of the fact. An engagement should come on a young girl as a surprise, pleasant or unpleasant, as the case may be. It is hardly a matter she could be allowed to arrange for herself . . . And now I have a few questions to put to you Mr. Worthing. While I am making these enquiries, you, Gwendolen, will wait for me below in the carriage.

GWENDOLEN [*reproachfully*]: Mamma!

LADY BRACKNELL: In the carriage, Gwendolen! [GWENDOLEN *goes to the door. She and* JACK *blow kisses to each other behind* LADY BRACKNELL's *back.* LADY BRACKNELL *looks vaguely about as if she could not understand what the noise was. Finally turns round.*] Gwendolen, the carriage!

GWENDOLEN: Yes, mamma. [*She goes out, looking back at* Jack]

LADY BRACKNELL [*sitting down*]: You can take a seat, Mr. Worthing. [*Looks in her pocket for notebook and pencil.*]

JACK: Thank you, Lady Bracknell, I prefer standing.

LADY BRACKNELL [*Pencil and notebook in hand*]: I feel bound to tell you that you are not down on my list of eligible young men, although I have the same list as the dear Duchess of Bolton has. We work together, in fact. However I am quite ready to enter your name, should your answers be what a really affectionate mother requires. Do you smoke?

JACK: Well, yes, I must admit I smoke.

LADY BRACKNELL: I am glad to hear it. A man should always have an occupation of some kind. There are far too many idle men in London as it is.

1. ***An Inspector Calls***, J. B. Priestley. Mr. Birling is a hard-nosed business man. He feels quite justified in sacking a young woman from his works because he sees her as a trouble-maker. He feels no responsibility for her welfare and totally rejects the suggestion that his action had any bearing on her later distress, or was in any way the cause of her suicide. The horrible nature of her death does not seem to affect him, or change his attitude in the least. He seems incapable of sympathy. His manner with the Inspector is over-bearing and self-important. He loses his temper easily when it seems that his authority is questioned.

Birling is supported in his attitude by Gerald, who takes the same view of a worker and seems, at this point, to be just as unfeeling as Birling. However Sheila and Eric respond differently. Eric believes that his father's action in dismissing the girl might well have started her on the path to despair. By taking this view Eric shows he has a greater imaginative grasp of how things affect people, and a greater sense of social responsibility. Sheila is very upset by the appalling manner of the girl's death and immediately relates the girl's experience to her own. While Sheila was enjoying herself the girl was suffering. Sheila's question, 'What was she like? Quite young?' shows her immediate identification with the girl as somebody very like herself. Her sympathy is immediate and strongly felt. Her feelings are that, had things been different, it could have been herself in that position.

Throughout, the Inspector is calm, matter-of-fact, and totally in charge.

2. ***The Importance of Being Earnest***, Oscar Wilde. These characters are not naturalistic in the way that those in the previous passage are. The dramatist's purpose is to present social types and manners in order to mock them. They are caricatures rather than characters.

Jack is the eligible young man about town, but serious, innocent and out of his depth with women. He is presented as devoted to Gwendolen, and is nervous, socially inept, and unsure of what to do in this situation. He speaks haltingly and has to be prompted into proposing. Gwendolen is a very assured young lady. She is determined to have a proper proposal, with Jack on his knees. She betrays no emotion, except satisfaction at the way Jack admires her, which she hopes will be publicly displayed. Her manner is brisk and business-like.

The relationship between Jack and Gwendolen is not a naturalistic one. They do not behave like real lovers. Their courtship is a mockery of the conventional forms of courtship between men and women of their class at the time the play was written (1894). This is shown in the way that Gwendolen states quite openly that she intends to accept Jack, but nevertheless expects him to go through the performance of getting down on his knees. It is all an elaborate little game. People like her brother do it often for practice. There is a suggestion that Jack should have practised too. Gwendolen stands for all the fashionable young women of the time

> **❝Do not think that 'caricature' is always bad and 'real' is always good.❞**

and Jack for all the rich young bachelors who allowed themselves to be bamboozled by them.

Similarly Lady Bracknell stands for the upper-class mother with a marriageable daughter, determined to acquire a husband of the right class for her. Gwendolen's desires are of no account. Lady Bracknell takes formidable command of the situation as she prepares to question Jack. It is in Lady Bracknell's remarks that Wilde's mockery of society is clearest because her statements are extreme, silly and comic. Wilde phrases them to be clever and funny rather than to sound as if a real person is speaking. No one in reality would say, 'Rise, sir, from this semi-recumbent posture' but it makes a wonderful line for an actress to bellow as she stands erect in exaggerated horror at the door. And no one would regard smoking as a man's 'occupation'. It is examples like this, throughout the speech of all the characters, which give this play its life and its point.

EXAM QUESTIONS

More questions are asked about character, development and relationships than any other type of question. Here are some examples.

1. Which do you think Shaw presents most vividly in **Pygmalion** – the women or the men? Write about how he portrays at least two women (Eliza, Mrs Higgins and Mrs. Pearce are the main ones) and at least two of the men (Higgins, Pickering, Freddy and Doolittle are those treated most fully) in your answer. (NEA)

You should write a paragraph or two on each of your choices, drawing on your knowledge of what Shaw gives the characters to say and do in the play. Try to say what has made each of them interesting, entertaining or believable to you. Finally make a judgement on whether the men are the more interesting characters or the women.

2. Trace the way Edgar's views and personality develop during the course of the play. (WJEC: **Strife**)

If you have made proper notes on each scene as you have gone along this is a fairly straightforward question. Use your knowledge of what Edgar says and does to describe how his personality changes. It is essential to do this and not just to say what happens.

3. In **Hobson's Choice** a business relationship gradually develops into a love relationship. Describe the steps by which this happens and show how love is connected with money in the play. (NI)

This question is asking you to relate character to ideas in the play. You are expected to look at the actions of Maggie and Will, their feelings and reactions towards each other throughout the play. Once again the work you have done making notes on each scene will be invaluable. As you describe their changing relationship you should note the way that money plays a part in it. For instance, the reason why Maggie picks Will in the first place, the difficulties and the way they make do at the beginning of their marriage, then the triumph at the end of the play. You will write a more successful answer if you include these ideas as you go along, rather than sticking in a paragraph about money at the end.

Other kinds of question that are asked about character include: what are their attitudes, what are their motives, whether you sympathize with them. You may be asked to put yourself in a character's shoes and write as though you were that character, as in the following question.

4. Look carefully at Mrs Birling's account of Eva Smith's behaviour at her committee. Put yourself in Eva's place. What do you think are her reasons for what she does and says, and what her feelings about it might be? You may write as Eva if you wish. (MEG: **An Inspector Calls**)

QUESTION, NOTES AND TUTOR'S ANSWER

1 ▷ QUESTION

The following question on *Macbeth* is answered below.

5. Read the following passage and answer the questions beneath it.

> LADY MACBETH: How now, my lord? Why do you keep alone,
> Of sorriest fancies your companions making,
> Using those thoughts which should indeed have died
> With them they think on? Things without all remedy
> Should be without regard: what's done is done.
> MACBETH: We have scotched the snake, not killed it:
> She'll close, and be herself, whilst our poor malice
> Remains in danger of her former tooth.
> But let the frame of things disjoint, both the worlds suffer,
> Ere we will eat our meal in fear, and sleep
> In the affliction of these terrible dreams
> That shake us nightly. Better be with the dead,
> Whom we to gain our peace, have sent to peace,
> Than on the torture of the mind to lie
> In restless ecstasy. Duncan is in his grave;
> After life's fitful fever he sleeps well;
> Treason has done his worst: nor steel, nor poison,
> Malice domestic, foreign levy, nothing,
> Can touch him further.
> LADY MACBETH: Come on;
> Gentle my lord, sleek oe'r your rugged looks;
> Be bright and jovial among your guests tonight.
> MACBETH: So shall I, love, and so, I pray, be you.
> Let your remembrance apply to Banquo;
> Present him eminence, both with eye and tongue:
> Unsafe the while, that we
> Must lave our honours in these flattering streams,
> And make our faces vizards to our hearts,
> Disguising what they are.
> LADY MACBETH: You must leave this
> MACBETH: O full of scorpions is my mind, dear wife,
> Thou know'st that Banquo, and his Fleance, lives.
> LADY MACBETH: But in them nature's copy's not eterne.
> MACBETH: There's comfort yet, they are assailable;
> Then be thou jocund. Ere the bat hath flown
> His cloistered flight, ere to black Hecate's summons
> The shard-borne beetle with his drowsy hums
> Hath rung night's warning peal, there shall be done
> A deed of dreadful note.
> LADY MACBETH: What's to be done.
> MACBETH: Be innocent of the knowledge, dearest chuck,
> Till thou applaud the deed.

(i) What do you learn of Macbeth from this passage? (6 marks)
(ii) What sort of relationship is shown between Macbeth and Lady Macbeth in this passage? (6 marks)
(iii) How has this relationship changed from earlier in the play? (8 marks)

2 ▷ NOTES

1. Read through the passage carefully.
2. Look at Macbeth's speeches and make notes on the thoughts and feelings he expresses. These notes only need to be a few words.
3. Make a second list noting Lady Macbeth's and Macbeth's reactions to each other.

4. Although these two questions carry an equal number of marks you will probably find more to say on the first.

5. Part (iii) refers to the rest of the play, so you must have read it all. It is not answered here.

3 SUGGESTED ANSWER

❝Many students lose marks by re-writing the passage in their own words. Have you really answered the question that was set?❞

(i) Macbeth is oppressed by a sense of danger; his mind is full of 'horrible imaginings'. He returns obsessively to thoughts of Duncan's death. Realizing how flimsy his hold on power is, he already feels that it is better to be with the dead, like Duncan, than to live under constant threat. He almost envies Duncan the peace of death for it seems infinitely preferable to the perpetual dread in which he lives. Neither by day nor by night can he rest easy: by day he fears the assassin even as he eats; by night he is plagued by 'terrible dreams'. Yet he will not surrender. He combats the fear with thoughts of more violence: Banquo and Fleance are particularly on his mind. He comforts himself with thoughts of their vulnerability. Night has become his element and he welcomes it with a grim satisfaction at the prospect of more dreadful deeds. These have become the dam that shores up his terrors.

(ii) There is still a clear bond of affection between Macbeth and his wife, but Lady Macbeth feels her husband slipping beyond her reach. She knows what afflicts his mind but seems powerless to draw him from the pit of his solitary brooding. Vainly she urges him to forget the past, but can only listen helplessly while Macbeth unburdens his guilt to her. She has no remedy for his state of mind and can only offer rather ineffectual comfort. Macbeth does respond to her appeal to keep up appearances among the guests, understanding the necessity for deceit even though he is disgusted with it. His fear of Banquo and Fleance strikes no chord with Lady Macbeth, consequently she no longer leads him. In the planning of this murder he is acting alone and without her knowledge. The force that she exerted over him has gone.

SUGGESTIONS FOR COURSEWORK

1. All the exam questions above are a suitable basis for a coursework unit.
2. Write a comparison of two characters in the same play or in two plays by the same dramatist or in plays by two different dramatists.
3. Make a study of a character as seen by two different dramatists, e.g. St. Joan in Bernard Shaw's play *St Joan*, *The Lark* by Jean Anouilh and in Shakespeare's *Henry VI*, where she is called La Pucelle.
4. You could write an imaginary encounter between two characters from different plays.

STUDENT'S ANSWER – EXAMINER'S COMMENT

Question

Examine to what extent the characters change and develop throughout Act 1 and then how far, and in what ways, they are developed throughout the play.

The opening of Act 1 of 'An Inspector Calls', reveals the scene of a wealthy family sitting around a table, modestly celebrating the engagement of their daughter. Although all the characters are present at the table, during this first act, one only obtains a firm impression of a few of them. As one progresses through the play, however, several of the characters change their attitude.

Mr. Birling's character is one which is established firmly in the reader's mind at the beginning of act one, and remains so throughout the play.

During this act, he immediately presents the impression of the dominating member of a wealthy family, as he endeavours to advise his son, and future son, as to how to get on, in the real world. He is dogmatic, and he puts on the impression he is very knowledgeable;

> 'And I say there isn't a chance of war'

and

> 'the Titanic...unsinkable, absolutely unsinkable.'

However, as it can be perceived from the ensuing play, and, in reality, the next thirty years, he was too sure of himself. Mr. Birling is also a 'hard-headed, practical man of business'; although perhaps too much so. His dedication to his arid conception of business causes him tobe narrow-minded, unable to meet the challenge, and needs of such people like Eva Smith, merely because it conflicts with his motto;

> 'For lower costs and higher prices.'

This shows he is certainly no humanitarian. He is smug; being contented with his social position and his family. However, as soon as the Inspector arrives, he feels threatened, and, in an attempt to win the Inspector's favour, he mentions his position and his connections;

> 'I was alderman for years – and Lord mayor two years ago.'

The inspector, however, begins to reveal his true character, in act one.

Mr. Birling is quite selfish and self-centred, which is revealed through his speech to Gerald and Eric;

> '...that a man has to mind his own business and look after himself and his own...'

However, further on in this act, it can be observed, he does not even care for 'his own', for he says to the Inspector, with relief:

> 'You didn't come here just to see me, then?'

He sticks by his selfish attitude, throughout the play; even after the Inspector left:

> 'There's every excuse for what both your mother and I did.'

This portrays also, his stubbornness.

Also, he cares only for the prospect of his knighthood, and nothing else:

> ' – and who here will suffer from that more than I will?'

His insensitivity is also portrayed towards the end of the play, when he says to Eric:

> 'You're the one I blame for this.'

Also, Eric, later on in the play says of him:

> 'Because you're not the kind of father a chap can go to when he's in trouble – that's why.'

This also shows something of Mr. Birling's character. Thus, Mr. Birling's main characteristics are established in act one, and are pursued throughout the rest of the play, remaining unchanged.

Good. Gives a clear impression of Mr. Birling through well chosen adjectives.

Good. Gives detailed evidence of the character of Mr. Birling through well selected quotations.

The writing now becomes rather disjointed, with short paragraphs and sentences simply stringing the quotations together. This fails to give a clear idea of the progression in the action of the play.

There could have been some illustration of Mr. Birling's unchanged attitude at the end of the play.

CHAPTER

THE
LANGUAGE
OF
DRAMA

VERSE AND PROSE
ATMOSPHERE
PAUSE
MOOD
TONE
FORMALITY
IRONY
COLLOQUIAL
   LANGUAGE
HUMOUR

GETTING STARTED

A number of exam questions may ask you to comment on the language of the play. Often this is in a short question based on an extract. We have already seen how the dialogue has a lot of information to convey about character, relationships and feelings. The dialogue can also create atmosphere, generate or intensify emotions and indicate tone. If you are studying a play in verse you should pay particular attention to the language. In any play, though, you should always think carefully about the kind of language used. Your knowledge of it will give depth to your comments on other aspects of the play.

ESSENTIAL PRINCIPLES

1 ▷ VERSE AND PROSE

Some plays, like Shakespeare's, are written in verse or, more usually, a mixture of verse and prose. *Verse* is generally reserved for the more serious and noble characters:

> THESEUS What say you Hermia? Be advised fair maid.
> To you your father should be as a God,

Prose is used for comic, unimportant or low characters:

> BOTTOM: First, Peter Quince, say what the play treats on; then read the names of the actors and so grow to a point.

By making these distinctions Shakespeare tells us important things about the nature of his characters.

In *A Midsummer Night's Dream* all the lovers, Duke Theseus and his bride, and the fairy king and queen, Oberon and Titania, are all given dialogue in verse. Bottom and his friends, the mechanicals, who provide the broad humour, speak in prose. When these comic characters present their play at court it has to be in verse. However it is not the serious blank verse of the higher characters but a jingling rhymed doggerel. Sometimes a character will have some dialogue in prose and some in verse to distinguish his moods and the seriousness of what he is saying. In *Henry IV Part 1* when Prince Hal is cavorting in the tavern with Falstaff he speaks in prose. When he shows his serious side, for instance with his father, the king, he speaks in verse. Falstaff, a comic character, speaks in prose whereas the king always uses verse. This technique of dividing dialogue between verse and prose is an easy way of distinguishing the status of the speaker or the importance and tone of the speech.

2 ▷ ATMOSPHERE

When a dramatist uses verse dialogue he can use all the qualities of poetry (see Ch.3). Atmosphere is easily created through verse. In *Julius Caesar* the atmosphere of the wild and dreadful night before Caesar's murder, when the skies seemed to drop fire on the earth and nature itself went mad, is vividly evoked. Throughout *Macbeth* the use of imagery connected with darkness and night helps to create the atmosphere of encompassing evil.

> *– Come seeling night,*
> *Scarf up the tender eye of pitiful day,*
> *And with thy bloody and invisible hand*
> *Cancel and tear to pieces that great bond*
> *Which keeps me pale. Light thickens, and the crow*
> *Makes wing to the rooky wood.*
> *Good things of day begin to droop and drowse,*
> *Whiles night's black agents to their preys do rouse.*

Lines such as these, as much as the appearance of the witches and the foul deeds committed, give the play its increasing sense of a world overwhelmed by dreadful wrong, a man lost in a miasma of evil doing. If you are studying *Macbeth* look through the play and notice how many of these references there are to blackness and night, and things associated with them. Make a note of them and memorize some of the lines.

In plays written in verse the language is vital in conveying mood, theme and action. You should look at some passages from the play (for instance Macbeth's soliloquies) in the same detail and in the same way as you would look at a poem.

Some prose dialogue also creates a very strong atmosphere. This can be so even when the language used is quite simple.

> PROCTOR: A fire, a fire is burning! I hear the boot of Lucifer, I see his filthy face! And it is my face, and yours, Danforth! For them that quail to bring men out of ignorance, as I have quailed, and as you quail now when you know in all your black hearts that this be fraud– god damns our kind especially, and we will burn, we will burn together.
> (*The Crucible*; Arthur Miller.)

The tension, guilt and hysteria of this language generates the atmosphere of a society that believes strongly in hell fire and damnation, for whom God and the Devil are real and present forces. This is created through the use of repeated phrases, through the images of Lucifer which Proctor conjures up and through the rhythm of the language.

3 ▷ PAUSE

The use of **pause** often creates a distinctive atmosphere. Harold Pinter frequently uses repetition, pause and silences in his dialogue. This brings a heavy feeling of tension and unease and makes his style very recognisable:

> ASTON: You make too much noise.
> DAVIES: But. . . but. . . look. . . . listen. . . listen here. . . I mean. . .
> [ASTON *turns back to the window*]
> What am I going to do?
> *Pause*
> What shall I do?
> *Pause*
> Where am I going to go?
> *Pause*
> If you want me to go . . . I'll go. You just say the word.
> *Pause* I'll tell you what though . . . them shoes. . . them shoes you give me. . .
> they're working out all right . . . they're all right. Maybe I could. . . get down.
> ASTON *remains still, his back to him, at the window.*
> Listen. . . if I. . . got down. . . if I was to . . . get my papers. . . would you. . .
> would you let. . . would you. . . if I got down . . . and got my. . .
> *Long silence.*

You have to hear this speech to appreciate the effect of all those hesitations. Read it aloud to yourself and notice the feeling of helplessness and threat. In any play, remember to look at the pauses. It is easy when you are reading to ignore them, but they are an important part of dramatic language because it is written to be spoken. Much can be conveyed in a pause or a silence. You will rarely come across pause used as much as in this example but it is only taking to great lengths an aspect of language that all dramatists use.

4 ▷ MOOD

Atmosphere affects all the characters onstage. Dialogue also has to express the passing **mood** of the characters. The atmosphere of **The Long and the Short and the Tall** by Willis Hall is tense and threatening, reflecting the harsh situation the soldiers find themselves in. The youngest, Whitaker, starts talking of his girl at home:

> WHITAKER: So we'd just walk along by the side of the river, like. Up as far as the bridge. Happen sit down and watch them playing bowls. Sit for ten minutes or so, get up and walk back. Just a steady stroll, you know. I never had much money – only my bus fare there and back sometimes – but it was . . . Oh boy! Oh you know – we had some smashing times together me and her.

The mood is soft and nostalgic. The images of the river, the men playing bowls, the familiar quiet sights of a peaceful England, contrast with the strangeness and the danger of the Malayan jungle that now surrounds them. Whitaker's boyish embarrassment about his feelings makes him speak haltingly and he is unable to express emotion except through exclamations such as 'Oh boy' and 'you know'. The tenderness of this passage makes his death all the more poignant.

We have already seen the power of verse to create an atmosphere of evil throughout **Macbeth**. The atmosphere of **Romeo and Juliet** is much more various. Here, for instance, is Juliet waiting for Romeo, after they have been married.

> **Come night, come Romeo; come thou day in night,**
> **For thou wilt lie upon the wings of night**
> **Whiter than new snow on a raven's back.**
> **Come gentle night, come loving, black-browed night,**
> **Give me my Romeo, and when he shall die**
> **Take him and cut him out in little stars,**

> *And he will make the face of heaven so fine*
> *That all the world will be in love with night*
> *And pay no worship to the garish sun.*

Juliet's mood is passionate, ecstatic. Shakespeare creates it through the many repetitions, so that her speech becomes almost a chant, an incantation. The usual associations of darkness are contradicted by the use of words like 'loving' and 'gentle', and by comparing Romeo to the day and to snow. Like those he is bright because, although he dare only come to Juliet's bedroom under cover of darkness, he brings joy. The final image of Romeo translated into a brightness which transforms the heavens is the most intense expression of Juliet's sense of her lover's beauty.

Moments before Romeo has killed Tybalt. Juliet knows nothing of this and her mood is in sharp contrast to what has gone before.

5 ▷ TONE

Closely allied to a character's mood is the **tone** of the dialogue. It is often quite difficult to decide on the tone of a speech. Try to imagine the words being spoken and then ask yourself what tone of voice the character is using. The tone shows the attitude of the character who is speaking. Tone can be serious, lighthearted, grave, teasing, formal, informal – there are many possibilities.

FORMALITY

One of the difficulties you may have arises from the way in which our way of speaking to others has changed. These changes in the **mode of address**, as it is called, affects tone.

In modern plays if we hear characters addressing each other as Mr. Brown and Miss Gardiner the formality of their tone indicates that they do not know each other well, or they are being very cold towards each other. Formality of address did not always indicate coldness or unfamiliarity. In **The Importance of Being Earnest** Jack and Gwendolen are calling each other Mr. Worthing and Miss Fairfax, even while Jack is proposing marriage. In the same situation in **She Stoops to Conquer**, written in the eighteenth century, Marlow and Kate call each other 'Sir' and 'Madam'. And in **The Way of the World**, written in the seventeenth century, the lovers, Mirabell and Millamant, never call each other by anything but their surnames. All these reflect the usual forms of address of the time.

In previous centuries it was common to call members of your family and intimate friends 'thee' and other people you were not familiar with 'you'. Shakespeare sometimes makes this distinction, but you have to be careful. He also uses 'thee' and 'you' quite indiscriminately. There is no rule – you have to listen to the tone and decide for yourself.

When thinking about tone it is important to take into account when the play was written and the social customs of the time.

IRONY

The most difficult tone to catch is the ironic one, because the character is saying one thing and meaning another. You are being asked to understand the meaning behind the words. We all use irony. For instance we say 'Oh! Great!', when it starts to rain just as we're setting out for a walk. In **The Taming of the Shrew** Petruchio calls Kate:

> *'pleasant, gamesome, passing courteous,*
> *But slow in speech, yet sweet as springtime flowers.*

Since she has just been shouting, screaming and fighting with him he cannot mean it. He is being ironic. There is another excellent example at the end of the passage from **Romeo and Juliet** used in the exam question at the end of this chapter.

Sometimes a character's words have a different meaning for the audience because the audience knows more about the situation than the character. This is **dramatic irony**. In **An Inspector Calls** Mrs. Birling speaks very forcefully against the young man who has got Daisy Renton pregnant. She says he must be made to face his responsibilities, whoever he is. She does not know that the young man in question is her son. But the audience has already guessed this, so they find her words ironic.

There can also be irony in the way events turn out. The witches predictions to Macbeth all prove true – but not in the way he expected. He believes he cannot be killed until 'Birnam wood be come to Dunsinane' but his enemies order their soldiers to camouflage themselves with leafy branches as they move on his castle and it appears as if the wood is moving. The prophecy, which he thought guaranteed his survival, has come true and he dies.

6 > COLLOQUIAL LANGUAGE

Most of us speak *colloquially*. It is the language we use when we are feeling easy, with friends, an off-duty language. Dramatists use it when they want to show a character as belonging to a certain class or part of the country, or to make the dialogue seem natural. Arnold Wesker's Ronnie does not speak in a cockney accent like his brother-in law, Dave. He is more educated and it shows in his speech. Even so he speaks colloquially:

DAVE: Jesus Christ it's heavy, its heavy. Drop it a minute

RONNIE: Lower it gently – mind the edges, it's a work of art.

DAVE: I'll work of art you. And turn that radio off – I can cope with Beethoven but not both of you.

RONNIE: What are you grumbling for? I've been shlapping things to and fro up till now, haven't I? (*I'm Talking About Jerusalem*)

Colloquial speech used to be used only for comedy. Nowadays so much of our speech is informal that modern plays conduct serious discussions in this kind of informal language.

7 > HUMOUR

We have already seen how *humour* can arise from situation, but much humour also arises out of the language used.

Some plays depend almost completely on the witty dialogue. For an example look back at the extract from *The Importance of Being Earnest* (see Ch.11). But humour in language does not have to depend on wit like Wilde's, or even jokes. In *Billy Liar* a lot of the humour is created by speech mannerisms, like Billy's father's who punctuates all his utterances with 'bloody':

GEOFFREY: More like one o' clock with your bloody half past eleven! Well you can bloody well start coming in of a night-time. I'm not having you gallivanting round at all hours, not at your bloody age.

Billy's girl-friend, Rita, uses 'rotten' in a similar manner:

RITA: Well, I'm going to see your rotten mother – I'll tell you that. My name's not 'Silly' you know. Either you get me that rotten ring back or I'm going to see your rotten mother.

Shakespeare was very fond of puns. A pun is a play on words that has two or more meanings. Here are two of the menservants at the beginning of *Romeo and Juliet:*

SAMSON: . . . I will show myself a tyrant. When I have fought with the men I will be civil with the maids – I will cut off their heads.

GREGORY: The heads of the maids?

SAMSON: The heads of the maids, or their maidenheads, take it in what sense thou wilt.

This is rather laboured patter, suitable for servants. It is a sixteenth century equivalent of the stand up comic and the straight man. The Elizabethans loved puns. They found them humorous and clever. Yet they could also be serious. Shakespeare would use puns in the most serious of situations. 'Ask for me tomorrow and you will find me a grave man', says Mercutio as he is dying.

If you are asked why you find a scene amusing, decide whether the comedy comes from the situation or the language or both. Look at the language for any exaggerated speech mannerisms, puns, or witty dialogue.

8 ⟩ SUMMARY

➤ Shakespeare, and other verse dramatists, use verse for serious characters and prose for low characters.

➤ Imagery creates atmosphere and mood. This applies particularly, but not solely, to verse plays.

➤ The use of pause and silence is important in dramatic language.

➤ Formality in language may be a question of period. This is important in deciding tone.

➤ Colloquial language may be used to make the play authentic or to show class or region.

➤ Humour is a product of language as much as situation.

ADDITIONAL EXAMPLES

Use these passages to test your understanding of what you have read in this chapter. Write down your own ideas before you read what I have written in the Key below.

1. What does the language of the following passage tell you about the characters? Look at the manner of the speech rather than the meaning.

> SIR TIMOTHY: But thank God, I'm not like thee, Nat Jeffcote. I sometimes think thou'st got a stone where thy heart should be by rights.
> JEFFCOTE: Happen I've got a pair of scales.
> SIR TIMOTHY: That's nowt to boast on. I'd as soon have the stone.
> MRS. JEFFCOTE: Beatice wants to speak to you, Alan.
> SIR TIMOTHY: Now my lass–
> BEATRICE: Father, I want to speak to Alan.
> SIR TIMOTHY: I'd like to have a word with thee first, Bee.
> BEATRICE: Afterwards, father.
> SIR TIMOTHY: Ay! But it'll be too late afterwards, happen.
> JEFFCOTE: Come, Tim, thou can't meddle with this job.
> SIR TIMOTHY: I call it a bit thick.
> BEATRICE: Please, father.
> MRS. JEFFCOTE: Come into the drawing-room, Sir Timothy. You can smoke there, you know.
> (**Hindle Wakes**, Stanley Houghton)

2. What is the mood created by this speech from the end of **The Glass Menagerie**? What features of the writing create that mood?

> TOM: Perhaps I am walking along the street at night, in some strange city, before I have found companions. I pass the lighted window of a shop where perfume is sold. The window is filled with pieces of coloured glass, tiny transparent bottles in delicate colours, like bits of a shattered rainbow. Then all at once my sister touches my shoulder. I turn around and look into her eyes. . . Oh, Laura, Laura, I tried to leave you behind me, but I am more faithful than I intended to be! I reach for a cigarette, I cross the street, I run into the movies or a bar, I buy a drink, I speak to the nearest stranger – anything that can blow your candles out! – for nowadays the world is lit by lightning! Blow out your candles, Laura – and so good-bye. .
> (Tennessee Williams)

1 ⟩ KEY TO THE EXAMPLES

1. **Hindle Wakes**. The first thing that the language tells you is that the play is set in the North of England, because of the use of words and phrases like 'nowt' and 'my lass' and the use of 'happen' for 'perhaps'. Secondly the way the characters 'thee' and 'thou' each other shows us that the time is probably the past, but not too distant past.

Sir Timothy and Jeffcote have the strongest dialect. Their down-to-earth speech contrasts with the women, especially Beatrice, who speaks very properly, even in this family situation. They appear to be self-made men who have risen from the working-class to positions of wealth and eminence. That Bee has had a very different childhood from her father's is shown in the way she talks.

These are things which the language tells you without considering the content of what is said.

Students often forget to consider imagery in prose.

2.   ***The Glass Menagerie***. The mood of this speech is one of sadness, of regret for the past, though not a wishing to return. It is a lonely, troubled speech, of a man who cannot escape the poignant memories of his sister.

The mood is created partly through imagery. There are the delicate images which remind Tom of Laura: the perfume and the glass, the rainbow – not a beautiful, coloured arch but one shattered. Laura herself appears to him almost as a wistful ghost or vision, without substance but always present. Tom's loneliness comes through his solitariness in a strange city at night. He always appears to be moving on, always in search of new companions. The urgency of that search, in a bar, or the movies, shows Tom's need to run away from the memories of his delicate and tender sister. He speaks of his reaction to his memories in a series of short phrases, 'I reach for a cigarette, I cross the street, I run into the movies'. This manner of speech recreates his mood of restlessness.

EXAM QUESTIONS

Many questions on language are small parts of questions.

1.   What are the differences in the way Mrs. Roberts and Enid talk to each other?(WJEC; on ***Strife***: Act II Sc. 1; 15% of marks)

2.   In this scene what are the differences between the way Lady Macbeth speaks and the way the other two speak which let you know that Lady Macbeth is mad? (NEA; on ***Macbeth***: Act V Sc. 1; 20% of marks)

3.   If you didn't know that Mitchem is senior to MacLeish, how could you guess it from the way each of them speaks? (WJEC on ***The Long and the Short and the Tall***, 10% of marks)

These questions ask you to look closely at a printed extract and notice something specifically in the language. Other questions will expect you to use your observations on language in talking about a character.

4.   Look carefully at what Helen says and how she says it in the speech which begins 'See yourself'. What does this speech tell you about Helen as a person? (WJEC; on ***A Taste of Honey***, 15% of marks.)

QUESTION, NOTES AND TUTOR'S ANSWER

1 QUESTION

Juliet is let down by all those closest to her. Look carefully at how each of them speaks to her here, and say what you think of each. How is your opinion influenced by their language as well as their attitude? Comment on the effect of all this on Juliet. (MEG)

CAPULET: Thursday is near; lay hand on heart, advise:
An you be mine, I'll give you to my friend;
An you be not, hang, beg, starve, die in the streets,
For, by my soul I'll ne'er acknowledge thee,
Nor what is mine shall never do thee good:
Trust to't, bethink you; I'll not be forsworn.
(*He storms out*)
JULIET: Is there no pity sitting in the clouds,
That sees into the bottom of my grief?

O, sweet my mother, cast me not away!
Delay this marriage for a month, a week;
Or, if you do not, make the bridal bed
In that dim monument where Tybalt lies.
LADY CAPULET: Talk not to me, for I'll not speak a word:
Do as thou wilt, for I have done with thee. (*She leaves*)
JULIET: O God – O nurse, how shall this be prevented?
My husband is on earth, my faith in heaven;
How shall that faith return again to earth,
Unless that husband send it me from heaven
By leaving earth? Comfort me, counsel me.
Alack, alack, that heaven should practice stratagems
Upon so soft a subject as myself!
What say'st thou? Hast thou not a word of joy?
Some comfort, nurse.
NURSE: Faith, here it is.
Romeo is banished; and all the world to nothing,
That he dares ne'er come back to challenge you;
Or if he do, it needs must be by stealth.
Then since the case so stands as now it doth,
I think it best you married with the County.
O, he's a lovely gentleman!
Romeo's a dishclout to him: an eagle, madam,
Hath not so green, so quick, so fair an eye
As Paris hath. Beshrew my very heart,
I think you are happy in this second match,
For it excels your first: or if it did not,
Your first is dead; or 'twere as good he were,
As living here and you no use of him.
JULIET: Speak'st thou from thy heart?
NURSE: And from my soul too:
Or else beshrew them both.
JULIET: Amen!
NURSE: What?
JULIET: Well, thou hast comforted me marvellous much.
Go in; and tell my lady I am gone,
Having displeas'd my father, to Laurence' cell,
To make confession and to be absolv'd.
NURSE: Marry, I will; and this is wisely done.
(***Romeo and Juliet,*** Shakespeare)

2 ⟩ NOTES

This is a complete question. It should take you about 40 minutes in the exam.
1. Read the passage carefully.
2. Look at Capulet's speech. Note down anything that strikes you about the form of the verse and the kind of language he uses. What is his tone? What impression do you get of him?
3. Do the same for Lady Capulet and the Nurse.
4. Note Juliet's reaction to each speaker.
5. Write four paragraphs – on Capulet, Lady Capulet, the Nurse and Juliet.

3 ⟩ SUGGESTED ANSWER

Capulet rages at Juliet. He is furious that she should not meekly accept the husband he has arranged for her. His daughter is his property to be given away to whomsoever he pleases. Although this seems an extraordinary attitude now it would be less so at the time when Shakespeare was writing. Even now brides are 'given away' in church by their fathers. Even when allowance is made for this historical difference, Shakespeare makes Capulet appear callous in the harsh way he speaks, never pausing for a moment to hear Juliet's fears or objections. He threatens and thunders, never seeking to persuade. His threats are real: Juliet knows he has the power to turn her friendless on to the streets if she does not obey him and marry Paris on Thursday. His temper is so great that he almost chokes on his words. The verse becomes very disjointed as a sign of his anger. Each line is broken up by pauses and the normal iambic rhythm disappears completely. In the line:

> ***An you be not, hang, beg, starve, die in the streets***

his voice seems to be rising in a crescendo of anger as he roars each awful word at his daughter. The manner of Capulet's speech, as much as what he is saying, robs him of all our understanding for his position: we feel only pity for Juliet suffering the onslaught of this tirade. He appears so unreasonable and tyrannical, a man so used to having his way that his temper immediately flares when he is crossed.

Lady Capulet can only follow her husband. The coldness of her manner is shown by her short, clipped phrases, which make her appear too fearful to contradict her husband. She cannot afford to have an independent opinion.

Left alone with Juliet, even the Nurse is cowed, though her natural talkativeness does not desert her completely. In her peasant's manner she can think of no other way than taking the easiest course in the present circumstances. Her tone is comforting, gentle and practical but she has no idea of Juliet's feelings. Since Romeo is miles away and can do her no harm, she thinks that Juliet had better make the best of a bad job. Morality does not enter her calculations. Clumsily she tries to manipulate Juliet's feelings, denigrating Romeo by calling him a 'dishclout' and praising Paris by comparing him to an eagle, just as earlier she had praised Romeo. For all her affectionate good intentions the Nurse appears despicable here, a base character, unable to rise to Juliet's needs.

Juliet's first reaction, if she cannot prevent or delay this marriage, is to see death as the only way out. Her passionate words are a counter-threat but once her mother leaves her she feels unable to cope with the situation she is entangled in. She is well aware that she is in danger of committing a mortal sin. In a wild despair she turns to the Nurse as her only comfort and as she listens to the Nurse's words she becomes quiet. By the time she answers her whole manner has changed, as if, in this short space, she has ceased to be a child and become independent. Her words:

> ***Well, thou has comforted me marvellous much***

are ironic. The Nurse has not comforted her at all. She hides her feelings and her intentions from the Nurse and determines to seek help from the only other person she can trust: Friar Laurence.

❝Note how the answer looks at the words as verse and at the way they sound when spoken. Have you done this?❞

SUGGESTIONS FOR COURSEWORK

1. All the questions above are suitable as a basis for a coursework unit.
2. Write a comparison of the kind of language used by two different characters in one play, or by two different dramatists. You would have to look closely at several passages.
3. Imitate the way a dramatist uses language. Write a dialogue or a speech for a character you have studied.
4. Make a study of humour in different plays, looking at language, situation and character.
5. Make a study of the way different dramatists use dialect.
6. Rewrite a piece of prose dialogue as verse.
7. Choose a passage of verse with a strong atmosphere and rewrite it as a prose description.

STUDENT'S ANSWER – EXAMINER'S COMMENT

Question

Choose two scenes from *Macbeth* that take place in darkness. What makes them effective? Look particularly at the language used.

Good. Points to Macbeth's fear as making the scenes effective.

Good. Explains the metaphor and chooses an appropriate quotation to the point.

Good. Identifies the language used to create atmosphere. Notices the personification.

This scene comes first in the play, so it should come first in the essay.

Good. Points out the imagery to do with night and tries to explain its effect.

The student's observation is good. However the discussion of language needs to be much more detailed and the imagery needs to be analysed more carefully.

The scene between Macbeth and Lady Macbeth before the banquet is one of the scenes that takes place at night and Macbeth refers to the night and darkness all through the scene. Lady Macbeth is trying to comfort him and turn his mind away from what they have done but Macbeth can only think about his terrible nightmares which come to him every night so that he can't get any sleep or rest from his guilty thoughts. One of the things that makes this scene effective is Macbeth's fear of night which brings the dreams that shake him. He uses the metaphor of being on a rack to describe his state.

'Them on the torture of the mind to lie
In restless ecstasy'

Later on he compares his thoughts to scorpions to show what mental agony he is in.

'O full of scorpions is my mind dear wife'

Although he is frightened of the night he wants it to come quickly so that Banquo can be killed. Shakespeare uses words like 'bat' and 'black Hecate' to create an evil atmosphere. Night is personified and Macbeth calls on it to come quickly. He speaks as though Night is going to do a murder.

'Come seeling Night
Scarf up the tender eye of pitiful day
And with thy bloody and invisible hand
Cancel and tear to pieces that great bond'

He describes the dark coming as 'light thickens' and as the good things of the day Fade and go to sleep the evil things of Night wake up to stalk their prey.

By mentioning these things Shakespeare builds a picture of evil which makes the scene very effective.

Another scene which takes place at night is the one where Macbeth is getting ready to murder Duncan. This scene begins peacefully with Banquo and Fleance going to bed and commenting on how dark the night is. When Macbeth appears they speak about the Weird Sisters, which together with the darkness gives a sinister feeling. When Banquo has gone Macbeth sees the vision of the dagger in the darkness. It seems he would not have seen it if it had been light because the night affects his imagination. In his speech Macbeth speaks of all the frightening things connected with night, like witchcraft, murder and death. Even before he has done the murder he is talking about bad dreams. He personifies wolf howling and then walking stealthily towards its prey like a ghost. Shakespeare uses these images to make the atmosphere effective.

READING
TO
UNDERSTAND:
NARRATIVE

**WHO IS TELLING THE
STORY?
TO WHOM IS THE
STORY TOLD?
HOW MANY STORIES
ARE THERE?**

G E T T I N G   S T A R T E D

We have all been familiar with reading stories from a young age. This probably makes the novel or short story section of the course the easiest to cope with. On the other hand, familiarity may also cause us to overlook obstacles. We have to remember that studying a novel or short story means looking at the question *how the story is told* as well as what it is about. This chapter will help you to ask how the story is told, and show you how to answer it.

ESSENTIAL PRINCIPLES

1 › WHO IS TELLING THE STORY?

A story can be told in the ***first person***. This is a grammatical term used to describe the use of 'I':

> *When I was nine years old I found myself completely alone in the world. The way that came about is very painful for me to recount.*

Alternatively it can be told in the third person. This term means referring to people as 'he' and 'she'.

> *Anne bent down and peered into the dark hole of the tunnel. She did not want to enter it. The enveloping blackness was the suffocation of her dream that could not be pushed away. She turned her head. It was day. She turned back and quickly went into the tunnel.*

A story written in the third person has a different effect from one written in the first person. If someone says something happened to them, personally, it may make the incident seem more real, and the listener may become more involved. Even so, more novels are written in the third person.

The word we use for story-telling is ***narration***. A story teller is a ***narrator***. Here are some questions to ask about narration:

(i) Is the story all told by one person?

(ii) Does the narrator have any part in the events of the story?

(iii) Is the narrator telling his or her own story?

(iv) How does the narrator know about the events?

(v) If the narrator is looking back on himself at a younger age, has his viewpoint changed?

All these things will alter the way in which the story comes across to the reader. The story of ***Wuthering Heights*** is told at first by Mr Lockwood, then it is taken up by his housekeeper Nellie Dean. One of the effects of having a second narrator take over from the first is to make the previous events seem distant. The events are moved back in time and yet another person is placed between the reader and the characters of the story. This allows the reader to accept the sometimes strange events and violent passions of the novel. Nellie Dean is a different kind of character from Mr Lockwood and so tells the story in a different way. Her viewpoint is that of a servant in the household of the major characters. It is because Nellie Dean plays a small part in the story she is telling that she knows what happened. Sometimes it seems that she should not be present at a private scene but we tend not to notice such intrusions when we are reading.

When the narrator is telling his own story, like Pip in ***Great Expectations*** or Scout in ***To Kill a Mocking Bird***, this difficulty does not arise. Both these narrators are looking back on their younger selves. This gives them the opportunity to comment on their own behaviour. In Pip's case he continually criticizes himself, regretting his earlier ingratitude to the good natured Joe.

One of the restrictions of a first-person narrative is that it can only be told from one person's point of view. Therefore, in most novels the story is told from the outside. The narration does not come through a person's voice at all. The author simply tells the story as though she knows everything that happened, even down to what all the characters are thinking. This method of story telling is most popular probably because the author then does not have to worry about how the narrator knows anything. Readers are accustomed to accepting a God-like knowledge in the author.

2 › TO WHOM IS THE STORY TOLD?

The story is, in the end, told to us, the readers. But some stories are told to a particular listener or a reader named or suggested by the narrator. Here are two examples of stories with special readers in mind:

(i) **A Diary**. Is this a private diary, supposedly written only for the person writing it? If so how does this affect the way it is written and our view of what we read?

(ii)   **Letters**. Stories written in the form of a correspondence between two people used to be popular. A letter assumes that one particular person is reading it and so is written to appeal to him or her.

In both these cases readers may feel in the privileged position of someone eavesdropping on intimacies.

When you are reading a novel it helps you to sort out who is telling the story and to whom if you ask the following questions:

➤ Is there a character in the book who is listening to the story? The character of the listener will affect the way the story is told.

➤ If there is no stated listener or reader what sort of person does the author *seem* to be addressing the book to?

If you can answer the question 'Who is the story told to?' as well as the question 'Who is telling it?' it may help you to understand the way in which it is written.

---

3 ▷ HOW MANY STORIES ARE THERE?

Just as many plays have subplots, novels often have several narrative lines. The separate strands of the story usually come together at some point. Often there is a linking idea or theme between the stories. For instance, in **Great Expectations** there are several strands which may appear at first to be unrelated: the stories of Pip, Miss Haversham, and Magwich. All these are connected, as we discover later on in the novel, by criminal activity. One of the ways of discovering the themes of a book is to look for links between the different threads of the story.

---

4 ▷ SUMMARY

➤ The type of narrator alters the way the story is told.

➤ First person narratives give an impression of intimacy to the reader, but they can only be told from one person's point of view.

➤ Third person narratives allow the author to know everything about all the characters. They can present several points of view.

➤ Where there is an imaginary person to whom the story is told this also affects the way it is told.

➤ Stories often have several strands linked by a common theme.

ADDITIONAL EXAMPLE

Use the following passage as an exercise to test your understanding of what you have read. Work out your own ideas before reading the Key below.

1.   What can you say about the narrator and narration of the following passage? (Look back at all the possible questions and decide which are appropriate to ask and answer here.)

When I came back from the East last autumn I felt that I wanted the world to be in uniform and at a moral attention forever; I wanted no more excursions with privileged glimpses into the human heart. Only Gatsby, the man who gives his name to this book, was exempt from my reaction – Gatsby, who represented everything for which I have an unaffected scorn. If personality is an unbroken series of successful gestures, then there was something gorgeous about him, some heightened sensitivity to the promises of life, as if he were related to one of those intricate machines that register earthquakes ten thousand miles away. This responsiveness had nothing to do with that flabby impressionability which is dignified under the name of the 'creative temperament'– it was an extraordinary gift for hope, a romantic readiness such as I have never found in any other person and which it is not likely that I shall ever find again. No – Gatsby turned out all right at the end; it is what preyed on Gatsby, what foul dust floated in the wake of his

> 66 **Don't confuse the 'I' of the story with the author.** 99

dreams that temporarily closed out my interest in the abortive sorrows and short-winded elations of men

(***The Great Gatsby***; F. Scott Fitzgerald)

1   **KEY TO THE EXAMPLE**

This is a narrative in the first person by someone who clearly has his own part in the story, but not the main part. He says the book is chiefly about Gatsby. The narrator's part seems to be mainly that of an observer who has watched some strongly emotional events for he speaks of 'abortive sorrows and short-winded elations'. Some of what he has witnessed has disgusted him and left him disillusioned with human nature: 'it is what preyed on Gatsby, what foul dust floated in the wake of his dreams'. These remarks, together with his earlier ones about wanting 'the world to be in uniform and at a moral attention' shows the narrator to be a principled person with scruples and concerned about decent behaviour. He also seems to have admired and appreciated Gatsby despite initially feeling scorn for him. This confession and the sense that he has principles makes us willing to accept the narrator's judgement. His authority for telling the story, the reason he knows what he does, is that he had 'privileged glimpses into the human heart', meaning that he was a confidante of Gatsby and possibly others too.

The narrator has no particular listener or reader in mind, but seems to assume that he is telling the story to someone fairly like himself: educated, decent and down to earth, with similar values to his own because he does not strive to justify what he says. He expects it to be accepted.

EXAM QUESTIONS

These questions show the kind of topics that you may be asked about. Read them carefully and work out how they could be applied to the novels you are studying.

The following question is on ***The Loneliness of the Long Distance Runner*** but it could be adapted to refer to any story told in the first person:

1. Alan Sillitoe lets Smith tell his own story. Do you think that this is a good or a bad idea? Use as evidence to support your opinion Smith's accounts of two or more of the following: his mates, the prison governor, the police, his family, Mr Raynor, the Match. (NEA)

Other questions may ask you about the character or point of view of the narrator, as in this question about Laurie Lee's ***Cider with Rosie***:

2. Throughout the novel the author describes himself as he once was. What view have you formed of his character? How far do you think the author wishes to praise himself or show up his faults? (N I)

Some questions may ask you to change the way the story is narrated and tell it from a particular character's point of view:

3. You have probably formed quite a strong opinion of Lacey in ***Samphire***, but he probably sees himself quite differently. Look at the story from his point of view and tell it his way.

QUESTION, NOTES AND TUTOR'S ANSWER

The following question shows you how to adapt Question 1 to a book you are studying. I have adapted it to ***To Kill a Mockingbird***.

1 ❯ QUESTION

In **To Kill a Mockingbird**, Harper Lee lets Scout tell her own story. Do you think this is a good idea? Use as evidence to support your opinion Scout's accounts of two or more of the following: her family, Boo Radley, Mrs Dubose, Calpurnia's church, the night outside the jail, the trial.

2 ❯ NOTES

1. List any general advantages and disadvantages you can think of to first person narrative.
2. Decide on the two or more events you wish to write about and jot down notes on Scout's part in each scene and any thoughts you have on the way it is told. Is it convincing? What difference does it make having it told by a child?
3. Use your general points for your opening paragraph.
4. Use the events of the book to bring out the points you have made in your opening paragraph.
5. The answer below is a long one. In the exam you will have 40 minutes to write your answer. You should try to write two or three pages.

3 ❯ SUGGESTED ANSWER

The advantage of allowing Scout to tell her own story is that it has the immediacy of any first-hand account. It is convincing because she herself has taken part in the events she is narrating. Readers feel involved because there is as little distance as possible between themselves and the narrator: they feel they know the person to whom all these things have happened. Scout is only a small child when the events of the story take place and this gives a second advantage. Because it is told through a child's eyes the story has the freshness of a child's point of view. However there is a disadvantage: Scout can only tell of things she has seen, or been told about, and this is occasionally awkward. She has to be present at events a child would not perhaps witness, or have conversations a child would not have.

We might feel that it is a disadvantage to have Scout as a narrator when Jem is ordered to read to Mrs Dubose as a punishment for destroying her camellias. It is not necessary for Scout to go with him. Atticus says, 'You don't have to go with Jem you know'. The author overcomes this by making Scout so devoted to Jem that it seems natural for her to accompany him, even though she finds it unpleasant.

Mrs Dubose is sick, old and a morphine addict. Jem is ordered to read **Ivanhoe** to her for two hours every afternoon for a month. Sitting beside Jem as he reads, Scout can obviously observe more than he. Without Scout's presence this part of the story would have to be told first by Jem to Scout. The detail and freshness of first-hand impressions would be lost. As Jem reads Mrs Dubose interrupts and corrects him but then Scout notices she has drifted off into a fit, which is horrible to watch. With a child's limited experience Scout is not aware of the cause; she simply recounts the events. Finally the alarm clock rings and they are sent away by Jessie the maid. Every day is the same. Eventually Scout realizes that the time before the fit starts and the alarm rings has gradually lengthened. Finally Mrs Dubose is conscious and cantankerous right up until they leave. The advantage of a child as narrator is that Mrs Dubose's behaviour is never questioned, a purpose beyond that of the whim of a nasty old woman is never sought. Her morphine addiction is only revealed to us when she dies a month later. Then we understand her behaviour and our sympathy with the character is the greater for being delayed: we always feel sorry when we say 'if only I'd known at the time'.

The author's purpose in including this episode is to contrast what is normally thought of as brave with the kind of courage Mrs Dubose showed in breaking her morphine addiction before she died. This is done through Atticus' admiration of her. He calls her a 'great lady'. He uses Mrs Dubose to teach Jem that courage is fighting even when you know from the start you're licked, which is exactly what he himself is doing in the case of Tom Robinson. By having a child as narrator the author is able to use the parent–child relationship to point a simple moral to the reader.

The difficulty of needing Scout to be present in situations where she might not be expected to be is cleverly overcome, indeed exploited, in the scene outside the jail the night before Tom Robinson's trial. Atticus knows there might be

Have you used the story to make points which answer the question? Many candidates lose marks because they just retell the story.

trouble. The previous night Scout and Jem overheard the Sheriff and other men predicting that some out-of-town folks might take the law into their own hands. Scout tells this part of the story as if she is somewhat baffled by the behaviour of Jem, who is four years her senior. When Atticus takes an extension cord and light bulb and goes out instead of going to bed Jem gets jumpy and prepares to follow him. Scout insists on going too, although she appears not to understand why. This lack of understanding means that the story can be told very simply. It also means that we, the readers, have to work out the significance of the events for ourselves, which helps to hold our interest and attention.

Jem, Scout and Dill find Atticus quietly reading outside the jail and are about to sneak quietly home when several car-loads of men arrive and confront him. In reply to their threats Scout hears Atticus say, 'Do you really think so', which she knows is his deadly question. This, Scout says, was too good to miss. She runs to Atticus. This action is the weakest point of the narrative. Even though Scout is presented as an impetuous, even wilful child, it does not seem a sufficiently strong reason for her to run out and risk punishment for not being at home in bed. On this occasion the author has not completely overcome the difficulty of getting the narrator on to the scene.

After that, however, the author uses Scout's age to enormous advantage. Firstly she defends Jem by kicking one of the men. It is only because she is a small girl that this does not spark off violence in retaliation. She has no idea of what is happening so she is not frightened. She launches into a conversation with Mr. Cunningham about his son and a law suit she has heard Atticus talking about. Finally her chatter defuses an ugly situation because it makes Cunningham and his gang look at Atticus as a person again and not an enemy or merely something in their way. The author uses the innocence of the child to comment on the morality and behaviour of the men.

Most of the time during this episode we feel we know more about the situation than Scout does. The author appears to describe the scene exactly as an eight year old would see it. We are left to draw the implications lost on a child. The language, though, is not that of a child, except when Scout speaks. We are told at the beginning that Scout is looking back on these incidents so the language used is that of an adult. Moreover Scout is presented to us as a bright little tom-boy, a precocious child who could read and write before she went to school. This allows the author to put her into situations and give her thoughts which might otherwise have been unconvincing.

SUGGESTIONS FOR COURSEWORK

1. Question 3 above might make a very good coursework unit, though any of them would be suitable.
2. Make a comparison of two different kinds of narrative.
3. Rewrite a third person narrative as a first person narrative, or the other way round.
4. Retell an episode in the form of letters.

STUDENT'S ANSWER – EXAMINER'S COMMENT

This is an early attempt to write about a novel.

Question

Write about Animal Farm. How does the author teach us about human society through the characters of the animals? (Write about at least 3 characters)

The story starts with a big meeting in the barn which is rather like a meeting in the House of Parliament. It first shows us how cruel and uncaring Jones seems to be. In the barn the animals start to complain about the humans and think of good ways to get rid of them. Major saying that there should be a rebellion against the humans and they should all be equal and run the farm themselves. This sounds like humans rebelling and trying to make things equal.

George Orwell the author teaches us about the human society in a totally different way to any other author by personifying the animals. In this way he shows us how humans think up what seem to be wonderful ideas and then because of greed they throw away all they have done. This is a very compact way of showing the human race as selfish, greedy and generally messing earth up by fighting and war.

Major is an old wise character who has spent much of his life in pigs sty. He provides the firm base on which the book is founded. He tells the animals that man is bad and he tells them that they should sing 'Beasts of England' as their national anthem. He portrays a wise human who has been around for a long time and knows that the world would be a better place if you make everyone equal which sounds very much like a communist idea.

Snowball came after Major as the second leader. He is a brave pig and he believes in what he does. He is not selfish and even thinks of a way to help the animals. He seems to show a good honest human that can get what he wants without having to use force.

Napolian is a rather nasty character. In the beginning, Major talks about how Jones has taken away the dogs puppies and the lambs and the calves. Everyone agrees that this is a dreadful thing to do. Then Napolian takes away the puppies which shows how selfish and what hypocrites people can be. He then uses power togain authority of the farm which is like many leaders in Europe and U.S.S.R. and all over the world have done. He overcomes Snowball by using his power but Snowball has no defences. He uses the puppies like secret police in Russia or Germany.

Boxer is portrayed as the good honest devoted worker. Without these people the world would fall to bits. Everyone relies on him to do all the work. He does all the work he is needed for and then he is sold for money. This shows the greed on the pigs behalf.

Mollie is a rather pretty mare who would rather be petted by humans than have to work. The pigs show how selfish people are in many ways. How they think that everything will work out and stay the same. They become lazier and even move into the farm house.

Good. Shows an understanding of the relationship between the events portrayed in the novel and society.

The second paragraph should be the introduction. It would be more effective if it mentioned that this is a 'fable' or an 'allegory'.

Good. Shows an understanding of the major characters of the novel.

Again, good linkage between events portrayed and society.

Here, and sometimes in other places, there is not enough detail of what each of the characters does. Specific events should be used as illustration.

PLOTS IN NOVELS

GETTING STARTED

When we read a novel or a short story it is frequently the desire to know what happens next that keeps us reading. Just like a dramatist, a novelist uses suspense, tension, conflict and surprise to keep us interested. If you have not yet read the chapter on plots in drama (Ch.10) you should do so to see how these elements work. In the exam you will be asked to recall what happened in the story and why it was important. But you should always try to do more than just tell the story. Telling the story will earn you some marks, but not very many. So from the beginning you must learn to ask what is significant about the events in the story you are reading. In other words you must ask not 'what' but 'how and why'. Make notes on each chapter as you read. Try to decide what has aroused or held your interest in each chapter. The sections that follow give you specific questions and ideas, first on the opening chapter and then on the rest of the novel.

AROUSING INTEREST
CHARACTER
SITUATION
SETTING OR ATMOSPHERE
COMEDY
DEVELOPMENT OF THE PLOT
THE ORDER OF THE STORY
ENDINGS

ESSENTIAL PRINCIPLES

<table>
<tr><td>

1 ▷ AROUSING INTEREST

</td><td>

Authors must arouse the interest of their readers and make them want to go on reading. How do they do it?

</td></tr>
</table>

CHARACTER

They can immediately introduce a character that we are fascinated by or sympathize with, like the Emperor Claudius in the first sentence of *I Claudius*:

> *I, TIBERIUS CLAUDIUS DRUSUS NERO GERMANICUS This-that-and-the-other (for I shall not trouble you yet with all my titles) who was once, and not so long ago either, known to my friends and relatives and associates as 'Claudius the Idiot' or 'That Claudius' or 'Claudius the Stammerer', or 'Clau-Clau-Claudius' or at best as 'Poor Uncle Claudius' am now about to write this strange history of my life;*

We do not have to like the character. Any strong reaction will do.

SITUATION

Another way is to plunge us into a situation that we then want to follow. This does not necessarily mean finding ourselves in the middle of a tense conflict on the first page. Consider the opening paragraphs of *To Kill a Mockingbird*:

> When he was nearly thirteen, my brother Jem got his arm badly broken at the elbow. When it healed, and Jem's fears of never being able to play football again were assuaged, he was seldom self-conscious about his injury. His left arm was somewhat shorter than his right; when he stood or walked, the back of his hand was at right-angles to his body, his thumb parallel to his thigh. He couldn't have cared less, so long as he could pass and punt.
>
> When enough years had gone by to enable us to look back on them, we sometimes discussed the events leading to his accident. I maintain that the Ewells started it all, but Jem, who was four years my senior, said it started long before that. He said it began the summer Dill came to us, when Dill first gave us the idea of making Boo Radley come out.

Already we are asking ourselves questions. Why was Jem's arm broken so badly? Who were the Ewells and what had they done to start it? Who was the peculiarly named person, Boo Radley, and what did he or she have to come out from? Because we are curious to know the answer to all these questions we go on reading.

SETTING OR ATMOSPHERE

A third way is to create a strong atmosphere or sense of place. This does not have to be an exotic place. Thomas Hardy begins *The Return of the Native* with a chapter describing a stretch of moorland in Dorset. It is not particularly beautiful. Nothing happens, no characters appear, but by the end of the chapter we are so immersed in the scene that it seems charged with significance. Dickens opens *Bleak House* with a similarly significant description. The first paragraph concentrates on mud, the second on fog:

> Fog everywhere. Fog up the river, where it flows among green aits and meadows; fog down the river where it rolls defiled among the tiers of shipping, and the waterside pollutions of a great (and dirty) city. Fog on the Essex marshes, fog in the Kentish heights. Fog creeping into the cabooses of the collier-brigs; fog lying out on the yards, and hovering off the rigging of the great ships; fog drooping on the gunwales of barges and small boats. Fog in the eyes and throats of ancient Greenwich pensioners, wheezing by the firesides of their wards; fog in the stem and bowl of the afternoon pipe of the wrathful skipper, down in his close cabin; fog cruelly pinching the toes and fingers of his shivering little 'prentice boy on deck.

And so it goes on. Dickens seems to draw us into the novel by creating the most unpleasant conditions that he can devise. He arouses our interest through distaste and imagined discomfort as much as through sympathy for the poor wretches who have to endure such weather. We also begin to suspect that this description has to do with more than simply weather. We read on to find out its significance.

COMEDY

Yet another way to keep the readers is to make them laugh, or at least smile:
I suppose that the high water mark of my youth in Columbus, Ohio, was the night the bed fell on my father.

That is the promising opening sentence of James Thurber's **My Life and Hard Times**. Promising because it suggests irreverent descriptions of hilarious situations. We read on.

How does the novelist arouse interest in the opening chapter of the novels you are studying?

2	DEVELOPMENT OF THE PLOT

Having aroused our interest the author must then keep it. The characters or the situation must develop just as in drama (again see Ch.10). One of our most basic interests is in other people, so the portrayal and development of characters is one of the novelist's strongest weapons. Another is the unfolding of a situation in a way that we recognize as a representation of life. Some of the ways that novelists have of keeping our interest are as follows:

(i) The development of *relationships* between characters. All novels involving courtship and 'romance' do this but there are many other kinds of developing relationships. For example there are family relationships and social relationships. Many novels include all these types. Think about whether – and how – relationships change from chapter to chapter in the novels you are reading.

(ii) The solving of a *problem* or a mystery. The detective novel is a popular form which uses this method. Other novels may incorporate less obvious mysteries as one part of the plot. For instance, who is Pip's benefactor in **Great Expectations**?

(iii) The development and resolution of a *conflict* between characters or groups. This may range from war between countries, through gang war, down to rivalry between individuals. The conflict does not have to be physical. The popularity of fights and trial scenes in literature (and on television) shows how potent the idea of conflict is.

(iv) The *overcoming of some difficulty* or disaster, as in many adventure novels.

(v) A *search* or discovery. Whether it is a search for lost empires, the discovery of penicillin or some kind of more personal inner quest.

These are just some suggestions. Most novels include many of these features at different points of the story. **Pride and Prejudice** includes a number of unfolding relationships, conflict, though never violent, between various characters, self-discovery by both Elizabeth and Darcy, and the overcoming of numerous difficulties on the way to fortunate marriage by Jane and Elizabeth.

How does the novelist maintain interest in the novels you are reading?

3	THE ORDER OF THE STORY

Remember that stories are constructed. An author decides not just what shall be told but the order of telling it. In life we learn things about people and events in a great jumble. We know that the lady next door is a nurse and we see her going to work regularly at the hospital. This gives us a particular view of her. Then suddenly we find out that she used to be a trapeze artiste in a circus and our view of her changes with a jolt. Just the same happens in novels; the author quite deliberately gives us information in a certain order. Our view of the characters may unfold smoothly, or we may be brought up short by an unexpected revelation, just as the novelist pleases. Ask yourself these questions.

(i) Is the story presented chronologically? That is, in the order in which the events happen?

(ii) If the story does not begin at the beginning, where does it begin? Why has the author chosen to begin at that point?

(iii) Does the plot move us back in time to some earlier point in the story? If so, how often and for what reasons?

(iv) Are we ever taken into the future and if so how is it done?

(v) Are we ever told things twice?

(vi) Are there any gaps or jumps in the story?

4   ENDINGS

The end of a story should show events brought to a conclusion which we feel is right and in keeping with what has gone before. Even when the end is a sad one we should feel that such an ending is justified. A sense of rightness has a lot to do with the themes and ideas of the book being worked out satisfactorily. Chapter 17 deals with this.

5   SUMMARY

➤ The first task of the novelist is to arouse our interest. This may be done through character, situation, setting or atmosphere and sometimes humour.

➤ The development of the plot maintains that interest through portraying characters and their relationships.

➤ Conflict, problems which have to be solved, struggle and discovery all help to maintain interest.

➤ The order in which the story is told is important for creating suspense, showing different points of view and developing our views about characters and events.

ADDITIONAL EXAMPLES

Use these examples as exercises to test your understanding of this chapter. Write down your own ideas before looking at the Key. The first two passages are openings, of a novel and a short story. Try to say what in them arouses our interest. What does the novelist do in the third passage to maintain interest?

1. Mr Tench went out to look for his ether cylinder, into the blazing Mexican sun and the bleaching dust. A few vultures looked down from the roof with shabby indifference: he wasn't carrion yet. A faint feeling of rebellion stirred in Mr Tench's heart, and he wrenched up a piece of the road with splintering fingernails and tossed it feebly towards them. One rose and flapped across the town: over the tiny plaza, over the bust of an ex-president, ex-general, ex-human being, over the two stalls which sold mineral water, towards the river and the sea. It wouldn't find anything there. The sharks looked after the carrion on that side. Mr. Tench went on across the plaza.

    (***The Power and the Glory***, Graham Greene.)

2. There was a man who loved islands. He was born on one but it didn't suit him, as there were too many other people on it, besides himself. He wanted an island all of his own: not necessarily to be alone on it, but to make it a world of his own.

    (***The Man Who Loved Islands***, D. H. Lawrence.)

3   .'Hymn number one-seven-five, "New every morning is the love". ' The navy blue covers of the hymn books, inconspicuous against the dark shades of the boys' clothing, bloomed white across the hall as they were opened and the pages flicked through. The scuff and tick of the turning pages was slowly drowned under a rising chorus of coughing and hawking; until Mr Gryce,

furious behind the lectern, scooped up his stick and began to smack it vertically down the face.

'STOP THAT INFERNAL COUGHING.'

The sight and swishsmack of the stick stopped the throat noises and the boys and the teachers, posted at regular intervals at the ends of the rows; all looked up to the platform. Gryce was straining over the top of the lectern like a bulldog up on its hind legs.

'It's every morning alike! As soon as the hymn is announced you're off revving up! Hm-hmm! Hm-hmm! It's more like a race track in here than an assembly hall! – hall – ringing across the hall, striking the windows and lingering there like the vibrations of a tuning fork.

No-one muffed. Not a foot scraped. Not a page stirred. The teachers looked seriously into the ranks of the boys. The boys stood looking up at Gryce, each one convinced that Gryce was looking at him.

The silence thickened. The boys began to swallow their adam's apples, their eyes skittering about in still heads. The teachers began to glance at each other and glance sideways up at the platform.

Then a boy coughed.

'Who did that?'

Everybody looking round.

'I said WHO DID THAT?'

The teachers moved in closer, alert like a riot squad.

'Mr. Crossley! Somewhere near you! Didn't you see the boy?'

Crossley flushed, and rushed amongst them, thrusting them aside in panic.

'There Crossley! That's where it came from! Around there!' Crossley grabbed a boy by the arm and began to drag him into the open.

'It wasn't me, Sir!'

'Of course it was you. '

'It wasn't, Sir, honest!'

'Don't argue lad, I saw you. ' Gryce thrust his jaw over the front of the lectern, the air whistling down his nostrils.

'MACDOWALL! I might have known it! Get to my room, lad!'

(***Kestrel for a Knave***; Barry Hines.)

---

1 ▶ **KEY TO THE EXAMPLES**

1. This is an interesting opening because it immediately provokes us to ask questions about the character and the situation he is in. Why is he looking for an ether cylinder? Why does he feel rebellious? A strong, exotic atmosphere is established by the blazing Mexican sun, vultures on the roof, the sharks. Mr Tench does not seem to fit in here but his gesture of rebellion is an ineffectual one: the piece of tarmac he feebly throws displaces only one of the vultures. Why isn't he able to do something positive? The vultures and the sharks, with their associations of death produce a tension and a strong sense of foreboding. The only other sign of humanity is an ex-human being.

2. The question raised here is will the man get what he wants: an island all of his own? It seems to be the opening of a search or a struggle to achieve that ambition.

3. The interest in this passage depends on the portrayal of Mr Gryce, the headmaster, his relationships with the other staff and the boys, and the tension produced by his anger. The beginning is also quite grimly comic with the description of the boys' chorus of throat noises which sound like racing cars. By comparing Mr. Gryce to a 'bulldog up on its hind legs' and by showing him smacking his stick down on the lectern while roaring furiously at the assembled school, Barry Hines creates a figure which is both funny and frightening. He conveys to us the trepidation of the boys as they stand silently, hardly daring to breathe. Even the teachers are affected by the tension. Mr Crossley appears almost as much in awe as the boys and panics when action is demanded of him. Then the blow falls on MacDowall. The tension is broken when he is carted off to await punishment.

    Notice how many of the sentences are very short. This is one of the ways tension is created. Another is by putting some of Gryce's words in capital

> ❝Did you note the character of Mr. Gryce, relationships and comedy? These are points that will gain marks.❞

letters to suggest his roaring. This device also adds humour. The fact that MacDowall is shown as being picked from the crowd indiscriminately – and probably unjustly – because Mr Crossley cannot confess that he does not know who did it, adds to our interest. It raises questions about the fairness of the behaviour of Gryce and Crossley. We sympathize with MacDowall. Perhaps we even sympathize with Mr Crossley. When we read the book these questions of fairness recur.

EXAM QUESTIONS

These are the kinds of questions you may be asked about plot:

1. Write about a book or books you have read in which conflict occurs between people or between the individual and authority. Show how the conflict develops. (LEAG)
2. Write about one book where natural or man-made disaster, e.g. fire, flood, storm or war, plays an important part in the story, explaining the part it plays. (LEAG)

LEAG, who set these two questions, ask very general questions that can be applied to a number of books. Other boards ask specific questions on set texts.

3. Trace how the rivalry between Jack and Ralph develops in ***Lord of the Flies***. (Part-question; WJEC)
4. By careful reference to any other one story from ***Modern Short Stories***, show the part played by violence.

Notice how all these questions widen the discussion of plot to include that of character or theme.

QUESTION, NOTES AND TUTOR'S ANSWER

Here is a question about ***Great Expectations*** but which can be applied to any novel.

1 ▷ QUESTION The openings of books, if successful, tell the reader what to expect. Quickly refresh your memory of Chapter 1 and then explore its power to draw you into the book. (MEG)

2 ▷ NOTES

1. This question is set for an open book exam so your first task is to look at the chapter to remind yourself of the work you have done on it.

    NOTE: The question says 'refresh your memory' and that is all you will have time for. Do not expect to be able to go into the exam room and write on a question like this without having prepared yourself.

2. Note that the question asks you to relate the chapter to the rest of the book. You should not, therefore, write just about the opening chapter.

3. Jot down notes on the general areas you want to cover before beginning to write. (Look back at the section on arousing interest) Use the following headings, expanding each one with detailed points and supporting evidence from the text:

    Character and situation of Pip;

    Character and significance of convict;

    Atmosphere of marshes;

Tension of situation;

Later significance of this meeting.

4.   Write your answer before reading the one below.

3 ⟩ SUGGESTED ANSWER

The opening chapter of ***Great Expectations*** introduces us to Pip, the central character and narrator of the story, and to the convict who so influences the course of his life. This meeting leads to Pip's 'great expectations' and many changes in his life.

The opening paragraphs arouse our interest in Pip by showing him to have survived while his mother and father and five of his brothers have died. As he is an orphan we feel sympathy for him. Almost immediately he is plunged into a terrifying situation which grips our attention.

The man who confronts him is a fearsome sight: wet, dirty with mud, shivering with cold and with a great iron on his leg. He strikes terror into Pip's heart not only by his appearance but also by turning him upside down and balancing him dangerously on the top of a high tombstone while he threatens him. All this, and the strangeness of the man, his looks and behaviour, further excites our interest and raises questions that we expect the novelist to answer. Why is he lurking in the churchyard? What has he done? Will he escape? His physical condition – filthy, cold, hungry and hunted – also elicits our sympathy, but his treatment of Pip, his dire threats of having Pip's heart and liver torn out and roasted whole, sets up an unequal conflict in which we hope Pip will not be harmed.

The place in which Dickens chooses to set the scene gives it a strong and eerily melancholy atmosphere. It is a raw afternoon on the 'dark, flat wilderness' of the marshes. The wind rushes in from the sea and the only living creatures to be seen are the scattered cattle. Pip is alone among the gravestones when suddenly the figure arises from among them. The convict's first words voice the threat to cut Pip's throat. It is a memorably dramatic scene. When Pip runs home across the marshes the lone figure outlined against the darkening sky is limping towards the gibbet – a further suggestion of crime and suffering, to be developed later in the novel. Everything in this scene is calculated to increase the atmosphere of grim mystery.

At the end of the chapter we are left wondering whether Pip will keep his meeting secret and if he will manage to return with the file and the food the convict has demanded. Our curiosity about the fate of both Pip and the convict has been awakened. We expect the meeting to have an uncommon effect on Pip's life, although we have to wait a long time before we see what it is.

The presence of a convict in the first chapter alerts us to one of the themes in the novel. A good deal of the book is concerned with crime and criminals and many of the characters are affected as well as Pip. Miss Havisham's plight is the result of a criminal deception; the same man affects Estella, the convict's child; Pip's sister, Mrs Joe Gargery, is maimed by Orlick, who also attacks Pip and represents unredeemable criminal brutishness; we see the effect of work among the criminal classes on Jagger and on Wemmick who has to become a different person to do his work; we are taken into the prison at Newgate.

A second theme is developed through the relationship of Pip and the convict. Pip's kindness as a child is rewarded with his 'great expectations', but these, perversely, lead him to behave badly, squander his money and neglect the good and faithful Joe. When Magwich re-enters the story Pip cannot, for shame, be unkind to the man who has done and promised so much. Pip loses the money which was intended to buy him the status of 'gentleman'. Nevertheless he learns how to be the true gentleman that Magwich wanted him to be.

66 Have you answered the question fully? You will lose marks if you do not refer to the rest of the book, as the question asked. 99

SUGGESTIONS FOR COURSEWORK

1. All the questions above are suitable as a basis for a coursework unit.
2. To satisfy the requirement of evidence of wider reading you could write a comparison of two opening, or closing, chapters.
3. Write a comparison of a chronological novel and one which uses 'flashback' to show how the use of the two techniques alters the way we read and learn about the action and the characters.
4. Write an alternative opening to a novel.
5. Rewrite an episode from a novel or short story as a play or a ballad.
6. Write a review of a novel you have read.
7. Rewrite a scene from a play as a passage from a novel, using one of the charac-

STUDENT'S ANSWER – EXAMINER'S COMMENT

Question
What is the role of the conch in *Lord of the Flies*?

> **Good. Correctly states the central importance of the conch.**

> **'At the beginning' is used twice. The first paragraph should make a general statement, leaving illustration or quotation to later paragraphs.**

> **Good specific detail from the story, linking the conch with an idea.**

> **Good. Identifies how attitudes towards the conch change as the story progresses.**

At the beginning of the book the conch is found by Ralph. It stays with Ralph and symbolizes his power and authority. As people begin to listen less to Ralph and more to fact they seem to disregard the conch.

> 'But there was a stillness about ralph as he sat that marked him out: there was his size, and attractive appearance; and most obscurely, yet most powerfully, there was the conch.'

At the beginning of the book the conch was used as a call for all the boys to come to the beach in order to discuss their position. It represented a meeting of civilised school boys waiting to organise things, vote on matters etc. All things that happen in the ordinary civilised world. Thus the conch gets associated with civilisation.

> 'This toy of voting was almost as pleasing as the conch.'

Here, William Golding is linking the conch with voting, one of the most civilised things that happens in the world. It's fair, democratic and far from barbaric.

Whenever anyone holds the conch they have power over everyone else. They have the right to express their wishes and rules are put forward. Thus through the conch rules are put forward and they make grand plans. Rules run parallel with civilisation. You need both and so the conch becomes the symbol of both.

As the story goes on the boys begin to forget the real world and they turn to hunting. Their grand plans dissolve and they begin to forget the rules. The conch begins to lose its power. First they tell Piggy to 'shut up' when he has the conch and the Jack starts to speak and call out when he hasn't got the conch.

> **There is not enough plot detail of how the conch came to represent order and civilisation. This continues throughout; few points are backed up by enough reference to events.**

'Jack! Jack! You haven't got the conch! Let him speak.'
Once the conch is disregarded so are the rules and
civilisation loses its foothold over the boys.
　　　'The Rules!' shouted Ralph, 'you're breaking the rules.'
From then on things go from bad to worse. The rules slip and
the conch loses it's meaning when Ralph and Jack split up
Jack says:
　　　'You haven't got it with you. You left it behind. See,
　　　clever? And the conch doesn't count at this end of the
　　　island.'
In the book the colour of the conch fades to white like the
fading of civilisation. In the end the conch is pure white.
Ralph begins to lose faith in the conch. Only Piggy clings to
the conch. He is the only one who is unaffected by barbarism
and so he is linked with the conch. They both stand for the
civilisation that was.
In the end the conch is shattered into a thousand pieces and
Piggy dies with it. Roger the hunter shattered both.

CHARACTERS

IN

NOVELS

GETTING STARTED

Just as with drama, a great many of the questions on novels are about character. Much of what was said in Chapter 11 about characters in plays also applies to novels. If you have not already done so you should study that chapter. The difference with the novel is that character is in the hands of the author and reader alone. The novelist has complete control over everything the character does, says, thinks, and all the external circumstances of the character's life. The reader's contribution is understanding and interpreting the text.

This chapter helps you to understand how novelists create characters. As you read, make notes about each important character under headings like those in the section below. If you do this for every chapter you will have a record of the characters' development and changing feelings throughout the novel.

APPEARANCE
  SHOWING PERSONALITY
  CONTRAST
  DRESS
SPEECH AND ACTIONS
SURROUNDINGS
THOUGHTS
INTRODUCING A
  CHARACTER
DEVELOPMENT
CHARACTER TYPES
NAMES
RELATIONSHIPS
AUTHOR'S ATTITUDE

ESSENTIAL PRINCIPLES

Some novelists give us detailed descriptions of the **appearance** of their characters, or at least of the main ones. Appearance is not character; but it is an indication, in some novels a strong indication, of character.

SHOWING PERSONALITY

Physical appearance can be used directly to show **personality**:

> Such a voice could only come from a broad chest, and the broad chest belonged to a large-boned muscular man nearly six feet high, with a back so flat and a head so well poised that when he drew himself up to take a more distant survey of his work, he had the air of a soldier standing at his ease. The sleeve rolled up above the elbow showed an arm that was likely to win the prize for feats of strength; yet the long supple hand, with its broad finger-tips looked ready for works of skill.

This is George Eliot's description of her hero at the opening of **Adam Bede** and she goes on to compare Adam with his brother Seth in a way that makes it clear that Adam's physical strength also denotes moral strength. His upright stance indicates a spiritual uprightness. The face and the eyes are frequently used to indicate personality: here George Eliot has used the whole body.

CONTRAST

Occasionally there is a **contrast** between the appearance and personality of a character:

> Mr Denny addressed them directly, and entreated permission to introduce his friend, Mr Wickham, who had returned with him the day before from town, and he was happy to say he had accepted a commission in their corps. This was exactly as it should be; for the young man wanted only regimentals to make him completely charming. His appearance was greatly in his favour; he had all the best part of beauty, a fine countenance, a good figure, and very pleasing address. The introduction was followed up on his side by a happy readiness of conversation. . .

This is our first introduction to Mr Wickham in **Pride and Prejudice** and if we are attracted by his appearance it is not surprising. One of the meanings of 'prejudice' is 'to form a judgement too hastily'. Jane Austen deliberately blinds us to Wickham's real character. It is part of her purpose to prejudice us in his favour so that we understand how her heroine is prejudiced. Later we, like her, discover that he is not what he appears to be and that is part of the meaning of the novel.

DRESS

The way characters **dress** may also be used to suggest character. At the beginning of **Tess of the d'Urbervilles** Tess is dressed in white as befits her innocent maidenhood. 'She was so modest, so expressive, she had looked so soft in her thin white gown', thinks the man who will become her husband. In **Oliver Twist** Dickens dresses the Artful Dodger in the clothes of a man. They are too big for him: he has to roll up the sleeves of his jacket. He is only a boy but his situation forces him to be 'street-wise' and act like a man. His clothes show how he has had to become prematurely adult. George Eliot contrasts the plain sensible dress of Dinah Morris with Hetty Sorrel's rose-coloured ribbons, which show her frivolousness (**Adam Bede**). Likewise in **Jane Eyre** Charlotte Bronte contrasts Jane's plain dark dress with Blanche's fashionable silks.

Think carefully and decide what the description of the characters' appearance is telling you about them.

2 ▷ SPEECH AND ACTIONS

Everything that was said about the speech and actions of characters in Chapter 11 also applies here. The novelist, however, depends only upon the reader's imagination, not on the actor's interpretation of the characters' words. A novelist can tell us that a character has a soft and gentle voice, or a firm, decisive walk. These details of the way in which characters **speak** and **act** add to the picture of them along with what they do and say.

You should note your reactions as you read and ask yourself what it is in the author's words that creates your reaction. You can see from the following extract from **Lord of the Flies** how much can be conveyed in a very short space:

Piggy took off his shoes and socks, ranged them carefully on the ledge, and tested the water with one toe.

"It's hot!"

"What did you expect?"

"I didn't expect nothing. My auntie -"

"Sucks to your auntie!" Ralph did a surface dive and swam under water with his eyes open; the sandy edge of the pool loomed up like a hillside. He turned over, holding his nose, and a golden light danced and shattered just over his face. Piggy was looking determined and began to take off his shorts. Presently he was palely and fatly naked. He tip-toed down the sandy side of the pool, and sat there up to his neck in water smiling proudly at Ralph.

"Aren't you going to swim?" Piggy shook his head. "I can't swim. I wasn't allowed. My asthma –" "Sucks to your ass-mar!"

The novelist, William Golding, has made all Piggy's actions careful, cautious and deliberate. Notice the way he arranges his shoes and socks. He enters the water somewhat nervously. He cannot swim. Taking off his shorts takes some determination. Entering the water makes him feel proud. His auntie obviously put a firm brake on all such activities and as a result he is physically timid. Notice too how his appearance – pale and fat – adds to this impression. Ralph, on the other hand, is presented as very competent in the water. He dives in, swims underwater with his eyes open and knows he must hold his nose when he turns over. His manner of speech is decisive, if boyish: 'Sucks to your auntie'. Twice he interrupts Piggy. Ralph's speech is also more educated than Piggy's: he speaks in complete, grammatical sentences, while Piggy's contains errors, such as the double negative in 'I didn't expect nothing' and the incomplete sentence 'I wasn't allowed'.

Even from these few sentences we have a clear initial impression of the character of the two boys from their speech and actions.

Take a short passage near the beginning of a novel, or where a new character is introduced, and look at it in detail. What you observe will probably be confirmed in later passages.

3 ▷ SURROUND-INGS

Many of our impressions of characters may be created by the **surroundings** in which the novelist places them. Our view of someone who is always seen in dark, dirty or unpleasant places, or always in the company of unpleasant people, like Fagin in **Oliver Twist**, is going to be affected by the nature of those surroundings. Adam Bede and Dinah Morris are always seen in clean and orderly surroundings so we associate them with those qualities. Remember, though, that a character's reactions to his or her surroundings is also important. Dickens refuses to let Oliver be contaminated by Fagin's world and so eventually he escapes. Nancy, although retaining some sense of what is good and right, is shown as having been immersed in that world for so long that she cannot accept the offer of escape when it comes.

These ideas are explored further in Chapter 16 on setting.

4 ▷ THOUGHTS

Novelists have the great advantage of being able to get inside a character's mind and describe their **thoughts** and feelings:

Poor Fanny! She sang little, and looked beautiful through that inappropriate hymn. . . . Brilliant she looked, and brilliant she felt, for she was hot and angrily miserable and inflamed with a sort of fatal despair. Because there was about him a physical attraction that she really hated, but which she could not escape from.

He was the first man who had ever kissed her. And his kisses, even while she re-belled from them, had lived in her blood and sent roots down into her soul. After all this time she had come back to them. And her soul groaned, for she felt dragged down, dragged down to earth, as a bird which some dog has got down in the dust.

(***Fanny and Annie***; D. H. Lawrence)

Notice how Lawrence moves from describing things that can be observed from the outside, 'looked beautiful', through things that can be guessed from her appearance, 'she was hot and angrily miserable', to things which only Fanny herself can know – 'And his kisses even while she rebelled from them had lived in her blood and sent roots down into her soul. . . . And her soul groaned for she felt dragged down. . . .'.

Sometimes writers clearly signal that they are moving inside a character's head by writing 'she thought' or 'he felt'. More often, like Lawrence, they gradually move from describing appearance or actions into describing thoughts and feelings. You should look out for these indications of a character's inner life for it is these that make the reader feel they really 'know' a character.

5 INTRODUCING A CHARACTER

We may be ***introduced*** to a character directly, through a description of appearance, actions and speech. Alternatively we may be introduced indirectly, through other characters' words, opinions and reactions to them. This happens most obviously when a narrator is used. (Look back at the passage quoted from ***The Great Gatsby*** in Ch.13.) But it can also accumulate through information given by other characters and their attitude:

"Why my dear you must know, Mrs Long says that Netherfield is taken by a young man of large fortune from the north of England; that he came down on Monday in a chaise and four to see the place, and was so much delighted with it that he agreed with Mr Morris immediately; that he is to take possession before Michaelmas, and some of his servants are to be in the house by the end of next week. "

"What is his name?"

"Bingley,"

"Is he married or single?" "Oh! single, my dear, to be sure! A single man of large fortune; four or five thousand a year. What a fine thing for our girls!"

Mrs Bennet, speaking here at the beginning of ***Pride and Prejudice*** has not even met Bingley yet she manages to convey a great deal of information about him, such as his status, his willingness to be pleased and take immediate action, and, most importantly, his significance for the other characters.

In the same novel Mr Collins is introduced through a letter he sends to Mr Bennet. When he arrives in the flesh he confirms the fatuous impression given by his letter.

How are the characters introduced in the novels you are reading?

---

6 DEVELOPMENT

Novelists show their characters in as many situations, and over whatever length of time, they choose. This allows them to ***develop*** characters, show them changing through their lives, or perhaps remaining constant as things change around them. We may find some of their behaviour unexpected. Before we dismiss it as unconvincing we must ask ***why*** the novelist portrays the character like this. Does it fit in with the larger purpose of the book? Look at all the different facets of a character which the novelist has chosen to display. Ask yourself why the novelist shows one character as always the same, while another changes.

Pip's character in ***Great Expectations*** goes through several stages, both in his own behaviour and his relationship with others. Joe, his kind and generous uncle, remains constant. Wemmick, the lawyer's clerk, has two distinct modes of behaviour, one for his work and one for home, which are never allowed to overlap. Each of these kinds of characterization tells us something. Pip develops because he has to learn what is true gentlemanly behaviour; Joe remains the same because he is the standard of goodness against which other characters are measured; Wemmick's dual personality represents the contrast between the debased values of the city and the better values of his domestic life. Dickens shapes each character differently because they fulfil three different functions.

Your notes on each chapter should record the **changes** in each developing character and the reason why those who do **not** change remain the same.

7 > CHARACTER TYPES

Despite the three different ways Dickens presents the characters of Pip, Joe and Wemmick, they are all fully developed, realistic characters. Some characters in novels are neither of these things. The animals in George Orwell's **Animal Farm** are obviously not realistic. They stand for certain characteristics. For instance, Boxer, the cart-horse, stands for the honest, unquestioning, hard-working peasant.

Characters who have only one or very few characteristics are said to be 'flat' or 'unrounded'. Most novelists employ such characters as part of their background.

Some characters have one characteristic exaggerated to such an extent that they become caricatures. George Eliot's Silas Marner is a caricature of a miser, poring over his gold and counting it every night, until he is suddenly given a child to care for.

All these character **types** can have a place in the author's scheme. The questions to ask are: Why have they been put there? What purpose do they serve?

8 > NAMES

In novels, as in plays, **names** can sometimes reveal a character's personality. We would expect a man called Gabriel Oak to be a sturdy, reliable person, with a good heart and true. He is probably a countryman. These characteristics, suggested by the oak tree, are all found in Gabriel Oak (in **Far from the Madding Crowd** by Thomas Hardy). Mr. Gradgrind is a hard, uncompromising person, totally lacking in sentiment, who believes only in facts and figures. His name has the right associations and the right sound for such a person.

Not all novelists use this technique. Think about the names of characters in the novels you are studying to see if they express anything of their nature.

9 > RELATIONSHIPS

Just as important as each of the characters in themselves are the **relationships** between them. These can be traced in the same way as individual characters. Look at the things they say and think about each other; how they act and react to each other; whether their thoughts about, and reactions towards, each other change. Sometimes the whole point of a book is shown through these changing relationships. The courtship of a couple is often used to show the novelist's ideas of goodness, propriety and virtue. When Rochester proposes to Jane, in **Jane Eyre**, neither she nor anyone else can believe that she, a mere governess, is the proper wife for him, a gentleman. When it is revealed that he is already married their relationship seems over, for Jane will not yield to his pleas to stay with him as his mistress. She abandons him but remains true to her love for him despite another offer of marriage. Rochester loses his sight while trying, but failing, to rescue his mad first wife from a fire. When he has suffered and expiated his sins he and Jane are reunited and the novelist finally allows them to marry. Jane's virtue and love earn her the reward of marriage. Marriage is often used as a reward for virtue triumphant or difficulties overcome.

Remember to record in your notes the characters' thoughts and feelings about each other, showing how they develop and how they express the novel's themes.

10 > AUTHOR'S ATTITUDE

An **author's attitude** to the characters is not always clear. Harper Lee obviously approves of Atticus in **To Kill a Mockingbird**: everything he does is presented to us in a good light and we are shown nothing bad about him at all; the whole town looks up to him. William Golding equally obviously disapproves of Roger in **Lord of the Flies** because he never does or says anything good and is shown as the initiator of evil. The other boys fear him but do not like or admire him.

Few judgements are as clear-cut as this. What, for instance, is Emily Bronte's attitude towards Heathcliff? He is adjudged at best uncouth and ill-tempered, and at worst wicked, by every other character in the novel, including Cathy who says she loves him as she loves her own soul. His actions reinforce these judgements. So why do I not despise him? Because Emily Bronte depicts him, with all his faults, with sympathy, understanding, and even admiration. His enormous love for Cathy and overwhelming pain at her loss is allowed to outweigh everything else. Through her attitude to this character the novelist displays her judgement, in this case of the importance of passion.

Always ask yourself: what is the author's attitude to the characters? What does it show about the author's judgement and values.

11 ▷ SUMMARY

➤ We learn about characters directly from their speech and actions and indirectly from their appearance, dress, surroundings and the opinions of others.

➤ The novelist's exploration of thoughts and feelings reveals the characters' inner life.

➤ Characters may be flat or rounded.

➤ Characters may develop or remain unchanged, according to their function in the plot.

➤ Relationships are developed in the same way as characters and may express the theme of the novel.

➤ The way the characters are presented and the language used to describe them shows the author's attitude to them.

ADDITIONAL EXAMPLES

Use these passages as exercises to test your understanding of this chapter. Write down your own thoughts before reading what I have written in the Key below.

1. What do we find out about each character in this passage. What is the author's attitude and what is your own response to the characters.

George turned the bean cans so that another side faced the fire. He pretended to be unaware of Lennie so close beside him.

"George," very softly. No answer. "George!"

"Whatta you want?" "I was only foolin', George. I don't want no ketchup. I wouldn't eat no ketchup if it was right here beside me. "

"If it was here you could have some. "

"But I wouldn't eat none, George. I'd leave it all for you. You could cover your beans with it and I wouldn't touch none of it."

George still stared morosely at the fire.

"When I think of the swell time I could have without you, I go nuts. I never get no peace."

Lennie still knelt. He looked off into the darkness across the river. "George, you want I should go away and leave you alone?"

"Where the hell could you go?" "Well, I could. I could go off in the hills there. Some place I'd find a cave. "

"Yeah? How'd you eat. You ain't got sense enough to find nothing to eat. "

"I'd find things George. I don't need no nice food with ketchup. I'd lay out in the sun and nobody'd hurt me. An' if I foun' a mouse, I could keep it. Nobody'd take it away from me."

George looked quickly and searchingly at him. "I been mean, ain't I?"

"If you don' want me I can go off in the hills an' find a cave. I can go any time."

"No – Look! I was jus' foolin' Lennie. 'Cause I want you to stay with me. Trouble with mice is you always kill 'em" He paused. "Tell you what I'll do, Lennie.

First chance I get I'll give you a pup. Maybe you wouldn't kill it. That'd be better than mice. And you could pet it harder."

Lennie avoided the bait. He had sensed his advantage. "If you don't want me, you only jus' got to say so, and I'll go off in those hills right there – right up in those hills and live by myself. An' I won't get no mice stole from me."

George said, "I want you to stay with me Lennie. Jesus Christ, somebody'd shoot you for a coyote if you was by yourself. No, you stay with me. Your Aunt Clara wouldn't like you running off by yourself, even if she is dead."

Lennie spoke craftily, "Tell me – like you done before. "

"Tell you what?"

"About the rabbits."

George snapped, "You ain't gonna put nothing over on me."

Lennie pleaded, "Come on, George. Tell me. Please, George. Like you done before. "

"You get a kick outa that, don't you? Awright, I'll tell you, and then we'll eat our supper . . . " George's voice became deeper. He repeated his words rhythmically as though he had said them many times before. "Guys like us, that work on ranches, are the loneliest guys in the world. They got no family.

(***Of Mice and Men***; John Steinbeck.)

2. What do you find interesting about these two characters?

Cabbage-Stump Charlie was our local bruiser – a violent, gaitered, gaunt-faced pigman, who lived only for his sows and for fighting. He was a nourisher of quarrels, as some men are of plants, growing them from nothing by the heat of belligerence and watering them daily with blood. He would set out each evening, armed with his cabbage-stalk, ready to strike down the first man he saw. 'What's up then Charlie? Got no quarrel with thee. ' 'Wham!' said Charlie, and hit him. Men fell from their bicycles or back-pedalled violently when they saw Charlie coming. With his hawk-brown nose and whiskered arms he looked like a land-locked Viking; and he would take up his stand outside the pub, swing his great stump round his head, and say 'Wham! Bash!' like a boy in a comic, and challenge all-comers to battle. Often bloodied himself, he left many a man bleeding before crawling back home to his pigs. Cabbage-Stump Charlie, like Jones' goat, set the village to bolting its doors.

Percy-from-Painswick, on the other hand, was a clown and a ragged dandy, who used to come over the hill dressed in a frock-coat and leggings, looking for local girls. Harmless, half-witted, he wooed only with his tongue: but his words were sufficient to befuddle the girls and set them shrieking with pleasure and shock. He had a sharp pink face and a dancer's light body and the girls used to follow him everywhere, teasing him on into cheekier fancies and pinning ribbons to his swallowtail coat. Then he'd spin on his toes, and say something quick and elaborate, uttered smoothly from smiling teeth – and the girls would run screaming down over the bank, red-faced, excited, incredulous, hiding in bushes to exclaim to each other was it possible what Percy just said? He was a gentle, sharp, sweet-moving man, but he died of his brain soon after.

(***Cider With Rosie***; Laurie Lee)

1. ***Of Mice and Men***. There are very few actions in this extract, so we learn about the characters almost entirely through their speech. George's words show him to be a rough, plain man but one who has sympathetic and tender feelings. That George cares for Lennie, even though he is a nuisance, is clear from the way he drops into telling the old story that Lennie wants to hear. He has been angry with Lennie but despite all the trouble Lennie causes, George is sorry to have hurt him. He knows the story will calm and comfort Lennie. George is also a practical man, realizing that a pup would satisfy Lennie's need for something to pet while being big enough to withstand Lennie's over-enthusiastic caresses. George changes from being glum about his own situation and resentful of Lennie's presence, to feeling sorry and wishing to make amends.

Lennie's words show us that he is affectionate to George but simple-minded and childlike in the way he tries to earn forgiveness. George can have all the ketchup, when there is any. His idea of going off to live in the hills is like a child's reaction to wrongdoing, with no realization of the difficulties he would encounter. He has a simple need to love things, but does not realize his own strength, unintentionally killing the mice he pets. Like a child he reacts instinctively to George's almost parental concern, sensing when he can get his own way. And like a child he loves stories and listens contentedly to George.

There is nothing in this passage to tell us directly the author's attitude to his characters so we have to deduce it from the way they are presented to us. The author's own language, in the few words and phrases of narration, is educated and much more sophisticated than anything George and Lennie would say: 'morosely' and 'looked quickly and searchingly' are too clever for them. Yet the educated author does not look down on his uneducated characters. He presents them seriously, not mocking their failings or showing them in a comic way. We therefore feel he is sympathetic towards them and understands their situation.

Because of this my own response to the characters is to feel sympathy. George's shouldering of responsibility for Lennie, despite the difficulties and the restrictions Lennie imposes on his own behaviour and pleasures, seems admirable. Steinbeck excites my sympathy for Lennie through his childlike qualities and his vulnerability.

2. **Cider With Rosie**. Both these characters are made interesting by making them unusual people with extraordinary mannerisms and appearance. Both provoke a strong reaction in other people.

Cabbage-Stump Charlie's unusual features are his devotion to his pigs and aggression to all men. His appearance – he is compared to a Viking – is a warning of his attitude to fights, which he seems to enjoy and practise as entertainment. His chosen weapon, the cabbage-stalk, is comic and so too is the language he uses – 'Wham! Bash! like a boy in a comic book'. Laurie Lee describes the villagers scampering out of his way or cowering behind locked doors to avoid the bloody results of Charlie's nightly excursions in search of victims or sparring partners.

Percy-from-Painswick is depicted as harmless but capable of creating as much of a stir as Charlie. Laurie Lee concentrates on his quaint dress, idiosyncratic speech and movements and his effect on the village girls. In his swallow-tailed coat trimmed with ribbons, his strange, balletic movements and rapid, shocking speech, he seems like a visiting entertainer rather than a half-wit from over the hill. But the final sentence of the extract quells the comedy and evokes pity for Percy.

EXAM QUESTIONS

A great many exam questions are asked about character, either in response to a passage printed on the exam paper, or in the book as a whole. A question might ask about:

➤ a character's thoughts and feelings;
➤ character development;
➤ relationships between characters;
➤ a character's part in the plot;
➤ characters in relation to the ideas, themes or background;
➤ the author's attitude towards the characters;
➤ your own response to the characters.

I have tried to touch on all these things in this chapter, but since questions of character are so much linked to **other** aspects of the novel you need to study these aspects, dealt with in other chapters. You cannot look at characters in isolation. Here are some examples of different types of questions:

1. Apart from Lewis and Benjamin and their parents, which character have you found particularly interesting? Write about him or her saying what you find of special interest. (**On the Black Hill**; Bruce Chatwin – MEG)

2. What kind of feelings do you have about Piggy from the beginning of the story to his death? You might like to consider one or two of the following questions:
   Why do you think that Golding decides to make him die in the novel? Could Piggy have possibly survived on this island without the children he was with? Was there something in Piggy's upbringing and character that made his death certain? What were his qualities? Were they needed on the island? What, do you think, would annoy others about the way Piggy talked and behaved? (*Lord of the Flies*; William Golding – WJEC)

3. Is there a family in one or more of the books you have read? Write about the family relationships as they exist and develop. (LEAG)

4. Elizabeth has developed and matured a great deal by the end of the novel. What do you think of her and the ways in which she has matured?
   Write about Jane Austen's portrayal of Elizabeth by considering particularly her relationships with and attitudes to the following during the course of the novel: her parents; her sisters; Bingley, Darcy, Wickham and Collins. (*Pride and Prejudice*; Jane Austen – NEA.)

QUESTIONS, NOTES AND TUTOR'S ANSWERS

1 > QUESTIONS

"Use this passage as a prose unseen, if you have not read the book."

The following questions, set by SEG on a passage from *Far from the Madding Crowd* are typical question on character in a given passage.

'Miss Everdene!' said the farmer.

She trembled, turned, and said 'Good morning. ' His tone was so utterly removed from all she had expected as a beginning. It was lowness and quiet accentuated: an emphasis of deep meanings, their form, at the same time, being scarcely expressed. Silence has sometimes a remarkable power of showing itself as the disembodied soul of feeling wandering without its carcase, and it is then more impressive than speech. In the same way, to say little is often to tell more than to say a great deal. Boldwood told everything in that word.

As the consciousness expands on learning that what was fancied to be the rumble of wheels is the reverberation of thunder, so did Bathsheba's at her intuitive conviction.

'I feel – almost too much – to think,' he said, with a solemn simplicity. 'I have come to speak to you without preface. My life is not my own since I have beheld you clearly, Miss Everdene – I come to make you an offer of marriage. '

Bathsheba tried to preserve an absolutely natural countenance, and all the motion she made was one of closing her lips which had previously been a little parted.

'I am now forty-one years old,' he went on. 'I may have been called a confirmed bachelor, and I was a confirmed bachelor. I had never any views of myself as a husband in my earlier days, nor have I made any calculation on the subject since I have been older. But we all change, and my change, in this matter, came with seeing you. I have felt lately, more and more, that my present way of living is bad in every respect. Beyond all things, I want you as my wife. '

'I feel, Mr. Boldwood, that though I respect you much, I do not feel – what would justify me to – in accepting your offer,' she stammered.

This giving back of dignity for dignity seemed to open the sluices of feeling that Boldwood had as yet kept closed.

'My life is a burden without you,' he exclaimed in a low voice. 'I want you – I want you to let me say I love you again and again!'

Bathsheba answered nothing, and the mare upon her arm seemed so impressed that instead of cropping the herbage she looked up.

'I think and hope you care enough for me to listen to what I have to tell!' Bathsheba's momentary impulse at hearing this was to ask why he thought that, till she remembered that, far from being a conceited assumption on Boldwood's part, it was but the natural conclusion of serious reflection based on deceptive premises of her own offering.

'I wish I could say courteous flatteries to you,' the farmer continued in an easier tone, 'and put my rugged feelings into graceful shape: but I have neither power nor patience to learn such things. I want you for my wife – so wildly that no other feeling can abide in me; but I should not have spoken out had I not been led to hope.'

'The valentine again! O that valentine!' she said to herself, but not a word to him.

'If you can love me say so, Miss Everdene. If not – don't say no.'
(***Far from the Madding Crowd***; Thomas Hardy.)

1.   What do you learn about Boldwood in this passage? (8 marks)
2.   What do you learn about Bathsheba's feelings from her reaction to Boldwood in this passage? (4 marks)

2 ▷ NOTES

1.   Read through the passage carefully.
2.   Go through the passage underlining everything relating to Boldwood and his character, feelings and behaviour.
3.   Write a substantial paragraph in answer to the first part of the question. Notice that there are 8 marks here, i.e. 40% of the total, so try not to miss anything.
4.   Go back and underline points about Bathsheba's feelings and reactions, then write a second paragraph in answer to the second part. There is less evidence in the passage so there are fewer marks. You should therefore write less.

3 ▷ SUGGESTED ANSWERS

66 **Have you described the feelings of each character and used the passage as reference? Some students lose marks by referring to the rest of the book instead of using the passage as evidence.** 99

1. Boldwood is overwhelmingly in love with Bathsheba. His voice betrays the depth of his feelings as soon as he speaks her name. He says he is forty-one and has been a confirmed bachelor, never thinking of marriage, until he saw Bathsheba. She has changed his life. He speaks of his love with great directness, his passion being so great that he cannot hide it. He is, in any case, unused to flattering people; he does not know, and does not want to know, how to proceed with a courtship in a gallant manner, although he speaks with dignity. All he wants, with great impatience, is for Bathsheba to be his wife. Until she does, he feels that his life is worthless. All other concerns have been driven out of his head and he can think of nothing else. He is determined that she shall not turn him down and is confident, given the evidence of the valentine which Bathsheba sent him, that he can win her. It is only her action which has led him to speak to her in this manner.

2. The intensity of Boldwood's voice makes Bathsheba tremble from the first words he speaks. She guesses what he has come to say, and is fearful, not knowing how to respond. She tries to give none of her feelings away in her face and stammers a non-committal reply. She feels very guilty about sending the valentine and wishes that she had not done so because it has stirred up Boldwood's feelings to a pitch she is incapable of dealing with. Realizing that this situation is all her own fault, she is paralysed and unable to reject him.

SUGGESTIONS FOR COURSEWORK

1.   You could write a coursework unit based on any of the exam questions given above.
2.   Write a completely new episode involving the characters of a novel you have read, making it fit in with the plot.
3.   Compare two characters from different novels by the same author. This would help to show evidence of further reading which is one of the requirements of the course.

4. Rewrite an episode from the point of view of one of the less important characters.
5. Write the diary of a character covering several chapters. Try to reveal the development of the character in what the diary says and the expression used.
6. Rewrite a dialogue between two or more characters as a scene from a play. Include stage directions to show the reactions of characters, tone of voice and movements.

STUDENT'S ANSWER – EXAMINER'S COMMENT

Question

Give your opinion of the character of Bathsheba at the opening of *Far from the Madding Crowd*.

> **Good. Points out an action which shows Bathsheba's vanity, then uses a quotation to support the point.**

> **Good. Points to something the character says herself which shows another aspect of her character.**

> **Good. A second characteristic illustrated through an action.**

> **Does not give any detail here.**

The first we hear of Bathsheba is when she looks in the mirror while in a prettily painted wagon. She seems to like herself the way she is. She didn't adjust anything.
'She simply observed herself as a fair product of nature in the feminine kind.'
In other words she was vain and liked her beauty too much.
She is also rather ungrateful, Oak pays her money but she hardly looked at him and certainly didn't thank him.
'She might have looked her thanks to Gabriel on a minute scale, but she did not speak there.'
So the impression we get of Bathsheba in the first chapter is not a favourable one especially in my view. I think she must have been spoilt, and told that she was beautiful over and over again.
From the next chapter we find out that Bathsheba likes money and fine things. While in the cow house she says,
'I wish we were rich enough to pay a man to do these things.'
Bathsheba likes luxury and I feel that at sometime she must have been quite rich.
In the next chapter we see Bathsheba as a bit of a tom boy when she's riding by Gabriel's hut.
'As if to assure herself that all humanity was out of view, then dextrously dropped backwards flat upon the pony's back, her head over it's tail, her feet against it's shoulders, and her eyes to the sky.'
Hardly lady-like! Bathsheba likes her fun and this introduces us that Bathsheba does what she feels like. She also likes playing games
'Now find out my name.' she said teasingly. This was said to Oak, He asked for her name and she plays upon him like a puppet.
But Bathsheba saved Oak's life and so she has some goodness in her, and I think she was concerned for him but covered it up when he came round.
It seems to me in chapter four she leads Oak's heart on a string like she did before. She runs after him and lets him go on as if she wanted to marry. Then she turns on him bluntly.
'I never said I was going to marry you.'

66 **This is talking about the character as though she were a person. In any case such personal reactions are not necessary.** 99

The conversation she has with Oak I seem to think that she finds it amusing. She doesn't love Oak and tells and so she's honest.
As her name suggests she is a bit headstrong. She does what she wants. I don't like her personally. She seems too sure of herself but underneath I think there is a nice young lady waiting to emerge.

66 **Nowhere are we told of Gabriel's reactions! The thoughts and feelings of another character are often very revealing.** 99

SETTING

GETTING STARTED

A novelist has to create in words all the sights and sounds of the characters' world. The setting of the novel can do more than produce atmosphere. It can be used to tell us about the feelings of characters and their relation to the world around them. Because the author creates the world in which the characters live, as well as the characters themselves, it is equally important in the ideas and structure of the novel.

The questions you have to ask are: what is my response to this world? Why has the author created it in this way? Different aspects of background and setting may be important at different points in a novel and, of course, all novels are different. This chapter shows you some ways of thinking about the background and setting of novels.

**ATMOSPHERE
MOOD
LANDSCAPE AND
WEATHER
SETTING AND
CHARACTERS
SOCIAL CONTEXT**

ESSENTIAL PRINCIPLES

 **1 ▷ ATMOSPHERE**

The mood of a whole book is often produced by the author's use of the background against which the story is set. There may be many different settings during the course of a novel. They all add up to give the general *atmosphere* of the book. An author who dwells on the dirt and misery of a setting, whether it be a rural hovel or urban slum will produce an atmosphere of hopelessness and oppression. - Graham Greene has become so well known for seedy, dirty, run-down settings in his novels that his typical setting has been given a name: Greeneland.

An author can move between widely different settings in a novel and yet produce a strong sense of place and a dominant atmosphere. In *The Mayor of Casterbridge* Thomas Hardy moves from the elegant Lucetta's drawing room at one end of the scale to the crowded slum of Mixen Lane, haunt of the undesirables of the town. He produces the feeling of life in the provincial market town of Casterbridge with its encircling countryside.

❝The examiners are looking for a personal response. What is your response to the author's setting?❞

The many descriptions of the town make us feel we know it in the same way we know a town that we have visited. The nature of the town is conveyed through references to its long history and remarks like this:

What an old-fashioned town it seems to be! said Elizabeth-Jane . . . it is huddled all together and it is shut in by a square wall of trees, like a plot of garden ground by a box edging.

Here the visual description of the town, especially the comparison to an enclosed garden, is also an indication of its nature: inward-looking and backward, a comfortable close-knit community shut off from the world. This sense of the place is important for the relationships between the characters and for the way in which we will view the downfall and exclusion from Casterbridge of Michael Henchard.

Other descriptions of settings in the same novel give a solemn atmosphere to the book which intensifies into tragedy: the strange, lonely Roman amphitheatre; the stone bridge over the river to which the unhappy resort.

Notice the settings of the novels you read. Do they produce a particular atmosphere? Of what sort is it? How is it related to the characters and themes of the novel?

2 ⬙▷ MOOD

Just as the setting can create a general atmosphere, so a particular environment can be used to convey the *mood* of a character. The red room in which Jane Eyre is shut up as a punishment is so oppressive that she falls ill. The room, with its dark furnishings and red hangings feels like a jail to Jane. Locked in this solemn, silent and chill room, the scene of Mr Reed's death, she waits as darkness falls:

Daylight began to forsake the red-room; it was past four o'clock, and the beclouded afternoon was tending towards drear twilight. I heard the rain still beating continuously on the staircase window, and the wind howling in the grove behind the hall; I grew by degrees cold as a stone, and then my courage sank. My habitual mood of humiliation, self-doubt, forlorn depression, fell damp on the embers of my decaying ire. All said I was wicked, and perhaps I might be so. . .

The mood created by the dreariness of the winter twilight in the cold, dark room and the sound of the rain and the wind, matches Jane's 'habitual' mood. The setting is an influence on Jane's mood and it is also a symbol of what she feels. The description of the scene attempts to produce in us the feeling that Jane has most of the time.

 **3 ▷ LANDSCAPE AND WEATHER**

Descriptions of the *landscape* and the *weather* are very effective in producing atmosphere and mood. Many people respond emotionally to the weather. In novels rain often figures in dismal scenes, as it did in the one above from *Jane Eyre*, sunshine figures in happy ones. Leafy lanes and green valleys are pleasant and comfortable; barren hills are grim. George Eliot uses a contrast of this kind in two settings, Loamshire and Stoneyshire, in **Adam Bede**. The most difficult and depressing events happen in Stoneyshire: the death of Hetty Sorrel's baby and her imprisonment. The setting is used to emphasize the meaning or moral that Hetty must suffer for the wrongs she has done.

We have already seen how Dickens uses fog in **Bleak House** (see Ch.14). The fog which literally envelopes the city evokes a powerful mood at the beginning of the book. It also stands as a symbol for the processes of the law which enmesh the characters throughout the story.

In **The Go-Between** by L.P. Hartley the mounting heat is used to denote mounting tension. Leo, the boy who narrates the story, frequently checks the rising temperature through the long, hot summer. The heat becomes oppressive. As it does so, the situation between the adult characters gathers to a storm. Leo is only imperfectly aware of what is going on; he is excited by the heat but when the storm breaks he is devastated. The weather is being used as a metaphor.

Can you find examples of landscape or weather being used to create a mood or being used as a symbol or metaphor?

4 ▷ SETTING AND CHARACTERS

There can be a distinct relationship between characters and the background against which they are set. Heathcliff belongs on the bleak, wild moors around Wuthering Heights: their character reflects his character. The Lintons live in the softer, more comfortable environment of Thrushcross Grange and are correspondingly gentler characters. The conflict in Emily Bronte's novel begins when Cathy deserts the first for the second. Why does she do it, because it seems from her character that she too belongs at Wuthering Heights?

A second point to note is the one already mentioned in the Chapter 15: setting can evoke in the reader a particular response towards a character. Henchard dying in a hovel evokes more pity than if he died in a good clean bed, particularly because we see him reduced to this from a position of wealth and strength. Read this passage and see what kind of response the setting creates. In **Tess of the d'Urbervilles**, Tess, abandoned by her husband, penniless, is grubbing up swedes for a living through the winter:

. . . the whole field was in colour a desolate drab; it was a complexion without features, as if a face from chin to brow should be only an expanse of skin. The sky wore, in another colour, the same likeness; a white vacuity of countenance. . . They worked on hour after hour, unconscious of the forlorn aspect they bore in the landscape. . . In the afternoon the rain came on again and Marian said that they need not work any more. But if they did not work they would not be paid; so they worked on. It was so high a situation, this field, that the rain had no occasion to fall, but raced along horizontally upon the yelling wind, sticking into them like glass splinters till they were wet through. Tess had not known till now what was really meant by that.

Many readers find the situation of the two girls very distressing. The awful conditions through which they work makes us respond with an increased sympathy.

When reading a novel you should note any connections between setting and personality. Then decide whether your response to a character is affected by the settings that the author puts him or her in.

5 ▷ SOCIAL CONTEXT

The society that the characters live in is just as important, and in some novels far more important, than the landscape or other surroundings. **To Kill a Mockingbird,** for example, contains people from all levels of society, from the shiftless and anti-social Ewells, through the poor but hard-working Cunninghams, to Aunt Alexandra with her land and her long family tradition. Alongside, yet inter-related, is the distinct society of the blacks. We get to know the town of Maycomb very well through its people. We know Thomas Hardy's Casterbridge not only through the

many descriptions of the town, but also the variety of the townspeople and their relationships.

Some novelists are very interested in society and use their novels to criticise
its faults. Dickens often displays the city as a place where villainy and hypocrisy
thrive. For example, he does this in both **Oliver Twist** and **Great Expectations**.
Jane Austen is interested in social relationships but only depicts the small section
of society, the upper middle-class, which she feels qualified to write about. Some
writers invent whole societies of their own, often setting them in the future, in
order to express their ideas. In **1984**, written in 1948, George Orwell invents a
state which had complete control over its citizens, with Thought Police to control
their thoughts. The television set becomes a two-way instrument, a camera as well
as a receiver acting as a spy in the corner of the room, transmitting details of
everyone's every action. Orwell was trying to show the dangers of allowing the
state to take over too much of people's lives. Aldous Huxley had similar intentions
when he invented the very different society in **Brave New World**.

When reading a novel, think about how important the social setting is. What
aspects of society has the novelist chosen to write about? Is the society shown in a
bad or a good light?

6 ▷ SUMMARY

➤ The setting of the novel is a whole, distinctive world, created by the novelist.

➤ Settings can produce the general atmosphere of the novel but also reflect a
character's particular mood.

➤ Landscape and weather are effective in creating atmosphere and reflecting
character.

➤ Landscape, weather and other aspects of setting may be used symbolically as
well as literally, to help convey a theme or idea.

➤ Settings may show character and may affect our response to a character.

➤ The social context is often important in conveying the author's views and criticisms of society.

ADDITIONAL EXAMPLES

Use these examples as exercises to test your understanding of this chapter. Write
down your own ideas before looking at the Key below.

1.   What kind of society is the novelist describing here?:

"Well, well, do as you like, Bessy," said Mr Tulliver, taking up his hat and
walking out to the mill. Few wives were more submissive than Mrs Tulliver on all
points unconnected with her family relations; but she had been a Miss Dodson, and
the Dodson's were a very respectable family indeed – as much looked up to as any
in their own parish, or the next to it. The Miss Dodsons had always been thought
to hold up their heads very high, and no-one was surprised the two eldest had married so well – not at an early age, for that was not the practice of the Dodson family. There were particular ways of doing everything in that family: particular ways
of bleaching the linen, of making the cowslip wine, curing the hams, and keeping
the bottled gooseberries; so that no daughter of the house could be indifferent to
the privilege of having been born a Dodson.
       (**The Mill on the Floss**, George Eliot).

2.   On a beautiful summer evening, under a chestnut tree, with the nightingales
      singing, Mr. Rochester proposes to Jane Eyre. Then comes the following
      passage. If you have not read the book, what does this passage suggest to
      you about Jane and Rochester's relationship? If you have read the book, your
      knowledge of the story will help you explain the meaning of this passage:

But what had befallen the night? The moon was not yet set and we were all in
shadow: I could scarcely see my master's face, near as I was. And what ailed the
chestnut tree? It writhed and groaned; while wind roared in the laurel walk and

came sweeping over us. "We must go in," said Mr. Rochester; "the weather changes. I could have sat with thee till morning, Jane. " "And so," thought I, "could I with you. " I should perhaps have said so, but a livid, vivid spark leapt out of a cloud at which I was looking, and there was a crack, a crash, a close rattling peal; and I thought only of hiding my dazzled eyes against Mr. Rochester's shoulder. The rain rushed down. He hurried me up the walk, through the grounds and into the house; but we were quite wet before we could cross the threshold. . . . Before I left my bed in the morning, little Adele came running in to tell me that the great horse-chestnut at the bottom of the orchard had been struck by lightning, and half of it split away.

(***Jane Eyre***, Charlotte Bronte)

KEY TO THE EXAMPLES

Look for symbols and metaphors in the action of the novels you are studying.

1. ***The Mill on the Floss***. The kind of society described in this passage is a small, settled village community. We know that the world is a narrow one because we are told it is a source of pride if one is looked up to by everyone in the parish and the next one to it. The wider world beyond that does not concern them. It is very conservative, always doing things in a particular way. Rural skills are still important: all the activities described – bottling, curing hams, winemaking – are those of the well-regulated country household in the last century. The family is comfortably off, though not wealthy. It is large, with a strong sense of family pride.

2. ***Jane Eyre***. From the way the weather changes we might expect that there is something wrong in the relationship between Jane and Rochester and their future will not go smoothly. The beautiful evening is destroyed by a terrible storm, rending apart the tree under which they have been sitting. This is a bad omen. It is as though the heavens are protesting at the event, the proposal, which has just taken place on this spot, and nature is signalling its disapproval of some wrong which has been done. Later we discover that Rochester is already married and he cannot marry Jane without committing the crime of bigamy.

    Charlotte Bronte is using the storm as an indication of the moral judgement on Rochester. (The thunderbolt is traditionally a sign of God's displeasure.) The description is of a real storm but it is equally a symbolic one.

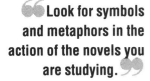

EXAM QUESTIONS

The first question below shows you the kind of material you could use in an answer. This question provides a useful model for two techniques:

➤ How to work out a number of paragraphs covering topics relevant to the question;

➤ How to refer to specific passages in your novel to illustrate your general points.

1.   What have you learned from the book of the similarities and differences between the various races on the island of Trinidad, and their ability to get on together? In your answer you may wish to consider some or all of the following:

> The customs of the different races;
>
> their attitudes to work;
>
> the position of women in their society;
>
> any other ideas suggested to you by the passage below:

Tiger sat on the step and watched night coming. The big thought he had postponed came back. It had happened when his parents had talked about Joe and Rita. At the time rum was in his head but now it was all clear. Why I should only look for Indian friend? What wrong with Joe and Rita? Is true I used to play with Indian friend in the estate, but that ain't that no reason why I must shut my heart to other people. Ain't a man is a man, don't mind if he skin not white, or if he hair curl. (*A Brighter Sun*, Samuel Selvon – SEG)

Each of the following questions is asking you to comment on the 'world of the book' and relate this to a particular feature: Dickens' moral view of the city; the nature of power in society; the society in relation to the individual character, respectively. To answer such questions you need to have noted as you read through the novel:

➤ the author's use of setting, and
➤ the relation between setting and character and ideas.

This will allow you to illustrate your answer in detail. Work out a plan for your essays in the same way as in the question above.

2. To what extent has your reading supported the view that Dickens sees London as a cruel, indeed nightmarish, city? (*Great Expectations*, Charles Dickens – MEG)

3. There are many glimpses of 'high society' before 1939 in this book. What impression do you have of their way of life and their power and influence? Use examples from the book. (*On the Black Hill*, Bruce Chatwin – MEG)

4. Hardy gives us a very detailed picture of Casterbridge in this novel. Show what you think is the importance of the town and its traditions in the story of Henchard. (*The Mayor of Casterbridge*, Thomas Hardy – MEG)

QUESTION, NOTES AND TUTOR'S ANSWER

The following question is from an open-book exam: the relevant passage is printed below. If you have not read the book, you can use the passage as practice for a prose unseen, answering the first two parts of the question but ignoring the part about the wedding. If necessary, look back at Chapter 2 for an explanation of unseens.

1 ▷ QUESTION Read again the beginning of Part Four, Chapter 1 of *Brighton Rock* by Graham Greene. What impression do you get from this passage of a Bank Holiday in Brighton in the nineteen thirties? What do you find particularly vivid in Greene's description and how does this scene, in your opinion, relate to the wedding which is about to take place?

It was a fine day for the races. People poured into Brighton by the first train. It was like Bank Holiday all over again, except that these people didn't spend money; they harboured it. They stood packed deep on the tops of trams rocking down to the Aquarium, they surged like some natural and irrational migration of insects up and down the front. By eleven o'clock it was impossible to get a seat on the buses going out to the course. A negro, wearing a bright striped tie sat on a bench in the Pavilion garden and smoked a cigar. Some children played touch wood from seat to seat, and he called out to them hilariously, holding his cigar at arm's length with an air of pride and caution, his great teeth gleaming like an advertisement. They stopped playing and stared at him, backing slowly. He called out to them again in their own tongue, the words hollow and unformed and childish like theirs, and they eyed him uneasily and backed farther away. He put his cigar patiently back between his cushiony lips and went on smoking. A band came up the pavement through Old Steyne, a blind band playing drums and trumpets, walking in the gutter, feeling the kerb with the edge of their shoes, in Indian file. You heard the music a long way off, persisting through the rumble of the crowd, the shots of exhaust pipes, and the grinding of the buses starting uphill for the racecourse. It rang out with spirit, marched like a regiment, and you raised your eyes in expectation of the tiger skin and the twirling drumsticks and saw the pale blind eyes, like those of pit ponies going by along the gutter.

In the public school grounds above the sea the girls trooped solemnly out to hockey: stout goal-keepers padded like armadillos; captains discussing tactics with their lieutenants; junior girls running amok in the bright day. Beyond the aristocratic turf, through the wrought-iron main gates they could see the plebeian procession, those whom the buses wouldn't hold, plodding up the down, kicking the dust, eating buns out of paper bags. The buses took the long way round through Kemp Town, but up the steep hill came the crammed taxicabs – a seat for anyone at ninepence a time – a Packard for the members' enclosure, old Morrises, strange high cars with family parties, keeping the road after twenty years. It was as if the whole road moved upwards like an Underground staircase in the dusty sunlight, a creaking, shouting jostling crowd of cars moving with it. The junior girls took to their heels like ponies racing on the turf, feeling the excitement going on outside, as if this were a day on which life for many people reached a kind of climax. The odds on Black Boy had shortened, nothing could ever make life quite the same after that rash bet of a fiver on Merry Monarch. A scarlet racing model, a tiny rakish car which carried about it the atmosphere of innumerable road-houses, of tootsies gathered round swimming pools, of furtive encounters in by-lanes off the Great North Road, wormed through the traffic with incredible dexterity. The sun caught it: it winked as far as the dining-hall windows of the girls' school. It was crammed tight: a woman sat on a man's knee, and another man clung on the running board as it swayed and hooted and cut in and out uphill towards the downs. The woman was singing, her voice faint and disjointed through the horns, something traditional about brides and bouquets, something which went with Guinness and oysters and the old Leicester Lounge, something out of place in the bright little racing car. Upon the top of the down the words blew back along the dusty road to meet an ancient Morris rocking and receding in their wake at forty miles an hour, with flapping hood, bent fender and discoloured windscreen.

2 > NOTES

1. Read through the passage carefully.
2. Make a list of as many *different* aspects of the scene as you can find.
3. Decide what the general atmosphere is and try to put a word to it – or several words if you think there is more than one element to it.
4. Make a second list of comparisons, images, particular expressions and anything else you find striking about the writing.
5. Look at the reference to brides and bouquets and think of what Pinkie's reaction to this might be.
6. Write three paragraphs:

> one on different aspects of the scene using your first list;
> one on what you find vivid in the description using your second list;
> one relating the passage to the wedding.

3 > SUGGESTED ANSWER

Brighton is full of people: they cram the trams, the buses, the taxis, and jostle in a seething mass along the seafront. There is an air of excitement from the multitude of people, all intent on enjoying themselves and winning money. Even the girls shut away from the crowds in the school grounds are infected by it. There is an enormous amount of noise, from the people themselves and from the traffic – car exhausts and overloaded buses straining their engines to climb the hill. A band plays with gusto and the sound gives a festive air. Even the private cars are crammed with people. Every conceivable vehicle, from ancient, unfashionable family cars to a zippy modern sports car, has taken to the road. All kinds of people, rich and poor, have taken the day off, for this is not actually a Bank Holiday, to attend the races. There is an air of teeming, tatty confusion, as people trail through the dust eating out of paper bags, and a sense that the normal rules of life have been relaxed and anything can happen.

The writing is made vivid by the numerous details, and through particular, unexpected features. The solitary negro, brightly dressed and smoking a cigar, is a

Have you given examples of vivid writing? Have you answered both parts of the question?

sufficiently unusual sight for the children to back away in alarm when he speaks. The band, is not, as you might expect, a regimental marching band, but a group of blind beggars. Greene notices how they guide themselves along the street by keeping one foot against the kerb. Many of the people in this extract are compared to animals. The band is like a group of blind pit ponies, the girls keeping goal are armadillos, the younger girls, ponies on the turf. The whole crowd is like a mass of insects moving mindlessly as if compelled by some force of nature rather than reason. These comparisons, particularly the last, are de-humanizing and vividly create the feeling of the crowd, where individuals are submerged and the mass takes on a life of its own. Further comparisons add to this effect. The noise of the crowd is like that of a machine: it 'rumbles'. The movement of the crowd is mechanical too, as if on a creaking escalator. Yet the sports car is alive: it 'worms' its way through the traffic. The sun, reflecting off it, seems to be giving a great wink, as though it is in the know about some of its rakish activities.

The woman in the car sings incongruously about brides and bouquets. The connection between this scene and the wedding is made through the song from the car. The words float down to Pinkie following in his battered old Morris and remind him of his marriage. He resents being in a situation where he has to marry Rose, but he must do it so that she cannot give evidence against him. The whole idea of marriage disgusts him. What is more, Rose is poor, unglamorous and innocent. She comes from the very background from which he is trying to escape. The sports car is a symbol of what Pinkie wants. He is envious of people who own scarlet racing cars and their life-style. It is ironic that the romantic and traditional song should come from the car, with its associations of smutty sexual encounters 'in by-lanes off the Great North Road'. The song is out of place in such a car. Pinkie wants nothing to do with brides and bouquets but he does want the car.

There is another, more general, connection between this scene and Pinkie's wedding. A wedding is usually a celebratory, festive occasion, as this scene is. Pinkie's wedding is grimly functional, performed in a bare, official room with only the two necessary witnesses present and without even a wedding ring. The only similarity with this scene is in the general seediness of the surroundings.

SUGGESTIONS FOR COURSEWORK

1. All the questions above are suitable as a basis for a coursework unit.
2. Choose a passage from a novel you are studying which uses the setting to convey any two of the following:
   > atmosphere
   >
   > a symbolic expression of a character's mood
   >
   > an expression of a theme
   >
   > a striking scene in its own right.
   Write about the use the author makes of the setting in the scene.
3. Write a comparison of the settings of two novels, or two different settings in the same novel and show how the author uses them.
4. Make a study of the social setting of the period when an author was writing. Show how it appears in a novel you are studying.

STUDENT'S ANSWER – EXAMINER'S COMMENT

This question involves the 'setting' of *Far from the Madding Crowd*.

Question

How does Hardy create an appropriate atmosphere and background to the events of the story?

> **Much better to refer to an event rather than a chapter number.**

> **Good. Refers in detail to the words used.**

> **Good. Identifies the atmosphere.**

> **The essay has moved away from the title. It is now concerned with the character's feelings rather than with atmosphere. Although this student contines to write well about the language, it is not until much later that he/she gets back to answering the question actually set! You cannot afford to ramble.**

> **Good. Points out the symbolic nature of the action.**

> **Good. Getting back to the atmosphere and background to the story.**

Hardy has many ways of capturing our attention and creating our emotions in chapters twenty eight and forty four.

At the beginning of chapter twenty eight Hardy describes the landscape: the words he uses are pump, radiant, clear and untainted. We can see that this is not unlike Bathsheba at this time – her body or her mind.

We obtain a feeling of warmness and self-indulgence 'bristling balls of gold' and 'luxuriant rays.' The branches caress Bathsheba, perhaps showing promises of what is to come. Hardy describes throughout the chapter Bathsheba's feelings: she ran 'literally trembling and panting' because of the danger she is in. Bathsheba is excited and therefore we feel much of this excitement ourselves, She is afraid of the sword and overwhelmed at the end which creates these emotions in the reader. Hardy is very keen to divulge Bathsheba's emotions so that we can understand and sympathize with her but it is noticeable that not once in the chapter does Hardy pinpoint Troy's feelings, so we imagine Troy as merely a figure and an object, not a person, who sets off the fire in Bathsheba.

Troy is ready and waiting, and when he produces the sword, it is introduced as a living thing which first may give us the idea that is an extension of his manhood. He then performs the 'cuts and thrusts' which are noticeably 'entering' movements. The exercises overall are a symbol of foreplay – a taste of what is to come for Bathsheba.

During the chapter, many phrases are used to describe the movement of the sword and its effect on Bathsheba. 'A rainbow' is a very good one because it symbolizes a mirage – something that is enchanting but soon disappears which is Troy's love and their marriage. It 'resembles a sky full of meteors close at hand', which shows that this was new to her, something alien and exciting. And finally 'like a twanged harpstring' which describes Troy;s sword arm. This is a strange simile for Troy, but perhaps Bathsheba thought she was in heaven!

Troy deceives her when he tells her the sword is blunt which is a symbol of their whole relationship.

The sword, as it moved past her, Hardy says, has left the shape of her which shows that at that time Troy had summed up her character totally and knew just what she wanted. It is because of this that Troy can go on to cut off the lock of her hair and remove the caterpillar from her bosom.

THEMES

AND

IDEAS

TITLES
CHARACTERS AND
    IDEAS
PLOTS AND IDEAS
ENDINGS
SIGNIFICANT EVENTS
CONTRASTING PAIRS
SETTING

GETTING STARTED

Some exam questions will test whether you understand what the book is about. That is not what the story is, but the ideas it expresses. Every author has an outlook on life which the story expresses. Some stories set out very clearly to put forward the author's point of view, even to teach or preach. Ideas may be aired through a character's thoughts or conversation. More often the author's ideas will be buried in the story. The themes will only emerge gradually as these ideas become clear. You will only be able to say what the book is really 'about' when you have finished reading and can see the pattern complete. This is why re-reading is essential. The second time through, you can pick up hints and indications you overlooked before because you did not realize their importance. That is not to say you should not be looking for themes from the beginning. As you read ask yourself, 'What seems to be important for this novelist?'.

ESSENTIAL PRINCIPLES

Every part of a novel can express its theme.

1 > TITLES

The title often gives a good idea of the themes of a novel. This is not surprising because in it the author may try to sum up in a few words what is important and significant in a book. Jane Austen is very good on titles: ***Pride and Prejudice*** and ***Sense and Sensibility*** tell us what her books are about before we begin to read. We expect to find in these novels characters who have the qualities mentioned in the titles and we do. We also find out what Jane Austen's verdict on these qualities is through her handling of the characters.

Do not, however, always expect the title to give you a clue to the theme. ***Oliver Twist*** tells us who, not what, the book is about.

An interesting exercise is to compose alternative titles which express the novel's theme.

2 > CHARACTERS AND IDEAS

Novelists show their views in the kind of characters they create and what befalls them. Which of the characters are condemned and shown in a bad light, which are approved of? The answers to these questions may show you the novelist's values. Among other things in ***Pride and Prejudice***, Jane Austen disapproves of Mr. Collins' pomposity, Mrs. Bennet's silliness, Lady Catherine's snobbishness, Mary's self-absorption and above all Wickham's selfish opportunism and deceit. All these characters are commented on adversely, sometimes openly, sometimes by implication. Elizabeth and Darcy are admired for their ability to learn. They are rewarded with wealth and happiness.

Another way novelists show disapproval is to bring characters to a bad end. Fagin, who throughout ***Oliver Twist*** has no pity for anyone, is mercilessly shown suffering in the condemned cell before he is hanged.

Some characters embody an idea so completely that they become types, or caricatures. Mr. Bounderby, as his name implies, is a walking example of a 'bounder', a Victorian word for a person without principles. Big Brother, in Orwell's ***1984*** is totalitarianism personified. (Look back at Ch.11 on character types and names in drama, for more examples of characters who embody ideas.)

3 > PLOTS AND IDEAS

Plots, unlike life, can be organized however the novelist wishes. Therefore, they can be specially tailored to show what the novelist thinks ought to happen. A novelist who wants to discuss the class system, for example, will construct a story that includes class conflicts. One who thinks that marriage is a good and necessary thing for women, like most nineteenth century novelists, will show events leading to happy and successful marriages. One who thinks, as the present day writer Fay Weldon does, that marriage is a poor deal for most women, will construct stories that show marriage in a poor light. George Orwell constructed a story, ***1984*** which he hoped showed the evil of totalitarian rule. The ideas came first; the working out of the plot, in which the individual is crushed by the state machine, is designed to demonstrate those ideas.

Ask yourself these questions about the novels you are studying. What is the purpose of the story? What works out successfully for the characters; what fails? What is shown to be good and what bad? Who wins the conflicts? Are we made to feel that the right side won?

4 > ENDINGS

Not all bad characters die or are punished in the end and not all good characters receive rewards. And by no means can all characters be divided neatly into good and bad – most are a mixture. In working out the plot the novelist may deliberately offend the reader's idea of what is fair in order to make a point. At the end of ***Of Mice and Men***, for example, Steinbeck has George shoot his friend Lennie. George does it quickly and cleanly, while Lennie is happily dreaming of the future, in order to save him from far worse. We see that it is not fair that Lennie should die; we also see that it is inevitable. Lennie is a simpleton in a hard world where there is no place for him. The author produces complex responses in his readers. Our recognition of the appropriateness of the end of the novel shows that we have understood Steinbeck's ideas, as expressed through the novel's plot and structure. Happy endings, or fairly happy endings should strike us in the same way, as justified and inevitable. It is right that Adam Bede and Dinah Morris should marry. But first Adam has to learn that his first choice, Hetty, is the wrong woman for him although Hetty is more beautiful. It is a painful lesson, but necessary, so that the book may reach the conclusion which we recognize as proper.

We may not always feel the ending is satisfying. At the end of ***The Mayor of Casterbridge*** Henchard dies just before Elizabeth-Jane finds him. Is this inevitable? Some people would say not. They grumble that it is artificial that Elizabeth-Jane should arrive just too late so that Henchard dies miserable and lonely. In fact, they grumble that Thomas Hardy does this kind of thing far too often. This criticism is really saying that Hardy does not express his ideas through his plots in a satisfactory way. The idea that Hardy is expressing by having Henchard die, is the folly of his strongly impetuous nature. He destroys what he loves right from the beginning when he sells his wife. All events point to the fact that Henchard cannot win, but the manner of his death also points to Hardy's deeply fatalistic view of life. Hardy is artistically right even if not completely realistic. His novel ends in a way that is appropriate to the scheme and ideas of the book even if this is not a way which is likely to happen in real life.

5 > SIGNIFICANT EVENTS

While endings are very important because they complete the pattern of the story, many other events in the story can be significant in stating the theme. These can often be seemingly quite small. In ***A Passage to India***, when Mrs. Callendar takes an Indian doctor's carriage without permission, it is significant because it shows the relationship between the races. In the same novel Mrs Moore finds a wasp on the coat-peg – not a very earth-shattering event:

> *Going to hang up her cloak she found that the tip of the peg was occupied by a small wasp. She had known this wasp or his relatives by day; they were not as English wasps, but had long yellow legs which hung down behind when they flew. Perhaps he mistook the peg for a branch–no Indian animal has any sense of an interior. . . There he clung, asleep while jackals in the plain bayed their desires and mingled with the percussion of drums. 'Pretty dear,' said Mrs. Moore to the wasp.*

This tiny event is made significant because it is used to show the difference between India and England. The distinctions which the English are used to do not seem to apply: the animals cannot be shut outside – indoors and outdoors do not seem to count; a peg and a branch are the same to the wasp. This implies that animals and people cannot be divided into separate categories. Mrs. Moore can see this. She calls the wasp a pretty dear, though most people – English people – would shoo it away or kill it. Later in the novel there is another reference to a wasp when a character tries to explain why, in the Hindu religion, even the life of an an insect is valuable. The little incident in this passage shows that Mrs Moore understands this instinctively.

Look out for such events as these. When apparently small things are mentioned several times they are usually significant in the novel's theme.

6 > CONTRASTING PAIRS

Many plots are built around contrasts and these are often instructive in revealing the author's ideas and the theme of the novel. ***Contrasting pairs*** occur frequently throughout literature and several have already been mentioned in the course of this book. In settings we have had the contrast of Wuthering Heights and Thrushcross Grange and of Loamshire and Stoneyshire (see Ch.16). In character we have had Kate and Bianca, Maggie Hobson and her sisters, (see Ch.11). In **The Mayor of Casterbridge** the impetuous Henchard is contrasted with the calm and methodical Farfrae: as Henchard falls so Farfrae rises, taking over Henchard's business and his house. Henchard's failure is the result of his character, which contains what is often called a 'fatal flaw'. Hardy uses the opposing character of Farfrae to expose Henchard's faults and to show how he could have behaved differently.

7 ▷ SETTING

Chapter 16 showed how the **setting** of a novel can create a particular atmosphere or a distinct world. The nature of this world, or atmosphere it generates, also shows the author's views. Dickens' city is cruel; Orwell's state is oppressive and all-pervasive; Graham Greene's world is degraded. There is a very general idea, found frequently in English literature, that the town or city tends to be bad and harbour vice, while the countryside is wholesome and good. This idea goes back to classical literature and the biblical paradise in the Garden of Eden and can be traced from Shakespeare down through Dickens and the nineteenth century and on to **Lark Rise to Candleford** and **Cider with Rosie**.

Apart from such general ideas, setting can give more specific indications of the ideas or themes of a novel. The opening of **A Passage to India** is a description of the city of Chandrapore where the novel is set. In the description the author, E. M. Forster, mentions much that is important for the rest of the novel. He begins:

Except for the Marabar Cave – and they are twenty miles off – the city of Chandrapore presents nothing extraordinary.

He then seems to forget the caves and goes on to the city where everything seems to be made of mud. This is where the Indians live. On a hill above the city the British, the rulers, live. The positions are significant – in fact everything is significant. The caves, which seem only to have been mentioned in passing, become the scene of the most important event in the novel. The mud becomes a symbol of life. The whole novel deals with the difficult relationships between British and Indian and the prejudices of oppressor and oppressed, westerner and oriental.

We cannot see the significance of everything immediately. We have to store the details in our minds and wait for the significance to be revealed. That is what we have to do all the time when we are reading.

8 ▷ SUMMARY

➤ Titles can sum up what a story is about.
➤ The author's ideas can be shown through the treatment of characters, particularly contrasting characters, and through comment on their behaviour.
➤ The events of the story, particularly the ending, show the author's concerns and judgements.
➤ The setting of the story can show the author's general outlook or point to the theme of the story.

ADDITIONAL EXAMPLES

Use these examples as exercises to test your understanding of what you have read in this chapter. Write down your own ideas before reading the Key below.

1.   This passage, from the end of **A Passage to India** restates the themes of the novel quite clearly. What are the ideas expressed in this passage?

'Down with the English anyhow. That's certain. Clear out, you fellows, double quick, I say. We may hate one another, but we hate you most. If I don't make you go, Ahmed will, Karim will, if it's fifty-five hundred years we shall get rid of you, yes, we shall drive every blasted Englishman into the sea, and then,'– he rode against him furiously–'and then', he concluded, half kissing him, 'you and I can be friends. ' 'Why can't we be friends now?' said the other, holding him affectionately. 'It's what I want. It's what you want. ' But the horses didn't want it–they swerved apart; the earth didn't want it, sending up rocks through which riders must pass in single file; the temples, the tank, the jail, the palace, the birds, the carrion, the Guest House, that came into view as they issued from the gap and saw Mau beneath them: they didn't want it, they said in their hundred voices, 'No, not yet, and the sky said 'No, not there. '

2. What ideas are being expressed in the following extract from **Animal Farm**? Why does George Orwell choose to present them through the characters of animals?

Major continued: 'I have little more to say. I merely repeat, remember always your duty of enmity towards Man and all his ways. Whatever goes on two legs, is an enemy. Whatever goes on four legs, or has wings, is a friend. And remember also that in fighting against Man, we must not come to resemble him. Even when you have conquered him, do not adopt his vices. No animal must ever live in a house, or sleep in a bed, or wear clothes, or drink alcohol, or smoke tobacco, or touch money, or engage in trade. All the habits of Man are evil. And, above all, no animal must ever tyrannize over his own kind. Weak or strong, clever or simple, we are all brothers. No animal must ever kill any other animal. All animals are equal.

'And now, comrades, I will tell you about my dream of last night. I cannot describe that dream to you. It was a dream of the earth as it will be when Man has vanished. But it reminded me of something I had long forgotten. Many years ago, when I was a little pig, my mother and the other sows used to sing an old song of which they knew only the tune and the first three words. I had known that tune in my infancy, but it had long since passed out of my mind. Last night, however, it came back to me in my dream. And what is more, the words of the song also came back–words I am certain, which were sung by the animals of long ago and have been lost to memory for generations. I will sing you that song now, comrades. I am old and my voice is hoarse, but when I have taught you the tune, you can sing it better for yourselves. It is called "Beasts of England". '

Old Major cleared his throat and began to sing. As he had said, his voice was hoarse, but he sang well enough, and it was a stirring tune, something between 'Clementine' and 'La Cucuracha'. The words ran:

> *Beasts of England, beasts of Ireland,*
> *Beasts of every land and clime,*
> *Hearken to my joyful tidings*
> *Of the golden future time.*
>
> *Soon or late the day is coming,*
> *Tyrant Man shall be o'erthrown,*
> *And the fruitful fields of England*
> *Shall be trod by beasts alone.*
>
> *Rings shall vanish from our noses,*
> *And the harness from our back,*
> *Bit and spur shall rust forever,*
> *Cruel whips shall no more crack.*
>
> *Riches more than mind can picture,*
> *Wheat and barley, oats and hay,*
> *Clover, beans and mangel-wurzels*
> *Shall be ours upon that day.*

**KEY TO THE EXAMPLES**

1. A Passage to India. The Indian and the Englishman who are talking in this passage want to be friends. They each feel affection for the other but they cannot be friends because the Indians want the British out of the country so

that they can rule it for themselves. Only then will individuals be able to come together. As it is everything around them in society, the whole way that life is organized in India, is a barrier to their friendship and understanding. Perhaps the Indians and the English can never come together because even the landscape, the rocks, seems to be against it, and the sky says 'No, not there'.

2.   ***Animal Farm***. George Orwell is using an old tradition when he chooses animals as his characters. Just as in Aesop's Fables they are used to stand for human characters. We understand that he is really writing about human society. By writing about animals he is able to simplify the characters, the events and the ideas, so that he can put them across more directly and with greater force. He also avoids stirring up our prejudices. We feel that animals are removed from us so we can view their activities dispassionately.

Major is addressing all the animals 'of every land and clime'. His speech is a rallying cry to unify them against their common enemy, Man. He has a vision of a better life for all, when the tyrant will no longer rule over them with cruelty. They will be their own masters and everyone will share in the good things of life. This is an ancient and long-felt desire of the animals, for it has come to Major in a dream of something he heard in infancy. Once Man has been conquered and overthrown, all the evils of his rule will be abolished and never allowed to return.

Major represents the visionary seer calling on his fellows to revolt. He could be any leader with a dream of the future, and the animals any group who feels themselves oppressed. The promises of the golden age to come are the promises that every leader makes: the wheat and barley that the animals will receive represent any unfulfilled desires. Because the animals' hatred for the present system is so great, Major says everything must be swept away. Revolutionaries generally want to break completely with the past. They cannot admit that anything is good, so everything must go.

Like other revolutionary thinkers, Major is sincere. He wants to better the lot of everyone and to make them all equal. He warns against backsliding in the future. The animals must not overthrow Man just to become like him. He sees that there is always the danger of the strong taking advantage of the weak. Orwell is saying that despite the sincerest intentions there is the danger that self-interest will prevail.

By the end of the book Major's revolution has suffered the fate that he foresaw. The pigs have taken the place of Man.

EXAM QUESTIONS

Here is a general question that allows you to write about the ideas in a story:
1.   What have you found to be enjoyable or interesting in a book or short story you have studied? You may wish to consider characters, events, setting or ideas. (LEAG)

You could answer this question by writing about how the characters, events and settings show the author's ideas, in the way discussed in this chapter. Other questions will ask about specific ideas in a novel:
2.   Printed below are the seven commandments set up by the animals in
Animal Farm after the revolution. Explain how these are changed or rubbed out and say what you think the importance of the commandments are in the story.
1. Whatever goes upon two legs is an enemy.
2. Whatever goes upon four legs or has wings is a friend.
3. No animal shall wear clothes.
4. No animal shall sleep in a bed.
5. No animal shall drink alcohol.

6. No animal shall kill any other animal.

7. All animals are equal.

(WJEC)

The temptation with this question would be to explain the changes by telling what happens in the story and forget to deal with the ***importance*** of what happens. You should use the events of the story as illustration of the importance of the commandments and to show Orwell's ideas.

Many questions on themes concentrate on the endings of stories, because that is when themes are shown most clearly.

3. Do you like happy endings to stories? Write about the final section of one or more novels or short stories and say how successfully you feel the ending, happy or not, is in bringing the story to a close. (LEAG)

4. Why, in the world of this book, must Lennie die? (MEG on ***Of Mice and Men***: John Steinbeck)

Look back at Ch.15 for hints on how to answer this question.

The following question asks about theme through character:

5. Dickens wrote in the preface to the novel that Oliver showed goodness surviving and finally triumphing. How good do you think Oliver is? Do you think he deserves to triumph in the end? (NI on ***Oliver Twist***)

QUESTION, NOTES AND TUTOR'S ANSWER

1 ▷ QUESTION

Explain the importance for the novel as a whole of Mr Bennet's remark: 'one cannot know what a man is by the end of a fortnight'. (NI on ***Pride and Prejudice***)

2 ▷ NOTES

1. This is part of a question, but an important part, carrying 40% of the marks for this question. You should try to write at least a page. In an exam you should spend about 20 minutes on it.

2. As preparation make a list of all the occasions in the novel when longer acquaintance causes one character to change his or her opinion of another.

3. Make a plan, perhaps along these lines.

(i) Remark applies generally. Note title.

(ii) Elizabeth's misconceptions–Wickham, Darcy.

(iii) Darcy's misconceptions–Elizabeth, Jane.

(iv) Other characters.

3 ▷ SUGGESTED ANSWER

❝ Do all your references to the book illustrate the central idea of the question, that it takes time to know someone? ❞

Although it is their new acquaintance with Mr Bingley which causes Mr Bennet to make this remark, the assertion applies less to Bingley than it does to other characters. As the title suggests, the idea of 'prejudice' is central to the novel. Several characters make a judgement after an initial impression, which proves to be unsound or inaccurate.

The theme is worked out most importantly through Elizabeth Bennet. Elizabeth is a lively and witty girl. She trusts to her intelligence to provide her with sound opinions of people and her judgement is often shown to be correct. She immediately dislikes and distrusts Miss Bingley and Mrs Hurst. Elizabeth's good-natured sister, Jane, accepts their friendliness at face value and points to their kindnesses to her, but Elizabeth is shown to be right. Elizabeth's opinion of Mr Collins is formed immediately on reading the letter which announces his visit. He appears to her to be pompous, complacent and foolish to a laughable degree. Again, she is proved right. It is all the more disconcerting, therefore, when in two important cases her prejudice leads her into errors of judgement.

On her first encounter with Mr Darcy she finds him proud and disdainful. She is piqued by his cool remarks about her appearance and his refusal to dance with her. This initial impression of Darcy is reinforced when she meets Wickham and hears the story of how Darcy deprived him of the living promised to him by Darcy's father. Because Wickham is pleasant and attentive, and, moreover, good-looking, Elizabeth believes his stories and sympathizes with him. Therefore, when Darcy unexpectedly proposes to her Elizabeth declares that she cannot marry a man who, as well as being insufferably haughty and ruining Jane's relationship with Bingley, has treated Wickham very badly. Elizabeth can hardly accept Darcy's version of the events. She is mortified when events prove her to be mistaken in her assessment both of Wickham and Darcy. Wickham's unprincipled behaviour towards her sister, Lydia, could have ruined her life. It is Darcy who arranges a financial settlement which persuades Wickham to marry Lydia. In making Wickham Lydia's seducer and Darcy the saviour of the family honour, Jane Austen shows how mistaken Elizabeth's first views are. And since even her intelligent heroine succumbs to such an error, we see how difficult it is to withhold judgement and form a true and fair view.

Darcy also makes mistakes. Blinded by his pride and reserve he fails to assess Elizabeth correctly at first. He judges her on her family status until her liveliness and wit compel him to look at her as an individual. He falls in love with her almost against his will. He also fails to understand the reticence of Jane's character and so advises his friend Bingley against marrying her, on the grounds that she lacks real ardour and is merely fortune-hunting. In both cases Darcy's error is based on giving undue weight to the value of position and fortune. However, unlike other members of his class – Lady Catherine de Bourgh, for example – he is willing to learn. Darcy, as well as Elizabeth, is shown as having to reserve his judgement on people.

The force of Mr Bennett's remark is lost on Mrs Bennett and her younger daughters. She and they persist in their silly and superficial opinions of people and never attempt to reach a right view. Jane is shown as always kind and good, but she errs in her reluctance ever to believe ill of anyone. Jane Austen makes her heroine fall into the same error as her mother and younger sisters but then gives her the wit and wisdom to overcome her prejudices and understand that you cannot know a man in a fortnight. The whole story is constructed around the misapprehensions which keep the hero and heroine apart. Only when they overcome them are they allowed to come together.

> 66 **Tell enough of the story to show that you know it in detail, but not so much that you wander off the point. Keep the question in mind.** 99

SUGGESTIONS FOR COURSEWORK

1. All the questions above are a suitable basis for a coursework unit.
2. Write a comparison of the closing chapters of two novels you are studying, showing the themes of the novel.
3. Make a study of several contrasting pairs of characters.
4. Write an alternative last chapter for a novel. Change the events in any way you like, but make the new ending
   (a) convincing in terms of the characters—would they behave like that?
   (b) appropriate to the themes of the novel. How are they treated in the new ending, in comparison to the original ending.
5. Have a group discussion on the themes of one or more novels and write a record of it.

STUDENT'S ANSWER – EXAMINER'S COMMENT

Question

What is the primary meaning of *Lord of the Flies*?

Good. Clearly states the argument of the essay in the opening sentence.

Good. Uses a direct quotation which exactly illustrates the point about Jack's feelings.

A good choice of incidents to illustrate the idea stated at the start of the essay. This is so throughout the essay.

The unfolding of the argument is not signposted in paragraphs which clearly indicate the progression of ideas. The paragraphs become shorter and shorter.

Much more detail is needed to explain events like Simon's murder and, a little later, the breaking of Piggy's glasses and the destruction of both Piggy and the conch.

The primary meaning of 'Lord of the Flies' is that which illustrates that fact that in any society, however big, once we are left up to our own means, without rules and regulations the standard begins to drop. So, the primitive spirit, which is present in each one of us, begins to get the better of us. The book illustrates this, throughout the steady decline of civilization amongst the marooned boys, progressing throughout the novel. The decline begins with the very first chapter, where Ralph tears off his clothes, and comparatively tears off a part of civilization.
'He kicked his shoes off fiercely and ripped off each stocking with its elastic garter.' It progressed then to apathy about necessities required, in order to be rescued or survive, on Jack's part. He became obsessed with the hunt, and killing. The passage reads:
> 'He tried to convey the compulsion to track down and kill
> that was swallowing him up.'
It began to decline steadily when the hunters led by Jack, painted their faces, and then later when the fire – a sign of civilization – was neglected in order to hunt and kill. This was an important point because it distinctly showed the two paths: one being the path leading to disorder, through the hunt and kill; and the other being the path leading to civilization, through the fire and rescue. he also indicated, that, at this point, only a handful of boys were following the latter path. Another important incident which showed the definite decline, was when Piggy's glasses were half broken, and so a part of civilization was broken. Simon said:
> 'One side's broken'
The path towards disorder was followed further as the boys began to succumb to the pleasures of the hunt. The passage reads,
> 'Ralph too was fighting to get near...The desire to
> squeeze and hurt was over-mastering.'
'The pig-run..,Ralph was content to follow jack along it.'
This latter quote was symbolic, in that it indicated that Ralph was content to follow Jack along the pit-run – the path to disorder; although he never continued any further.
Then the group separates, which is an important part in the book because Golding thus shows that when a society crumbles, the different parts cannot exist humanely. Jack said.
> 'I'm going off by myself.'
Gradually things become worse, as Simon is murdered, by the evil he knew was the source of the fear, and so religion and reason are wiped off the island of the other boys.
Then in chapter ten it is evident that the evil rules, when the hunters steal Piggy's glasses – a symbol of civilization – and so civilization diminishes. The quote, talking of Jack, read,
> 'He was chief now in truth...from his left hand dangled
> Piggy's broken glasses.'
Piggy, a sign of common-sense and intellect, Ralph a sign of authority, and the coach, a symbol of order and rule, still remained and so a thread of civilization still existed at this point.

THE
LANGUAGE
OF
PROSE

COMPARISONS
CONTRASTS
ASSOCIATION
WORDS
REPETITION
SENTENCES
DIALOGUE

G E T T I N G   S T A R T E D

Some questions will ask you how an author achieves particular effects in a passage of prose. Many of these will be part-questions on a passage printed on the exam paper. Even so, they may carry up to 40% of the marks for that question. In answering these questions, some of the terms and techniques used in writing about the language of poetry are useful. Although we cannot look at a whole novel, or even a short story with the close attention we would give to a poem, it is worth looking at some passages closely to see how the language works. The chapter on language in drama (Ch.12) also contains sections that can be applied to prose.

ESSENTIAL PRINCIPLES

1 > COMPARISONS

As in poetry, **comparisons** help to make prose writing vivid and interesting. Prose writers do use metaphors, but they are far more likely to use similes. (If you have forgotten the meaning of these terms, look back at Chapter 4. If you have not read that chapter you should do so.)

Charlotte Bronte shows the cold, hard and inhuman characteristics of Mr Brocklehurst in **Jane Eyre** by comparing him to an inanimate thing:

. . . presently beside Miss Temple, who herself had risen, stood the same black column which had frowned on me so ominously from the hearthrug at Gateshead.

At other times he is compared to 'black marble' and a 'black pillar' with a face like a 'carved mask placed above the shaft by way of capital'. These comparisons help to create the physical appearance of Mr Brocklehurst and a sense of his towering, forbidding presence. They also tell us a lot about his nature, which is solemn and unfeeling. Notice how all the comparisons are similar. Novelists often cluster images in this way. D. H. Lawrence, writing of the boy in **The Rocking Horse Winner**, uses two contrasting similes about his eyes. When he is winning and things are going well his eyes are like blue fire; when he is sick and exhausted from seeking the name of the Derby winner on his rocking-horse his eyes are like blue stones. The whole condition of the boy is summed up in the difference of his eyes, fire for life and stones for death. Lawrence is a writer who uses many comparisons, quite a lot of them metaphors. These are often quite brief. 'A bomb of rage exploded in her breast' is his telling description of a woman's anger. Later he speaks of 'the risen viper of the little elderly woman' (**The Blue Moccasins**).

When you are reading ask yourself whether the author is making comparisons. Work out what the character or thing is being compared with. Then think about what effect this comparison creates for the reader.

2 > CONTRASTS

Few writers use **contrast** as deliberately as Dickens does at the opening of **A Tale of Two Cities**:

It was the best of times, it was the worst of times, it was the age of wisdom, it was the age of foolishness, it was the epoch of belief, it was the epoch of incredulity, it was the season of Light, it was the season of Darkness, it was the spring of hope, it was the winter of despair. . .

The mention of two contrasting qualities together helps to emphasize them both. Black stands out against white, light against dark.

When you read notice the way that writers use contrast. Ask yourself what effect it creates.

3 > ASSOCIATION

Prose works very strongly through the kinds of **associations** which the words arouse in the reader. We have already looked at the kind of feelings we get from associations to do with the weather (see Ch.16). We have also seen how names like Gabriel Oak have certain associations which novelists sometimes use to help characterization (Ch.15). Many words carry these kinds of associations. Some words work on us very strongly: 'gloom' carries unpleasant associations, 'rainbow' pleasant ones. Poets use such associations very freely and deliberately – again you should look back at the chapter on figurative language (Ch. 4). Prose writers use them more sparingly.

When you are asked to say how a writer creates atmosphere or makes the writing vivid, look at the pleasant and unpleasant associations of the words used.

4 >	WORDS

> 66 **Use your dictionary whenever you are in any doubt about the meaning of a word.** 99

There is a tendency to think that it is adjectives and adverbs that make description lively:

He looked scornfully (*adverb*) down his aquiline (*adjective*) nose. Languidly (*adverb*) she raised a slender (*adjective*) arm to the bell-pull and he glanced suspiciously (*adverb*) round the room.

We can get tired of this sort of writing very quickly. Of course good writers do use adverbs and adjectives in a striking and original way, but not usually in quantity. It is often the single well-placed word that strikes us:

A bell began to toll with a *peremptory* clang. (Thomas Hardy)

Suddenly Piggy was a-bubble with *decorous* excitement. (William Golding)

We must expect writers to use unusual words that we have to look up in the dictionary.

Liveliness in the writing can just as frequently be a product of verbs:

I *hurled* myself across the room, *seized* him round the chest, *squeezed* as hard as I could to prevent his escape, and then *flung* him with a dextrous twist of my wrist towards the nearest chair. (*My Family and Other Animals* by Gerald Durrell)

The vigour of this sentence comes from a succession of verbs which re-create the actions for us rather than simply describe them.

Look at all the kinds of words the writer uses and be especially attentive to unusual words or words used in an unusual way.

5 >	REPETITION

This is one of the prose writers' most useful techniques for heightening atmosphere, creating tension, or simply giving an increased importance to what is being said. We have already had an excellent example of the *repetition* of a single word many times in Dickens' passage on fog (see Ch.14).

We do not expect a high degree of patterning in prose, so patterns rapidly become obvious and we can quickly feel that they are overdone. Nevertheless arrangements in threes is a favourite device:

You must be admired, you must be courted, you must be flattered – you must have music, dancing and society – or you languish and die away.

says Eliza of her sister Georgiana in *Jane Eyre*. The weight of her scorn is increased by the thrice stated phrase and the three frivolities that Georgiana relishes. A little later Mrs Reed recalls Jane's childhood behaviour and her distaste is expressed through a similar method of listing three items of Jane's conduct:

I could not forget your conduct to me, Jane – the fury with which you once turned on me; the tone in which you declared you abhorred me the worst of anybody in the world; the unchildlike look and voice with which you affirmed that the very thought of me made you sick . . .

Repetition is not always in threes of course, nor is it always used for unpleasant statements or adverse criticisms like these.

Look out for repetitions, not just of the same word, but of the same kind of phrase as in the example above. Ask yourself why the writer uses them, and whether they are successful.

6 >	SENTENCES

> 66 **Notice how writers use sentences and then follow their example in your own writing.** 99

Different kinds of *sentences* give different effects. A succession of short sentences might give speed, urgency, or might show simplicity and directness. Long sentences bring intricacy and complexity in thought, feeling or situation. When a short sentence comes after a long one it is usually emphatic or dramatic:

Never listen when they tell you that Man and the animals have a common interest, that the prosperity of the one is the prosperity of the others. It is all lies.

says Major, in *Animal Farm* and we can imagine the dramatic pause before he snaps 'It is all lies'.

Notice the kinds of sentences which writers use in describing different situations and how they vary them. Think carefully about what this variation adds to the effect of the writing.

7 ❯ **DIALOGUE**

If a writer uses a great deal of **_dialogue_** it makes for a quite different style from that of one who uses more passages of action, explanation and description. In the extract from **_Of Mice and Men_** in Chapter 15, the author gives little information in his own voice because he uses so much dialogue. This gives more prominence to the voice of the characters and we feel we come to know them more directly.

Notice how much dialogue a writer uses and how the voices of the characters vary, as in dramatic dialogue.

8 ❯ **SUMMARY**

➤ Prose writers use comparisons and associations in the same ways but usually not to the same extent as poets.

➤ Contrast and repetition are used to emphasize effects.

➤ Differences in style depend on:

the kind of words used;
the kind of sentences;
the amount and kind of dialogue.

All these need to be looked at carefully.

ADDITIONAL · EXAMPLE

Use the following passage to test your understanding of what you have read in this chapter. Try to say what makes it a vivid piece of writing. Write down your own ideas before reading the Key below.

The creepers and the bushes were so close that he left his sweat on them and they pulled together behind him. When he was secure in the middle he was in a little cabin screened off from the open space by a few leaves. He squatted down, parted the leaves and looked out into the clearing. Nothing moved but a pair of gaudy butterflies that danced round each other in the hot air. Holding his breath he cocked a critical ear at the sounds of the island. Evening was advancing towards the island; the sounds of the bright fantastic birds, the bee-sounds, even the crying of the gulls that were returning to their roosts among the square rocks were fainter. The deep sea breaking miles away on the reef made an undertone less perceptible than the susurration of the blood.

Simon dropped the screen of leaves back into place. The slope of the bars of honey-coloured sunlight decreased; they slid up the bushes, passed over the green candle-like buds, moved up towards the canopy, and darkness thickened under the trees. With the fading of the light the riotous colours died and the heat and urgency cooled away. The candle-buds stirred. Their green sepals drew back a little and the white tips of the flowers rose delicately to meet the open air.

Now the sunlight had lifted clear of the open space and withdrawn from the sky. Darkness poured out, submerging the ways between the trees till they were dim and strange as the bottom of the sea. The candle-buds opened their wide white flowers glimmering under the light that pricked down from the first stars. Their scent spilled out in to the air and took possession of the island.

(**_Lord of the Flies_**, William Golding)

1 ❯ **KEY TO THE EXAMPLE**

One of the things that we can notice about this passage is the appeal that it makes to the senses. Firstly there is the heat, so intense that Simon leaves sweat on the creepers as he brushes past them. Colours are emphasized: the green candle-buds contrast with the white flowers; the tropical brightness of birds is depicted in words that describe not their hue but their dazzling effect on the eye –'gaudy', 'fantastic', 'riotous'. The brightness of the day contrasts with the dimness of the night lit only by the pin-pricks of the stars.

Sounds are mentioned, but not distinguished from each other. They are simply 'bee-sounds' and 'bird' sounds, as though they all merge as one, except for the cry of the gulls. Even this grows fainter as the evening comes. Underneath them all is the murmuring of the sea. In an exceptional simile Golding compares this to blood in the veins, which is more of a sensation than a sound. The image works, however, because the sound of the word 'susurration' is onomatopoeic. The sound echoes the sense (it means whispering or murmuring), and conveys the distance and lowness of the sound of the sea. Finally there is the overwhelming scent of the flowers.

The coming of the evening is described with verbs that seem to make the landscape and vegetation active and give it will and purpose. The evening 'advanced', the colours 'died'. the sunlight is purposeful: it 'slides' up the bushes and 'withdraws' from the sky. The darkness is active: it pours from the sky. Most of all, the candle-buds seem to possess a will and a strength of their own. The sepals 'drew back' and the flowers 'rose to meet the air'. When they open, their scent takes possession of the island. By using verbs in this way Golding gives a strange vibrancy and life to the island which seems appropriate to the tropical setting.

EXAM QUESTIONS

In the chapter on Setting (Ch.16) the exam question answered demanded some close attention to the way Graham Greene created the scene. That is the way in which work on language is incorporated into other questions. Look back at that question to see what was said about how Greene made the writing vivid.

You may be asked about tone:

1. Jane Austen writes in both a sarcastic and an amusing way. Give 2 examples of both sarcasm and humour and comment on what makes these lines convey their tone. (Extract from **Pride and Prejudice** - *NEA*)

The most usual type of question on language is the one that asks you to examine how the atmosphere is created in a particular passage:

2. Would you agree that this is a particularly powerful and horrible scene? What makes it so? Consider both what is happening and the way the author has written it. (Extract from **After First Death** by Robert Cormier- MEG)

The instruction to look at the way the author has written the passage is a useful reminder not to say only what is happening. Do not rely on always having such a reminder written into the question. Be on the look out for 'how' questions. The use of this word indicates that you should write about the author's use of language–the way the passage is written, as well as what it is about.

3. (i) How does Dickens create the feeling of discomfort that the passengers on the Dover Mail suffered?
    (ii) How does Dickens make you feel something mysterious or dangerous could happen? (Extract from **A Tale of Two Cities** - NEA)

4. Using the whole passage, show how the writer makes use of sounds in creating the atmosphere of assembly. (Extract from **Kestrel for a Knave**, Barry Hines. - WJEC)

The passage referred to here is printed in Chapter 14 If you have not read the book you could use the passage as practice for a prose unseen. You could also use the following question in the same way if you have not read **Oliver Twist**. Unseens are explained in Chapter 2.

QUESTION, NOTES AND TUTOR'S ANSWER

1 ▷ QUESTION   How does Dickens convey the atmosphere of the condemned cell? (NI 30% of marks)

They led him through a paved room under the court, where some prisoners were waiting till their turns came, and others were talking to their friends, who crowded round a grate which looked into the open yard. There was nobody there, to speak to *him*; but as he passed, the prisoners fell back to render him more visible to the people who were clinging to the bars: and they assailed him with opprobrious names, and screeched and hissed. He shook his fist, and would have spat upon them; but his conductors hurried him on, through a gloomy passage lighted by a few dim lamps, into the interior of the prison.

❝What kind of imagery is Dickens using here?❞

Here, he was searched, that he might not have about him the means of anticipating the law; this ceremony performed, they led him to one of the condemned cells, and left him there – alone.

He sat on a stone bench opposite the door, which served for seat and bedstead; and casting his bloodshot eyes upon the ground, tried to collect his thoughts. After a while he began to remember a few disjointed fragments of what the judge had said: though it had seemed to him at the time, that he could not hear a word. These gradually fell into their proper places and by degrees suggested more: so in a little time he had the whole, as it was delivered. To be hanged by the neck, till he was dead.

As it came on very dark he began to think of all the men he had known who had died upon the scaffold; some of them through his means. They rose up, in such quick succession he could hardly count them. He had seen some of them die, – and had joked too, because they had died with a prayer on their lips. With what a rattling noise the drop went down; and how suddenly they changed from strong vigorous men to dangling heaps of clothes!

Some of them might have inhabited that very cell – sat upon that very spot. It was very dark; why didn't they bring a light? The cell had been built for many years. Scores of men must have passed their last hours there. It was like sitting in a vault strewn with dead bodies – the cap, the noose, the pinioned arms, the faces that he knew, even beneath the hideous veil – light, light!

At length, when his hands were raw with beating against the heavy door and walls, two men appeared: one bearing a candle, which he thrust into an iron candlestick fixed against the wall: the other dragging in a mattress on which to pass the night; for the prisoner was to be left no more alone.

Then came the night – dark, dismal, silent night. Other watchers are glad to hear the church-clocks strike, for they tell of life and coming day. To the Jew, they brought despair. The boom of every iron bell came laden with the one deep hollow sound – Death. What availed the noise and bustle of cheerful morning, which penetrated even there to him? It was another form of knell, with mockery added to the warning.

2 ▷ NOTES

1. Read through the passage carefully
2. As you go jot down a list of effects. For example:
   Entrance to cell through crowds yelling and screaming – Gloomy passage, dim lamps – Alone – Stone bench, heavy walls, iron candlestick, etc.
3. Arrange these effects roughly under headings
   - (i) Entering cell
   - (ii) Conditions
   - (iii) State of mind
   - (iv) Ghosts
   - (v) Dark/light
   - (vi) Sounds.

   This listing and arranging does not have to be done neatly and carefully. It is a rough guide so that things are grouped together. This will make your finished writing more organized and easy to read.
4. As you write, remember to mention Dickens to show you realize all these effects are deliberate parts of his method.

3 > SUGGESTED ANSWER

The atmosphere of the condemned cell is created through descriptions of the conditions of the cell and its past inmates and through insights into Fagin's state of mind.

Dickens allows the shadow of the place to which he is going, to fall over Fagin even before he enters the cell. He is led like a trapped animal, through crowds of prisoners and people all yelling and screaming their hatred of him.

The prison and the cell are described in words calculated to evoke a sombre atmosphere. The passage is 'gloomy' the lamps 'dim'. Everything in the cell is hard and comfortless: a stone bench, iron candlestick, heavy walls and door. Dickens dwells on the fate of Fagin's victims who have passed through this cell before him. They rise like ghosts in his mind, trussed, blindfolded, ready for the noose, and the sight is horrifying. Horrifying too is the picture of living men transformed into mere things: Dickens compares them to a heap of clothes. The repetition of the phrase 'hanged by the neck' emphasizes the awful finality of Fagin's fate.

Dark, with its associations of evil deeds and nightmare, is always strongly suggestive. Dickens twice says it is 'very dark' and opposes this to the craven desire for light. Three times the word appears, suggesting Fagin's mounting panic. Sounds are also used to create the atmosphere. First, in Fagin's imagination, there is the rattling noise of the drop; outside the night is dismally silent, broken only by the sound of the bell, bringing the hour of death closer. The words used to describe the bell, 'iron' and 'hollow', add to the prevailing gloom. When the sounds of morning do break in they are presented as a mocking contrast.

SUGGESTIONS FOR COURSEWORK

1. All the questions above are a suitable basis for a coursework unit.
2. Make a comparison of the language used by two different novelists by looking closely at several passages.
3. Choose a passage with a strong atmosphere and rewrite it as verse.
4. Write a piece in imitation of the style of a novelist you admire.
5. Study the way a novelist achieves his effects by using the techniques mentioned in this chapter.

STUDENT'S ANSWER – EXAMINER'S COMMENT

Question

What techniques does Hardy use in his description of Fanny's journey to Casterbridge Union?

> **Good. States clearly the two techniques – descriptive words and sentence construction – that the student is going to concentrate on.**

> **Good. Gives a clear example of sentence and describes its effect.**

```
The techniques Hardy use create a vivid, and memorable
description of her journey. he uses a lot of strong
descriptive words and he constructs the sentences in such a
way, that, in reading it we mimic the movements of Fanny.
For example, he makes his sentences long, with several pauses
in them, causing the reader to stumble over them, as Fanny
would be painstakingly stumbling over each and every step.
For example,
     'At length her onward walk dwindled to the merest totter,
     and she opened a gate within which was a hay-stack.'*
```

❝Another good example with relevant comment.❞

❝Good. Mentions the descriptive words used, and their effect.❞

❝The writing has now degenerated into almost a series of notes. You must write in proper continuous prose.❞

❝Good. Notices the use of symbol.❞

❝A few techniques missed – but those identified are ably discussed. However, the essay is rather disorganized, as shown by the need to mark sentences which should have come earlier in the essay.❞

It seems impossible to read these sentences quickly, not only because the descriptive words would seem misplaced, but also, because of the length, and punctuation of the sentences. Another instance, where Hardy mimics the movements of Fanny by his sentence construction, is in describing:

'with a quickened breathing...'

The ensuing sentence, is not only long, but also broken up by frequent commas, causing the reader to breathe frequently, thus emphasizing Fanny's state of breathing. The descriptive adjectives, verbs, and adverbs also add emphasis; for example:

'slowly walked', 'feebler', 'dwindled', 'small mincing steps', 'she sank',

They all create a vivid picture of her movements.

*and also:

'Her friend moved forward slowly...half her weight being thrown upon the animal.'

**The chapter describes her journey, and emphasizes at the beginning, the little hope she has, through the words:

'shutting out every speck of heaven.'

and,

'a distant halo.'

Thus, it implies there is no hope, except in Casterbridge but she adds:

'Perhaps I'll be in my grave by then.'

Implying she has little hope, either. However she struggles on using physical aids, crutches, and her strength of character, and will. Although, when she reaches the bridge, even her mental state gives up.

'Hopelessness had come at last.'

When everything seemed lost, a stray dog, helped her on her way. Symbolically, the dog seems like a 'Jesus' figure coming to her help in her greatest despair, and pulling her through. Also, as Jesus was rejected, so too was the dog, by the men in the union house, when they arrived:

'I stoned it away.'

So Fanny did reach the union house, although she did not live long enough to keep her engagement with Troy, for she died in childbirth.

I N D E X